Zero Waste Cooking

by Rosanne Rust, MS, RDN

for
dummies®
A Wiley Brand

Zero Waste Cooking For Dummies®

Published by: **John Wiley & Sons, Inc.,** 111 River Street, Hoboken, NJ 07030-5774, www.wiley.com

Copyright © 2022 by John Wiley & Sons, Inc., Hoboken, New Jersey

Published simultaneously in Canada

For general information on our other products and services, please contact our Customer Care Department within the U.S. at 877-762-2974, outside the U.S. at 317-572-3993, or fax 317-572-4002. For technical support, please visit https://hub.wiley.com/community/support/dummies.

Wiley publishes in a variety of print and electronic formats and by print-on-demand. Some material included with standard print versions of this book may not be included in e-books or in print-on-demand. If this book refers to media such as a CD or DVD that is not included in the version you purchased, you may download this material at http://booksupport.wiley.com. For more information about Wiley products, visit www.wiley.com.

Library of Congress Control Number: 2021951059

ISBN 978-1-119-85044-1 (pbk); ISBN 978-1-119-85045-8 (ebk); ISBN 978-1-119-85046-5 (ebk)

SKY10031867_121021

Contents at a Glance

Introduction 1

Part 1: Adopting a Food Waste Strategy 7
CHAPTER 1: Doing Your Best to Waste Less 9
CHAPTER 2: A Side of Sustainability: Putting Food and the Environment
into Context 21
CHAPTER 3: Getting Your Head in the Zero Waste Game 41

Part 2: Waste Not, Want Not in Your Kitchen 49
CHAPTER 4: Setting Up Your Kitchen for Zero Waste Success 51
CHAPTER 5: Storage Strategies to Help Reduce Your Personal Food Waste 61
CHAPTER 6: Managing Your Zero Waste Grocery Budget and Staying Healthy 77
CHAPTER 7: Sample Meal Plans: Zero Waste Ideas in Action 103

Part 3: Zero Waste Recipes 113
CHAPTER 8: Guest-Pleasing Starters 115
CHAPTER 9: Anytime Egg Dishes for All 131
CHAPTER 10: Leveraging Leftovers for Nutritious Soups and Salads 143
CHAPTER 11: Wasting No Time or Money on Dressings, Sauces, and Toppings 159
CHAPTER 12: Simple Sides for Busy Times 171
CHAPTER 13: Barnyard, Seaside, and Vegetarian Main Dishes 185
CHAPTER 14: Oh, the Pasta-bilities! 211
CHAPTER 15: Creating Delicious Handhelds with What You Have on Hand 229
CHAPTER 16: Anytime Sweets and Savory Snacks 241
CHAPTER 17: Crafting Mocktails, Smoothies, and Cocktails 253

Part 4: The Part of Tens 269
CHAPTER 18: Ten Uses for Leftover Eggs, Ripening Produce, and Scraps 271
CHAPTER 19: Ten Ways to Use Stale Bread 279
CHAPTER 20: Ten Ways to Use Up Dairy Before It Spoils 287
CHAPTER 21: Ten Ways to Reduce Waste from Restaurant Meals 293

Appendix: Metric Conversion Guide 301

Index 305

Recipes at a Glance

Starters and Apps

Chicken Parmesan Stuffed Mushrooms....................................117
Lemony Salmon Patties...119
Ham Fritters..120
☺ Layered Bean Dip..121
☺ Creamy Veggie Dip...123
☺ Basic Cream Cheese Dip..124
☺ Roasted Grape Tomatoes with Feta....................................125
☺ Texas Caviar..126
☺ Pizza Rolls...127
☺ Stuffed Greek Bread...129

Egg Dishes

☺ Egg Muffin Cups...135
Fajita Eggs...136
Leftover Steak and Eggs...137
☺ Cheesy Veggie Crustless Quiche......................................138
Basic Egg Strata..139
☺ Basic Frittata..140
Potluck Egg Bake..141
Easy Cheese Soufflé...142

Soups and Salads

Homemade Stock..145
Empty-the-fridge Chicken Vegetable Soup with Egg Noodles..............146
Beef Stew with Potatoes, Carrots, and Peas............................147
Beef Chili..148
Kitchen Sink Chicken Chili..149
Wedding Soup with Spinach...150
Bean Soup with Diced Pork...151
☺ Mixed Produce Salad with Farro.....................................152
Protein-packed Waldorf Salad..153
Salmon Spinach Salad with Sliced Grapes...............................154
☺ Chopped Salad with Lemon Vinaigrette...............................155
Tuna "a la Niçoise" Salad...156
☺ Nutty Mixed Salad with Beans, Beets, and Goat Cheese...............157

Dressings, Marinades, Sauces, and Toppings

- Citrus-mustard Salad Dressing 161
- Everyday Vinaigrette Dressing. 162
- Go-to Honey Dijon Salad Dressing 163
- Easy Basic Marinade 164
- Basic Cream Sauce. 165
- Quick Canned Tomato Pasta Sauce 166
- Versatile Pesto 167
- Aquafaba Fluff 168
- Apple-Ginger Chutney. 169

Side Dishes

- Roasted Veggie Trio. 173
- Garlic Broccoli. 174
- Roasted Bell Peppers 175
- Zucchini with Caramelized Onions 177
- Chickpea Artichoke Grain Bake 178
- Roasted Carrots with Honey Glaze 179
- Cheesy Herbed Rice. 180
- Kicked-Up Cannellini Bean Salad. 181
- Black Bean and Edamame Salad. 182
- Beans and Rice 183
- Baked Apples 184

Main Dishes

Whole Roast Chicken 190
Chicken with Orzo, Artichokes, and Zucchini. 192
Foil-pack Greek Chicken with Olives, Feta, and Peppers 193
Teriyaki Chicken Tenders. 195
Spiced Chicken over Rice. 196
Chicken-Stuffed Baked Potatoes 197
Grilled Marinated Flank Steak. 198
Skillet Meatballs 200
Spice-rubbed Pork Tenderloin with Roasted Sliced Grapes 201
Slow Cooker Pulled Pork 202
Roast Pork Loin with Apples and Onions 203
Broiled Salmon Fillet. 204
Baked Fish with Herbed Bread Crumbs 205
Foil-baked Tilapia with Peppers 206
- Moroccan Veggie Skillet 207

🕓 Spicy Tofu Broccoli Bowl..208
🕓 Lentil-stuffed Zucchini..209

Pasta Dishes

🕓 Broccoli Bits and Bell Peppers with Linguine 217
🕓 Vegetable Lasagna...218
🕓 Penne Bake with Veggies 220
Smoked Salmon Pasta with Asparagus....................................221
Garlic Linguine with Clams...222
Pasta with Roast Vegetables and Salmon.................................223
🕓 Pasta with Chickpeas...224
🕓 Veggie-Roast Pasta Primavera..225
Bow Ties with Turkey and Peas...226
🕓 Roasted Tomatoes and Bell Peppers with Penne 227
Angel Hair with Shrimp and Spinach......................................228

Handhelds

Mushroom Turkey Burgers...232
Pork Pita Pockets with Cucumber Sauce 233
Flexible Quesadillas 234
Fajitas with Avocado Cream 235
Pork Tacos with Peppers, Onions, and Lime Crema.....................236
Fish Tacos..237
Bagels with Smoked Salmon and Cream Cheese 238
Seafood Salad Sandwich 239

Sweets and Snacks

🕓 Peanut Butter Yogurt Fruit Dip 243
🕓 Basic Muffins..244
🕓 Fruit Cobbler..245
🕓 Add Anything Scones..246
🕓 Black Bean Brownie Bites...247
🕓 High-Fiber Waffles..248
🕓 Basic Bean Dip 249
🕓 Roasted Pumpkin Seeds...250
🕓 Individual Pizzas..251
🕓 Pear and Goat Cheese Flatbread 252

Drinks

🍶 Mocktail Lemonade with Mint 256
🍶 Mocktail Sangria with Citrus 257
🍶 Mocktail Long Island Iced Tea 258
🍶 Berry Smoothie 259
🍶 Green Smoothie 260
🍶 Tofu Smoothie 261
🍶 Basil-infused Sparkling Water 262
🍶 Cranberry-Rosemary Cocktail 264
🍶 Infused Vodka 265
🍶 Pimm's Cocktail 266
🍶 Special Whiskey Sour Cocktail 267
🍶 Vegged-Up Bloody Mary Cocktail 268

Table of Contents

INTRODUCTION 1
   About This Book. 1
   Foolish Assumptions. 3
   Icons Used in This Book 3
   Beyond the Book. 4
   Where to Go from Here 4

PART 1: ADOPTING A FOOD WASTE STRATEGY 7

CHAPTER 1: **Doing Your Best to Waste Less** 9
   What Is Zero Waste Cooking? 10
      Using food and ingredients wisely 10
      Shopping for what you need and storing it properly. 10
      Making the most of scraps and leftovers. 11
   Adopting a Zero Waste Mindset 12
   Benefiting from a Zero Waste Approach 13
      Saving green while going green. 14
      Enjoying better nutrition and health 14
      Helping the planet. 17
   Getting Started: How to Waste Less Food Today 19

CHAPTER 2: **A Side of Sustainability: Putting Food and
the Environment into Context** 21
   Boiling It Down: Defining Sustainability 22
   Sustainability in Agriculture: Economic, Environmental,
   and Social Concerns 23
      Meeting your needs and the needs of your grandchildren. 23
      Using natural resources efficiently 24
      Feeding the world 24
   Considering Conservation along the Food Supply Chain 25
      Ecological management of pests. 26
      Pasture management, cover crops, soil conservation,
      and quality 27
      More food with fewer resources. 27
      Upcycling. 27
   Concerning the Environmental Impact of Food Waste 28
   From Farm to Fork: Understanding Where Your Food
   Comes From. 31
      Organic farming is superior. 32
      Technology and agriculture don't mix 33
      Eating less meat is better for the planet 34

Bringing It Home: Deciphering Package Icons and Labels 36
USDA Certified Organic....................................36
Free-from labeling......................................37
So-called plant-based products...........................39
Carbon footprint labels..................................40

CHAPTER 3: **Getting Your Head in the Zero Waste Game**.......41
Doing Your Homework: Analyzing Your Food Waste Habits........42
Keeping the Environment and Your Wallet in Mind...............43
When shopping: Will I use this?............................43
When storing: What's the best way to preserve my food? 45
When cooking: How can I better use scraps and leftovers? 46
Repeat after Me: Practice, not Perfection 47

PART 2: WASTE NOT, WANT NOT IN YOUR KITCHEN 49

CHAPTER 4: **Setting Up Your Kitchen for Zero
Waste Success**.................................... 51
Taking Inventory of the Food in Your Kitchen....................52
Finding out what's in your fridge and freezer 53
Unpacking your pantry....................................53
Cruising your countertop 54
Cracking the Code: Deciphering What Product Dates
Really Mean 55
Giving Back to the Earth: Creating a Composting Strategy.........58

CHAPTER 5: **Storage Strategies to Help Reduce
Your Personal Food Waste** 61
Making Smart Decisions for Your Pantry Storage..................62
Choosing less packaging...................................62
Repurposing containers...................................63
Ditching plastic bags for reusable options 64
Keeping it airtight 65
Using reusable food coverings 66
Considering shelf life: The first in, first out system 66
Using Your Fridge and Freezer Efficiently 67
Cool rules for you and your appliance........................68
Optimizing your fridge's storage zones 69
Knowing what freezes well.................................71
Buy Less, Store It Right, and Use It All 75
Making the most of what you buy and cook....................75
Storing the trimmings.....................................75

CHAPTER 6: **Managing Your Zero Waste Grocery Budget and Staying Healthy** 77

Meal Planning Made Easy 78
  Consulting your calendar: Determining when and what to eat at home 78
  Considering the ingredients already in your kitchen 79
  Making a solid grocery list and sticking to it 79
Aligning Zero Waste with Budget-Conscious Buying 82
  Making smarter bulk buys 83
  Deciding where to shop 84
  Shopping the specials and BOGOs 85
  Enjoying canned and frozen produce 85
Versatile Foods to Keep You Healthy 86
  Making the most of legumes 86
  Getting the most out of grains 89
  Picking produce 93
  Making smart meat and dairy selections 95
  Using dairy to enhance meals 99

CHAPTER 7: **Sample Meal Plans: Zero Waste Ideas in Action** 103

Touching on Zero Waste Meal Plan Basics 104
  Using one ingredient in multiple recipes..................104
  Prepping and cooking extra servings 104
  Getting creative with leftovers 105
Sample Meal Plans: Ready-Made with Flexibility 106
  Week 1 sample meal plan 107
  Week 2 sample meal plan 108
  Week 3 sample meal plan 109
  Week 4 sample meal plan 111

PART 3: ZERO WASTE RECIPES 113

CHAPTER 8: **Guest-Pleasing Starters** 115
Sharing Small Plates to Make a Meal 115

CHAPTER 9: **Anytime Egg Dishes for All** 131
How to Tell Your Quiche from Your Frittata 132
Easing into Egg Recipes with an Omelet 133

CHAPTER 10: **Leveraging Leftovers for Nutritious Soups and Salads** 143
Putting Stock in the Benefits of Homemade Stock 144

CHAPTER 11: **Wasting No Time or Money on Dressings, Sauces, and Toppings** 159

Flavorize and Tenderize 160

CHAPTER 12: **Simple Sides for Busy Times** 171

Getting Creative Sides to the Table.................................172

CHAPTER 13: **Barnyard, Seaside, and Vegetarian Main Dishes**...185

Prepping and Carving a Whole Chicken.........................186
Making Bread Crumbs 188

CHAPTER 14: **Oh, the Pasta-bilities!** 211

Pasta Basics 212
Name that pasta shape 212
Pasta cooking instructions...213

CHAPTER 15: **Creating Delicious Handhelds with What You Have on Hand** 229

Keeping It Fresh: Working with More than Just Sliced Bread 230
Enjoying Handhelds for Breakfast 231

CHAPTER 16: **Anytime Sweets and Savory Snacks**.............241

Zero Waste Add-ins and Swaps..242

CHAPTER 17: **Crafting Mocktails, Smoothies, and Cocktails**.....253

Setting up Your Bar and the Pour....................................254

PART 4: THE PART OF TENS...269

CHAPTER 18: **Ten Uses for Leftover Eggs, Ripening Produce, and Scraps**....................................271

Feed Crushed Egg Shells to Your Plants.........................271
Freeze Egg Whites 272
Add Any Extra Egg Yolks 272
Seal and Gloss with an Egg Wash 273
Mix in Finely Chopped Veggie Scraps..............................274
Roast or Sauté to Stretch Wilting Veggies 275
Use Veggie Scraps to Create New Soups 275
Dry Leftover Herbs, Veggies, or Fruit 276
Turn Droopy Fruits and Veggies into Slaw or Chutney 277
Dye Eggs with Leftover Onion Skins.................................278

CHAPTER 19: Ten Ways to Use Stale Bread 279
    Fresh Bread Crumbs. 280
    French Toast. 281
    Crostini for Appetizers 282
    Pappa al Pomodoro 282
    Bread Pudding. 283
    Croutons for French Onion Soup 283
    Stuffing or Southern Dressing. 284
    Roasted Tomatoes with Bread and Cheese. 285
    Panzanella 285
    When All Else Fails. 286

CHAPTER 20: Ten Ways to Use Up Dairy Before It Spoils 287
    Replacing Buttermilk. 288
    Making Oatmeal 288
    Thickening Stews and Sauces 289
    Baking 289
    Breading Foods 289
    Making a Soft Cheese 289
    Tenderizing Raw Chicken and Other Meats. 290
    Yogurt Helps Ensure Crispy, Moist Chicken or Fish 290
    Beyond Cooking: Milk Baths and Facials 291
    Feed Me, Seymour: Fertilizing Plant 291

CHAPTER 21: Ten Ways to Reduce Waste from Restaurant Meals. 293
    Order Wisely. 294
    Box Up Leftovers Big and Small 294
    Actually Eat What Food You Bring Home. 295
    Combine Leftovers to Create a New Meal. 295
    Turn Extra Takeout into a One-Bowl Wonder 295
    Fill Omelets with Leftover Meats or Veggies 296
    Add Pasta to Leftover Restaurant Sauces 296
    Stuff a Baked Potato with Doggie Bag Goodies 297
    Make Takeout Leftovers into Tasty Nacho Toppings. 298
    Level Up Grilled Cheese Sandwiches with Yummy
    Bits of Leftovers. 298

APPENDIX: METRIC CONVERSION GUIDE. 301

INDEX. 305

Introduction

Up to 40 percent of the food produced doesn't get eaten. This is a waste of not only food but also all the resources it took to produce, process, and deliver that food.

Food and food systems have deep cultural roots, playing a major role in our lifestyles, celebrations, and livelihoods. My experiences interviewing and counseling people about what and how they eat offers me important insights into their "whys," too. In some cases, food is a comfort, part of an identity, or simply a basic need. In other cases, diet is a form of medical therapy — in that dietary change can improve a medical condition or help manage a disease. In addition, changes in food choices are now made with the environment in mind. But for any of that to work, the individual must accept, and sustain, the change.

My philosophy about food and eating habits is one of reason. For dietary changes to have any impact — whether on your body, your budget, or the environment — those changes must be reasonable and doable. Extreme measures are rarely sustainable. Zero waste cooking can save you money and may even improve your nutrient intake. It also has a positive impact on the environment, reducing the overall methane emissions that result from the food waste that goes from your kitchen to landfills. This book aims to help you reduce your food waste, no matter what you eat.

About This Book

This book aims to help and encourage you to waste less food.

Many zero waste cooking books adopt the notion that to have a positive impact on the environment, you must focus almost entirely on eating more plants and removing animal products from the diet. This book doesn't. The notion that everyone can (or wants to) adopt a vegetarian diet is simply unrealistic. Instead, this book encourages you to give more thought to what you eat, and what you throw away, while you begin to adopt a budget-friendly diet that balances your use of a variety of foods with less waste and less harm to the environment.

The goal of this book isn't to shame you into overhauling your diet, tell you what to eat, or make you feel guilty about your food choices. Rather, my goal in writing this book is to share some facts about how food waste impacts the environment and why reducing food waste is important, help you understand where your food comes from, provide information on food safety and nutrition, and ultimately help you get started with zero waste cooking.

Reducing food waste is a big challenge for the whole world, so this book is here to help you keep things in perspective. Practice and progress, not perfection, is the expectation.

When I wrote the recipes in this book, I used easy-to-find ingredients and also tried to provide recipes in which you can easily swap in similar ingredients you have on hand that you need to use up (or that you prefer). In most cases, a similar ingredient will result in just as tasty and successful of a dish — especially if it leads to you wasting less food. As you read the recipes, keep these conventions in mind:

>> Oven temperatures are listed in degrees Fahrenheit.

>> A "pinch" of salt is assumed to be ⅛ teaspoon. "Salt to taste" suggests your judgement in how much you salt the food.

>> All eggs are large.

>> Flour used is all-purpose flour, but feel free to use gluten free, whole wheat, or any other replacement flour.

>> When fresh meat or vegetables are listed in a recipe, cooked can often be substituted.

>> Canned or frozen vegetables and fruits can replace fresh.

>> All milk is 1% fat, but whole, 2%, or nonfat milk can be used instead. Of course, if you don't tolerate cow's milk, feel free to use a milk alternative such as soy milk.

>> I created the recipes using plain nonfat Greek yogurt, light sour cream, and light cream cheese, but regular plain yogurt, regular fat sour cream, and regular cream cheese can be used as substitutes.

>> I recommend using freshly ground peppercorns from a peppermill, but regular ground pepper is also fine to use.

>> Dried herbs can be used in place of fresh.

🍅 The small tomato icon indicates the recipe is vegetarian or contains no meat, but it may contain eggs or dairy.

To make the content more accessible, this book is divided into four parts. You don't have to read from beginning to end but can turn to any part — or any chapter — at any time and reference back and forth as often as you need. I put a lot of heart and research into writing this book so, of course, I think every word is important, but some pieces of information aren't essential, but are there to help you understand the overall food waste topic. These details appear in sidebars (shaded gray boxes), and you can feel free to skip them without missing any key zero waste cooking information.

Within this book, you may note that some web addresses break across two lines of text. If you're reading this book in print and want to visit one of these web pages, simply key in the web address exactly as it's noted in the text, as though the line break doesn't exist. If you're reading this as an e-book, you've got it easy — just click the web address to be taken directly to the web page.

Foolish Assumptions

In writing this book, I made some assumptions about you:

- » You have an interest in cooking, saving money, staying healthy, and wasting less.

- » You want to be a good steward to the environment, and you feel overwhelmed with all the "stuff" in your life.

- » You have access to a kitchen, with a refrigerator-freezer, stove top, oven, and possibly a microwave, and have basic cooking tools.

- » You have basic cooking skills, you're busy, and you aren't interested in getting too fancy in the kitchen.

- » You want to reduce your food waste, do more with the ingredients you have on hand, and get more creative with recipes.

If this sounds like you, then you're in the right place!

Icons Used in This Book

Throughout this book, icons in the margins highlight certain types of valuable information that call out for your attention. Here are the icons you'll encounter and a brief description of each.

TIP

The Tip icon marks shortcuts that can save you time or money or make zero waste cooking easier.

REMEMBER

Remember icons mark the information that's especially important to know. If you're short on time, siphon off the most important information in each chapter by skimming through to look at these icons.

TECHNICAL STUFF

When I get into the weeds of the subject matter, you'll see the Technical Stuff icon. This icon marks information that is a bit more technical, so if you aren't into it, you can skip over these sections without missing out on the major focus of the chapter.

WARNING

Look out! The Warning icon tells you about information that could relate to your safety. It marks important information that may save you headaches or prevent you from being misled.

Beyond the Book

In addition to the abundance of information and guidance related to zero waste cooking that I provide in this book, you get access to even more help and information online at Dummies.com. Check out this book's online Cheat Sheet. Just go to www.dummies.com and search for "Zero Waste Cooking For Dummies Cheat Sheet."

Where to Go from Here

The joy of For Dummies books is that you can start anywhere. If you're already on a zero waste journey and just need an idea for dinner tonight, then go straight to the recipes in Part 3. From starters to soups to sides to sweet and savory snacks and more, Chapters 8 to 17 have you covered. For quick zero food waste tips, just head straight to Part 4.

If you're just beginning to research the issue of food waste, then start at the beginning in Part 1. Your kitchen is just one part of the food waste issue, so Chapters 1 and 2 look at the bigger picture of the food supply chain. If you're the type of person who likes to sit and think things through before you take action, then head to Chapter 3 where I get into the details that help you assess your current food waste so you can take a good look at your habits.

For more about organizing your kitchen for zero waste, check out Chapters 4 and 5.

As a registered dietitian, I had to include some information in the book about nutrition. I created all the recipes with both health and the optimal use of ingredients to reduce food waste in mind. If you want to find out more about staying healthy on a budget, head to Chapter 6.

And if meal planning is your jam, Chapters 7 offers four weeks of meals that help you waste less by making the most of your shopping list.

I hope this book changes your perception of food and the environment and your role in it. I hope it's a reference that you can count on to help you make the most of what you have by creating healthy meals that minimize food waste.

1

Adopting a Food Waste Strategy

IN THIS PART . . .

Find out how adopting a zero waste cooking method benefits you and the environment.

Learn the basics of kitchen organization so you can begin zero waste cooking.

Understand what sustainability really means.

Discover zero waste action steps that fit your lifestyle.

IN THIS CHAPTER

zero waste

» Discovering the benefits of zero waste cooking

» Understanding the framework of food and environment

Chapter **1**

Doing Your Best to Waste Less

A n estimated 30 to 40 percent of the food supply in the United States is wasted due to loss (never delivered or prepared) and waste (thrown away). That's more than 130 billion pounds of food per year! Hard to imagine, right? Maybe not when you consider how every day, shoppers are enticed to buy food in bulk but often end up throwing away the excess. Or how, all too often, diners bag up restaurant leftovers only to let them languish in the fridge (or, worse yet, in their car's back seat), and then throw them out, packaging and all. What do these examples have in common? Good intentions, yes. But also, unnecessary waste.

Many of us may not even realize how often we waste food, nor the impact that waste can have on our communities. When you make a concerted effort to avoid waste, you won't be throwing away money or nutrition. Reducing your food waste has the potential to have a positive impact on your health, your budget, and the environment. This realization makes it even more convincing to work on wasting less, and that effort begins at home.

What Is Zero Waste Cooking?

Zero waste cooking is a strategy to reduce food waste. It's about using all the food that you purchase, grow, or have access to, and leaving behind as little food and packaging as possible. It's something to feel good about as you save money and reduce your impact on the planet.

REMEMBER

Zero waste cooking is *not* about perfection or self-righteousness. Neither is it about becoming vegetarian or eating less meat. Be wary of statements about avoiding meat and dairy when in the context of zero waste cooking. The goal of zero waste cooking is to reduce all food waste.

Zero waste cooking is about adopting a philosophy to waste less food in your household no matter what your dietary choices are (of course I still want you to make mostly healthy ones!). It's about learning how to grocery shop more mindfully and efficiently to maximize your food and your food budget. It's also about having a plan for the food you buy and storing food properly.

Using food and ingredients wisely

In the United States and many parts of the world, we're blessed with an abundant food supply. We travel to grocery stores, expecting all the food and ingredients that we desire to be there. (Skip to Chapter 2 to learn more about the food supply chain and where your food comes from.) We expect our apples and tomatoes to be blemish-free and our food to be fresh and appealing. We purchase what we need (and sometimes more than we need) and bring it home to store on our shelves or refrigerator or freezer. You could say, we're a little spoiled.

To create a zero waste kitchen, you simply begin by being more thoughtful about your purchases. You then start to rethink your leftovers and plan out how you're going to prepare every ingredient that goes into your shopping cart. You also may have some second thoughts about perfect produce, realizing that a small blemish here or there doesn't impact the safety or nutrition of the food.

Shopping for what you need and storing it properly

Zero waste cooking focuses on shopping for what you *need*, not what randomly "looks good." Grocery stores strategically set up their shelves and displays to entice you to buy more. They place seasonal items at your eye level, and companies pay a premium for the best shelf placement. But shopping only for what you need will ultimately help reduce your food waste. You'll find lots of tips and strategies for sticking to your food budget and grocery list in Chapter 6.

A good shopping list makes trips to the grocery store more efficient. Your list should include everything you need to create meals for the next week or two. You might break your list into a big order or a few smaller orders, so think of your list as a running inventory as well. These are planned purchases that fit your budget and meal planning. Chapter 4 helps you analyze what you have, what you don't use or need, and what may be ending up in your garbage can too often. Here are a few reminders to get you started:

>> **Use a list.** Consider a digital app or keeping a running list on your smartphone.

>> **Delay a purchase.** When you see that tantalizing endcap, tell yourself to make a note and think about it for your next trip. This will eliminate an impulse buy but not deny the possibility of putting the item into your cart next time.

>> **Don't overspend.** Have a budget in mind before you go and keep a rough total as you shop.

>> **Choose quality over quantity.** In most cases, it's worth paying more for a high-quality food product (say, cheese) than getting a larger portion of it (more than you may need or be able to use).

>> **Store food properly.** Once you bring the food home, storing it properly helps preserve its quality and safety longer, thereby helping you reduce food waste. Chapters 4, 5, and 6 offer you lots of ideas and tips for making food and ingredients last longer. You may be surprised to find out what those best-by dates really mean, or why you shouldn't store avocadoes near bananas.

Making the most of scraps and leftovers

There are two kinds of people: those who love leftovers (usually the cooks of the house!), and those who say, meh. I hope this book inspires you to look beyond reheating a plate of turkey and mashed potatoes or a bowl of chili and instead create completely new dishes with those previously cooked ingredients.

As a wise cook once said, "Cook once; eat thrice." Making use of leftovers, as well as doing some batch cooking, will save you both time and money. It'll also take some of the day in, day out stress out of preparing dinner every night.

TIP

You don't have to eat trendy foods to eat a well-balanced zero waste diet. Avocadoes may be all the rage, but they're not the be-all and end-all for nutrition (and they spoil rapidly). No *one* food holds that health halo. It's the totality of your diet through the week that impacts your nutrition status and your environmental footprint. Healthy food doesn't have to be fancy or expensive.

The meal planning ideas in Chapters 6 and 7 use the concept of creating a grocery list with common ingredients that you can use in various ways through the week to make different meals.

REMEMBER

Some foods simply taste better the next day or two. Dishes like chilis, soups, casserole dishes, or lasagna, for instance, get even better after they sit for a while, allowing all the flavors to come together. You won't regret making extra servings when you cook those dishes.

Adopting a Zero Waste Mindset

You probably picked up this book because you want to waste less in your kitchen and you care about the environment. The goal of the book is to help you get started and maintain a mostly zero waste lifestyle (*mostly* because, hey, nobody is perfect). While Chapter 3 gets into the nitty-gritty of creating a zero waste mindset, an overarching theme throughout the book is "progress, not perfection." As you wrap your mind around the idea of wasting less food, the book addresses several things:

>> How the idea of sustainability fits into a zero waste mindset (see more in Chapter 2)

>> The three pillars of sustainability in agriculture and how they allow for the efficient use of natural resources to feed hundreds of millions of people

>> How various sectors of the food supply chain conserve resources and work to reduce food waste

>> How to analyze your personal food waste habits and create a plan to waste less

>> How to choose foods with both your budget and health needs in mind

>> How to organize a zero waste kitchen

>> How to plan meals, waste less, and cook delicious meals

You may wonder why I cover things like sustainability, the food supply chain, and the U.S. agriculture system that brings you your food. Well, it's important to know how the environmental piece of reducing food waste fits into the larger picture of where food comes from. There's a lot of conflicting information about the "best diet," the many sources of greenhouse gas emissions, and how various sectors impact the environment. Hopefully, this information will give you more to think about.

REMEMBER

Many things impact climate change. This book assumes that the more than 333 million people in the United States have a variety of food budgets and circumstances. This book was written with the broad spectrum of food budgets and food availability, both rural and urban, in mind. The recipes and meal planning strategies I include were designed for everyone — not just those with a specialty grocer down the block — so they can enjoy eating for good health and learn how to waste less.

Benefiting from a Zero Waste Approach

Zero waste cooking can save you money, improve your diet quality, and help the environment. You could say it's a win-win-win! You may be reading this book because you want to do your part to support a healthy planet, or maybe you want to waste less and save money, but you may not be aware that a zero waste approach may also indirectly improve your health. How? Well, there's money savings in taking a little bit of time to work on your grocery shopping strategy and use of leftovers. And when you become more mindful of food storage, meal planning, and using up fresh fruits and vegetables, you actually end up increasing your consumption of those nutrient-rich foods. Read on, dear reader.

The Environmental Protection Agency (EPA) estimated that, in 2018, 63 million tons of food were wasted, with 40 percent of that coming from households like yours and mine. Check out apps such as Too Good To Go that help connect people in need with surplus food supplies that they can purchase at deeply discounted rates.

Wasting food isn't just an environmental issue; it's a social issue, too. It's estimated that about 10 percent of U.S. households are food insecure at some time during the year. And hunger and undernourishment throughout the world continue to be a major concern.

TIP

Feeding America is an organization that works to reduce food waste and hunger by matching excess food from national food and grocery manufacturers, retailers, government agencies, shippers, packers and growers, and other organizations, with the food banks that need it most. Many agricultural organizations donate milk, meat, and eggs to local food banks and community organizations as well. To get involved, check with your local food bank or go to www.feedingamerica.org/take-action.

Saving green while going green

Sure, you want to save the earth, but don't forget that creating a zero waste kitchen is also going to save you money. All that food waste adds up to more than $160 billion each year (retail and consumer waste). Some estimate that this equates to about $1,500 a year per household. Whew! That's lot of missed meal creations.

Just think about all the fun experiences you could buy with the money you're going to save on your zero waste journey. Or maybe you can donate some of that money to a worthy charity of your choice.

TIP

One way to start working on this right away is to designate a "food scrap bowl" to keep in your refrigerator. This bowl or container can hold things that you normally might throw away (old bananas, carrot tops, bruised fruit, dried-out tomatoes). After a few days, check out what you have and head to Part 3, where you'll find recipes that are especially versatile for cooking with bits and scraps.

TIP

Consider using a community-supported agriculture (CSA) system to purchase seasonal produce from local farmers. The way this works is locally grown produce is shipped to your door weekly, which can save you money on your food bill and saves gas and transportation. You could even split it with a friend or neighbor.

Another great way to save money is by buying "ugly" or imperfect produce. Your local grocer may have a reduced-price shelf. There are several companies that funnel less-than-perfect produce from processors to sell directly to consumers at discounts, too. Keep in mind that farmers and food manufacturers are also always working toward reducing food waste. For instance, a bruised apple doesn't get bagged, but it goes into the apple juice or applesauce line at the packaging plant. Find more ideas in Chapter 6.

Enjoying better nutrition and health

Using a CSA may also inspire you to enjoy a wider variety of food, but so can simply adopting a zero waste kitchen strategy. Fruits and vegetables are often the items that get forgotten in the refrigerator. Sure, you had big intentions for them when you put them into your grocery cart, but then, oops, a few too many days go by.

When you adopt a better shopping strategy, you'll soon find you're getting more creative and seeking out more recipes to use up the food and produce items you have. In the end, that's a win for nutrition — and the planet!

My nutrition philosophy is to educate about food and nutrition, guide people in how their food choices may impact their personal health and lifestyle, and then allow them to make choices within that framework.

As you make the most of what you have and you create a plan going forward, your overall diet will likely, coincidentally, improve as well. Consider times when you ordered takeout and would forgo cooking what was in the fridge. A zero waste mindset can give you that little nudge you need to rethink some food waste decisions, saving you money and improving your diet. Maybe you still order takeout, but you make a firm plan to cook up the previously planned meal the next day. Another win!

Sharing the plate

Full disclosure: I'm an omnivore. I enjoy a variety of food, and my diet has the framework of a Mediterranean DASH diet (check out the latest edition of *DASH Diet For Dummies*). This is what works for both my health and my eating preferences.

Instead of pressuring fellow omnivores to avoid meat, I'd rather encourage them to add more vegetables and grains to their dishes, so in this book, I try to offer a variety of recipes that may appeal to many palates. In Part 3, you find many plant-based recipes, such as the Penne Bake with Veggies, Bow Ties with Peas, Lentil-Stuffed Zucchini, and the Mushroom Turkey Burgers. Of course, you may find Roast Pork Loin with Apples and Onions, Grilled Marinated Flank Steak, and Foil-pack Greek Chicken with Olives, Feta, and Peppers to be appealing as well.

Smaller portions of meat can share the plate with fruits, vegetables, grains, and dairy products. Saturated fat is what is most linked to disease. Saturated fat isn't just found in meat, however; it's also found in coconut and palm oils, ghee, butter, and processed baked goods.

Balanced eating

With the wide range of information (and misinformation) out there about diet and nutrition, we've lost sight of simple, balanced eating. Including a variety of foods in your diet, especially fruits, vegetables, beans, and grains, defines balanced eating.

As the surrounding sections point out, there are many benefits of zero waste cooking. You've got to find that sweet spot, where you're balancing your plate, wasting less food (and perhaps getting more creative), and, of course, enjoying what you eat, too!

If reducing the environmental impact of food waste and your diet and behaviors is your primary goal, that's great. However, I don't recommend abandoning health guidelines. Including a vegetarian dish once or twice a week isn't about shaming meat; it's about adding more variety and nutrition to your diet.

Pros and cons to plant-based eating

Eating more plants is good for your health. We know that a diet rich in fiber and low in saturated fat supports heart and brain health and may reduce the risk of some cancers. In addition to reducing disease risk, adding these foods may even help you live longer. That's good reason to try adding more vegetables and beans to your diet.

Beans are truly a superfood and definitely a food-to-include if you want to shift to plant-based eating. They're an affordable source of protein and an excellent source of fiber, and they provide iron, folate, potassium, and magnesium. In fact, the U.S. Dietary Guidelines recommend that you include 3 cups of legumes every week. Check out Chapter 6 for more information about incorporating them into your diet.

FROM ZERO WASTE TO MORE TIME AT THE TABLE

As you think about ways you can reduce food waste and incorporate more grains, beans, nuts, fruits, and vegetables into your diet, consider this: Eating this way may help you live longer.

Author Dan Buettner is a National Geographic Fellow whose work identified five areas in the world where people live the longest, healthiest lives: Okinawa, Japan; Sardinia, Italy; Nicoya, Costa Rica; Ikaria, Greece, and Loma Linda, California. The common ground in each culture is a plant-based diet, connections with family and friends, laughter, and daily physical activity. For example, in Sardinia, they eat a diet focused on whole grains, vegetables, beans, and goat's milk. They include meat as a flavor enhancer and accent to plant-based dishes. They also enjoy a Pecorino cheese made from sheep that supplies high levels of omega-3 fatty acids. They stay close with their family, enjoy shared meals and red wine, laughter with friends, and regular walks.

This sort of lifestyle is worth considering, no matter where you live! Slow down, prepare more meals to share with family and friends, laugh, and take a walk after dinner.

Helping the planet

Reducing your food waste may also help mitigate climate change because food is the single largest category of material placed in municipal landfills. When food rots, it produces methane, a greenhouse gas (GHG) that is related to climate change. Landfills are the third-largest source of human-related methane emissions in the United States.

REMEMBER

When you throw away food, you're also throwing away all the energy and emissions from the production, packaging, and delivery of that food.

WARNING

So what about eating less meat to save the planet, you ask? I recently read a magazine article that claimed that eating one less serving of beef a week for the year could be equivalent to driving 348 fewer miles. Statements like that are questionable. I have no idea how the author came to that conclusion (because no proven algorithms exist for it), but I often see "meat shaming" as a tactic to help save the environment. The article went on to say that ruminant animals are the "worst offenders" when it comes to greenhouse gas emissions and advised that the reader look for third-party certifications such as Animal Welfare Approved. These types of statements are misleading and without context. In addition, while animal welfare is important, it doesn't have a direct impact on greenhouse gas emissions.

REMEMBER

Agricultural systems are quite complex, as is the entire food supply chain. In any large system, there's always a need for ongoing reevaluation and improvement. This book doesn't aim to address all aspects of climate change and greenhouse emissions and the environment. As consumers, we're responsible for the choices in our own households. You do you.

Food waste and animal welfare are separate topics. However, in my experience, when people use terms such as *factory farming* and *animal welfare,* they're often taking a particular vegetarian-leaning stance. Large livestock farms in the United States are generally managed by people whose families have owned the land for many decades — which may not be what comes to mind when you hear the term *factory farm.* They're large, family-owned farms. I maintain that most of the beef, veal, pork, lamb, and poultry that you find at your local food markets were raised and slaughtered as humanely as possible.

REMEMBER

As a registered dietitian, I advise on nutrition and healthy lifestyle habits. Specific choices are yours to make; my goal is to share the science (as the body of evidence in how diet impacts health) and to help you keep all the chatter about food, diet, the planet, and health in perspective.

THE CONSCIENTIOUS OMNIVORE: JARGON OR ADVOCACY?

The term *conscientious omnivore* was likely coined about 15 years ago. Perhaps a former vegetarian, who wanted to feel good about eating meat, thought that making statements about "only eating ethically raised meat" would make them feel good.

After visiting more than a dozen farms, including a large beef operation and a small grass-finished beef farm, the farmers I've met take caring for the land and their animals very seriously. My definition of conscientious omnivore is one whose diet focuses on legumes, vegetables, fruits, and grains (that is, plant foods) but can include small amounts of meat and dairy, too.

- From a clinical nutrition standpoint, a diet high in fiber that is balanced for carbohydrate, protein, and fat (mostly healthy monounsaturated fats), and is limited in sugar and sodium, is related to the lowest disease risk. Fresh beef, pork, and poultry are good sources of protein and provide a lot of important nutrients, including B vitamins (thiamin, B6, B12, and niacin) and minerals (phosphorus, iron, zinc, and selenium). Animal foods do contribute cholesterol to the diet, but when you're eating small portions, it's not an issue.

- From an ethical standpoint, livestock is raised for food by farmers and ranchers who know what they're doing and raise and harvest animals in an ethical manner.

- From an environmental standpoint, being a conscientious omnivore can lower your overall food waste, reducing what ends up in landfills.

A vegan, on the other hand, may feel differently, and that's okay, too. It's important to keep in mind that there are a few different agendas here: health, the environment, and animal welfare. This book focuses on reducing food waste in your kitchen, not the ethics of eating or not eating meat.

I cover more about agriculture and sustainability in Chapter 2, but to set the record straight: It's your choice to be either an omnivore or an herbivore. In both cases, you can have a positive impact on your food budget and the environment when you waste less food (and switching to a zero waste kitchen may also improve your health).

Getting Started: How to Waste Less Food Today

You already have this book in hand, so you likely have already given some thought to your food waste habits. Perhaps you know what you waste but aren't sure how to change. Or maybe you know you can do better but aren't sure exactly how much you waste or where to start. No worries. This book meets you wherever you are in your food waste journey. Maybe the topic just sparked your interest, and you want to learn what zero waste cooking is all about. Or maybe you're already on a food waste journey and need more inspiration and tips to keep going. This book is here for you. Peruse from chapter to chapter and feel free to dog-ear it up!

REMEMBER

This book isn't going to guilt-trip you into literally wasting "zero" amounts of food or scraps. You don't have to be a perfectionist. My hope is to send you upon a journey toward zero waste. Like the Tortoise, slow and steady wins the race. Every small amount of food diverted from landfills can help the environment — and certainly your pocketbook.

Wherever you are on this journey, wasting less food starts with better understanding about what you throw away and why. For example, one of the reasons you may discard foods is reliance on best-by dates marked on packages. Those dates do relate to peak quality, but they're not food safety indicators. So, yes, you can still eat many foods past the best-by dates. Find out more about this in Chapter 4.

Walk over to your kitchen trash bin and take a look.

>> Is it filled with vegetable peels and coffee grinds, or whole pieces of rotten fruit or leftover cooked food?

>> Do you fill a kitchen garbage bag more than once a week? Or every day?

>> Do you find that you habitually throw away certain food items due to expiration (produce, bread, dairy)?

Now peek inside your refrigerator.

>> Are you storing food optimally?

>> Are there containers shoved to the back?

>> Is there fruit or spinach rotting in a drawer?

What about your pantry or wherever you keep dry goods?

>> Are there boxes or cans that you've had a long time and haven't used?

>> Are the foods dry, clean, and well-sealed? Are the packages in good physical condition?

>> Do you still stock snacks that are no longer your child's favorites?

>> Do you have enough rice and ramen to feed an army?

Depending on your answers, you may need to focus your efforts in one or more of the following areas:

>> If your kitchen trash can is heavy with rotten bananas, Thursday's uneaten leftovers, or moldy bread, then it's time to coordinate a shopping list and meal plan and utilize your freezer. Head to Chapters 5, 6, and 7.

>> If you found long-forgotten take-out leftovers pushed to the back of your fridge, then it's time to evaluate take-out orders or consider a weekly fridge check. Find related tips in Chapter 21.

>> If your produce drawer contains more slime than fruit, then an evaluation of storage habits is in order. Find storage guidelines in Chapter 5.

>> If your household of two always ends up with a bag of 4 or 5 extra buns, consider individual buns from the bakery instead next time.

>> If you've stockpiled more cereal in your pantry than you can eat in a year, then it could be time to mark that item off your grocery list and walk away from those tempting end cap sales.

REMEMBER

A little planning goes a long way! Smart shopping, storage, and food prep not only reduces your food waste, but it saves you money and helps save our planet. Once you put some of the ideas in this book into practice, come back here and revisit these questions to see you far you've come.

Chapter **2**

A Side of Sustainability: Putting Food and the Environment into Context

You may be wondering, "Why do I need to learn about sustainability or what farmers and ranchers do in a zero waste cooking book?" Arming yourself with a little background about sustainability, food waste data, and how your food gets from a farmer's field to your local market can help you understand your role to reduce food waste at home.

In this chapter, you find out about the food supply chain, the challenges that farmers and ranchers face, as well as some of the exciting technological advances of modern agriculture that make farming more efficient and eco-friendly, and bring more varieties of nutritious food to the table. This chapter also helps you understand how to interpret some of the hype and claims you often see on food packaging so you can skip the food fear and guild trip and avoid unnecessarily wasting the fruits of so many farmers' labor.

Boiling It Down: Defining Sustainability

Sustainability is a broad term that's important to just about every industry today, from businesses to technology to social and environmental sciences. According to Merriam-Webster, *sustainable* generally means "capable of being sustained." In the case of sustainable farming, it's defined as "of, relating to, or being a method of harvesting or using a resource so that the resource is not depleted or permanently damaged."

The fact is, farmers have been thinking about sustainability for a long time. The dozens of farmers I've met all have a passion for caring for their land, wildlife, air, and water. They view sustainability as producing crops and livestock in an efficient way that preserves the environment while maintaining the well-being of their animals, land, families, and the community around them. This is done in part by using advanced specialized veterinary healthcare, genetic technology, and advanced nutrition for plant crops and animal production.

REMEMBER

If farmers from the past didn't care for the soil and the land, there wouldn't be arable land available today to grow crops on. Keep in mind that sustainability encompasses more than just the environment. It's the intersection of environment, economics, and social responsibility. The work of bringing food to your table isn't sustainable if it isn't also economically viable.

However, you don't have to look far to read or hear statements that demonize ingredients — or worse, demonize the farmers and ranchers who work hard to grow and cultivate our food. The topic of sustainability has garnered a lot of attention over the past several years. Concerns are often encompassed within the context of scientific, economic, and political stances. Like just about every topic these days, a lot of misinformation and disagreement exists.

These are challenging times for the world. Food waste contributes greenhouse gasses to the environment and is part of the climate change issue. You and I can start by making changes in our own kitchens, but it's also important to understand a little about what sustainability in agriculture looks like and the roles of all the other players. Many people, across all food-related industries, are working to manage the nexus between food and climate to feed a growing population while also protecting the planet.

Sustainability in Agriculture: Economic, Environmental, and Social Concerns

Big-picture sustainability encompasses concerns for the environment as well as social equity and economic viability. Without one, you can't have the other. For the purpose of this book, I introduce these pillars in terms of food production and procurement.

Meeting your needs and the needs of your grandchildren

Today's world looks very different than it did in the 1960s. Global population has almost reached 7.9 billion people in 2021. That's about 6 billion more people than in the 1920s and double the people of the 1960s. That's a lot of mouths to feed. The need for water is also at a critical junction in many areas of the Western United States, including California, which produces about 50 percent of the fruits and vegetables brought to market year round. In addition, about a third of the world live in poverty with limited access to energy, water, or food. So, you see, focusing on sustainability is as important to humanity as it is to the planet.

We also now consume more resources than ever. Urban areas consume more power than rural settings, but we all use resources to light buildings, power appliances, and heat offices and schools. It's estimated that we use more resources each year than we put back. However, farmers are pretty efficient.

According to the International Food Information Council's (IFIC) 2021 Food & Health Survey, 42 percent of the 1,014 consumers surveyed (ages 18 to 80) believed their food choices have a moderate to significant impact on the environment. However, the perceived factors (sustainably sources labeling, recyclable packaging, non-GMO labels, locally grown) that those surveyed equate with "environmentally sustainable" don't necessarily relate to actual sustainability practices and may not be well regulated or defined. Opinions vary by generation as well. About 54 percent of Baby Boomers and Gen X say it's "at least somewhat" important that the food they buy is environmentally sustainable, whereas 61 percent of Millennials say it's "very/somewhat" important. Those surveyed agreed that it's difficult to know whether a food choice is environmentally sustainable, with 53 percent agreeing that if it was easier to understand the environmental sustainability in food products, it would influence the choices they make. That, my friends, is part of the goals of this chapter and this book — to help you understand the bigger picture.

From a personal perspective, it's important to understand how to conserve in your own household so that your grandchildren will continue to reap the benefits of safe and adequate housing and food.

Using natural resources efficiently

An environmentalist may see the environment as separate from humanity. However, farmers consider themselves stewards of the environment as they protect their land while producing food for people to eat.

While many people have a romantic image of who a farmer is, the reality is that today's farmers have a broad understanding of natural resources, the biogeo-chemical nature of the earth, and the integrity of the biosphere. In other words, they're scientists!

Modern farmers understand that a sustainable food system must remain within the planetary boundaries without irreversible impacts to the ecological systems. Even though the resources utilized to grow and produce food are sometimes under scrutiny, ultimately farmers are working toward increased production while using fewer resources (less land and water).

In fact, agriculture has to produce enough food for 10 billion people by 2050, while using fewer resources. This will require a team effort across the globe for innovation and partnership.

Regenerative agriculture is a relatively new term used to describe a holistic, principles-based approach to farming and ranching that focuses on the health of the ecological system, not just the production of crops or food. It may include a plan for cow grazing to restore pastures and grasslands. When animals graze, they add nutrients back into the soil, helping capture the carbon released. You may find a lot of different commentary surrounding this term; however, some of the practices used in regenerative ag aren't new. Many U.S. farms have adopted processes that support this idea over the years, including no-till farming and utilization of cover crops. By limited or non-tilling of land, a farmer can maintain a more nutrient-rich soil. Planting cover crops helps maintain soil erosion and build organic matter.

Feeding the world

The economist understands sustainability to mean there are finite resources and income to generate enough food for human consumption. This should cue us that it's important for nations to consider ways to transition to more viable food systems and encourage consumers to change some of our personal habits. As the saying goes, you can't keep repeating the same actions and expect a different result. Working toward a more sustainable food system could require reducing the overall demand of food and a shift in resources. I mean, how many flavors of potato chips do we really need?

Many scientists, economists, and industries are working toward improving agricultural systems globally. For instance, the World Economic Forum was established in 1971 as the International Organization for Public-Private Cooperation, to help shape global, regional, and industry agendas. Improving global sustainability in agricultural practices is part of their mission. They believe it will be vital to adopt technology, use more data to drive outputs, and recruit many more young people to the farming profession.

Other sustainability options include finding new ways to grow or create food in environments outside of the farm. While the idea of "lab food" may not feel comfortable, innovators are discovering amazing ways to conserve resources and make something out of almost nothing (see the later section "Upcycling").

REMEMBER

Encouraging less-intensive use of resources and improvements in the economic access to food are potential solutions for sustainable agriculture. Questions about how to feed the world are important, even if there isn't universal agreement on the best solutions. However, the goal of this book isn't to tell you what to start or stop eating. It's simply to work on what we, as consumers, have control of in our personal little worlds and waste less food in our kitchens.

Considering Conservation along the Food Supply Chain

If you picked this book up, you likely care about the environment. While this book's focus is on reducing your personal food waste at home, it's useful to step back to look at the big picture. What do we know about food and the environment? How are farmers and industry helping to conserve? Individuals and groups are working in multiple ways to produce adequate food, control the use of natural resources, and reduce waste across the food supply chain. This section covers a few of those ways.

Ecological management of pests

Imagine spending hundreds of hours preparing the land and planting crops across hundreds of acres. Then imagine losing all of that crop to bugs. To the farmer, this means a huge loss of time, income, and resources. To the consumer, it can mean higher prices at the grocery store or shortages of certain foods or ingredients.

Agroecology is the study of the relation of agricultural crops and the environment. Farmers are applying ecological principles to pest management. This is a win-win situation because it ensures high productivity while causing no harm to the environment. The word *pesticide* may conjure up devilish images of chemicals and evil, but in reality, responsible pesticide use actually helps the environment.

The media shares a lot of information about pesticides, their use, and their toxicity levels. Those used by both conventional and organic farmers are safe when applied appropriately. The miniscule "residues" that are sometimes left behind have no proven adverse effects on human health. Also, herbicides are a specific type of pesticide designed to kill specific weeds. *Pesticide* is the broader term of a chemical designed to kill weeds, insects, fungus, larvae, or bacteria. Farmers are motivated to use minimal amounts of pesticides because they're both expensive and time-consuming to apply.

PESTICIDES: THE DOSE MAKES THE POISON

The Environmental Working Group (EWG) is a popular nonprofit activist organization with a $12 million budget, heavily supported by the organic industry. A majority of toxicologists believe that the EWG overstates the health risks of chemicals.

Each year, the EWG publishes a "Dirty Dozen" list, warning consumers about consuming certain fruits and vegetables because of pesticide residue. However, their testing is done only on conventionally grown produce and doesn't test USDA Certified Organic produce (which allows an approved list of natural pesticides, but not synthetic ones). They also don't communicate the context of the residues, measured in parts per million (a part per million can be visualized as a single grain of sugar among 273 sugar cubes). Every chemical has a predetermined safe level of application. The pesticide residues found by the EWG are nowhere near a hazardous tolerance level according to the U.S. standards (No Observable Adverse Effect Level, or NOAEL, is the scale in which the highest tolerable level of a pesticide where no adverse effect is identified).

Pasture management, cover crops, soil conservation, and quality

Farmers use a lot of strategies to reach production and conservation goals. Every farmer manages their land differently depending on its geography. Careful consideration about the application of nutrients determines the health of the soil and overall production. Many farms have a "no till" or minimal tillage philosophy. Soil type and climate determine the type of tillage strategy. The less tillage, the less water erosion, and more carbon storage (which helps offset greenhouse gas emissions). Cover crops, planted after row crops are harvested, help with soil conservation as well as natural pest management. *Crop rotation* (rotating what you plant in various fields from one crop to another on an annual basis) allows for different plants to release different nutrients into the soil.

More food with fewer resources

When it comes to agriculture, sustainability is about growing enough food to meet humanity's need while enhancing the quality of the land, water, and air. Of course, this also has to be economically viable and promote the well-being of farmers and society.

Like so many aspects of our life, farming looks different than it did 30 years ago. Due to urban sprawl today's farmers are challenged to grow more food on less land. To do so, they use a lot of different technology to better manage their fields and crops. They call it "smart farming" (see the section "Technology and agriculture don't mix").

Upcycling

You likely have heard the term *upcycling* as a way to take a discarded byproduct from one industry and reuse it to make another product that's better than the original. But did you know that food can be upcycled, too? If you've ever enjoyed a spent grain pizza at a local microbrewery, you experienced an upcycled meal. Upcycling is taking food, or a food byproduct, and turning it into something edible. Beer manufacturers recycle their grain, creating flour, pasta, and bread products with safe, leftover raw material.

The first person who decided to make sausages, fruit jam, or banana bread may not have thought they were "upcycling," but it was a great food waste strategy. Industry is now using byproducts that are safe to eat (that were previously wasted) to create other products. For instance, the fruit pulp left after pressing fruit for juice can be used to add nutrition to snack bars. In fact, there's currently a whole industry focused on creating packaged foods from upcycled ingredients.

Because food is made from carbon, oxygen, and nitrogen, out-of-the-box-thinkers are discovering ways to literally create nutrition out of thin air. In the 1960s, NASA came up with the idea to feed astronauts using a type of bacteria known as *hydrogenotrophs* to transform the carbon dioxide (CO_2) the astronauts exhaled into protein. Today, more scientists are evaluating this "carbon capture" process, including a company called Air Protein that seeks to solve a decades-long challenge about creating protein from CO_2.

Cattle farmers upcycle, too, by using grocery store food waste to create ingredients for animal feed. No, they don't hand-feed a cow a candy bar or slice of old bread, but they take foods like them that are past their use-by dates (as well as waste like vegetable trimmings, food pulp, and nut hulls) and grind them up and add them to other feed material. That feed is then carefully analyzed for specific macro and micronutrients, to provide the specialized nutrition profile that meets the animal's needs. Animal science experts call this a circular bio-economy (our backyard chickens did the same — pecked at our moldy bread or rotting vegetables then created new nutrition via eggs!).

Concerning the Environmental Impact of Food Waste

While food spoilage is one of the biggest reasons people throw away food, many Americans throw away perfectly good, safe, and consumable food. In addition, the water and energy used to produce the food is also wasted. Food that sits in landfills results in the production of nitrogen pollution, and it emits methane, a greenhouse gas. According to the U.S. Environmental Protection Agency (EPA), food waste accounts for about 6 percent of human-caused greenhouse gas (GHG) emissions. Therefore, preventing food waste can be one potential solution to slow global warming.

REMEMBER

There's a lot of conflicting data regarding the role agriculture plays specifically in GHG emissions. While agriculture plays a role, according to the EPA it accounts for a small portion of all emissions compared to the transportation industry (see Figure 2-1). Planes, rockets, trains, buses, and automobiles generate the largest amount of GHG emissions, along with the energy and industry sectors, accounting for about 80 percent of all emissions (see Figure 2-2). Also, carbon dioxide accounts for 80 percent of GHG emissions, with methane accounting for 10 percent.

According to a report from the Food Waste Alliance, about a third of the world's food is wasted. The Food and Agriculture Organization of the United Nations defines *food waste* as "the decrease in the quantity or quality of food resulting from decisions and actions by retailers, food service providers and consumers." This can include not shelving produce that's less than desirable in shape, size, or color. Or pitching foods that are beyond the best-by date or are leftover in both restaurant and household kitchens (see Chapter 4 for more on best-by dates).

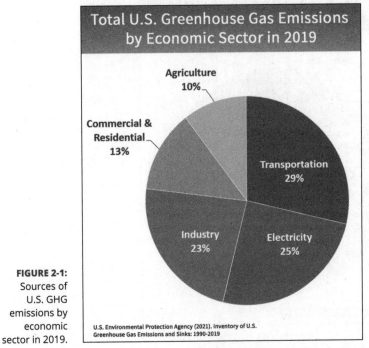

Total U.S. Greenhouse Gas Emissions by Economic Sector in 2019

Agriculture 10%

Commercial & Residential 13%

Transportation 29%

Industry 23%

Electricity 25%

U.S. Environmental Protection Agency (2021). Inventory of U.S. Greenhouse Gas Emissions and Sinks: 1990-2019

FIGURE 2-1: Sources of U.S. GHG emissions by economic sector in 2019.

Courtesy of U.S. Environmental Protection Agency

While it's estimated that the world wastes 1.4 billion tons of food, the United States wastes more than any other country. In 2018, the U.S. generated 63 million tons of food waste from commercial, institutional, and residential sectors, according to the EPA's 2018 Waste Food Report. That also includes food that's never eaten. Interestingly, it's estimated that with the increase in takeout, and food eaten at home during the 2020 pandemic, more food was wasted in 2020 and 2021.

TIP

Every sector has a role to play in reducing food waste. The goal of this book is to help you understand why it's important to reduce food waste and what part you can play by changing some of your personal food waste habits.

There's good and bad news. Over the years, it's been a challenge to track food waste. In 2018, the EPA revised its food measurement methodology to better capture where excess food goes through the food system. The bad news is that we wasted much more food in recent years compared to 1960 (63 million tons in 2018 compared to 12.2 million tons in 1960). The good news is that only 56 percent of the food waste generated in 2018 went to landfills, compared with 100 percent going to landfills in 1960.

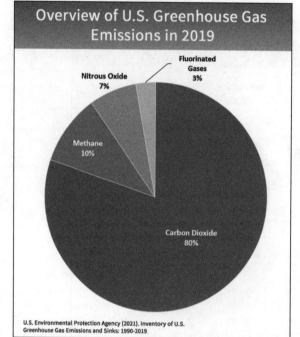

U.S. Environmental Protection Agency (2021). Inventory of U.S. Greenhouse Gas Emissions and Sinks: 1990-2019

FIGURE 2-2: Overview of GHG emissions in 2019.

Courtesy of U.S. Environmental Protection Agency

By 1980, the U.S. began working on diverting food waste from landfills and using it for energy (converting food waste to usable heat, electricity, or other fuel), to feed animals, or for composting. We've made progress in waste management, but we still have a way to go to reduce overgeneration of food waste.

REMEMBER

Food security is also a global issue. More than 800 million people in the world are hungry. You can find out more about donating food in Chapter 1.

GMOs AND YOU

Most of the foods we eat today were created through traditional breeding methods. Genetically modified organisms (GMOs) are widely misunderstood due to misinformation or lack of information. Images of "frankenfoods" are shown on the Internet giving an image of scary, unnatural interference with our food supply. A *genetically modified organism* refers to a precise form of plant breeding that uses *genetic engineering* (or bioengineering) to create a new seed or plant. Traditional plant breeding takes much more time than GE and makes it a difficult to make specific changes in the plant.

How does genetic engineering work? In simple terms, a scientist identifies a desirable trait in one plant or organism and transfers it to the plant or organism they want to improve.

Perhaps it's better to understand what GMOs aren't. There are currently only 10 approved GMOs in the U.S. market: field corn, canola, soy, alfalfa, sugar beets, Arctic apples, potato, squash, papaya, and cotton. About 70 percent of the GM crops produced in the U.S. are consumed by livestock animals. Some people worry that animals who have eaten the GM crops will produce food that's somehow genetically modified. That's not how it works. GMOs have never been found in the milk or meat of animals fed genetically modified feed.

Many experts say that implementing bioengineering in agriculture has the ability to help reduce the use of pesticides, reduce GHG emissions, and support overall agriculture-related environmental conservation. Plant scientists have discovered amazing ways to produce hardier plants that can withstand draught, inhibit pests, have shorter growth cycles, allow for more food to be grown on less land and erosion — all factors that reduce the overall carbon footprint.

From Farm to Fork: Understanding Where Your Food Comes From

Getting food to the grocery store is a complex and labor-intensive process involving several systems that begins with agricultural production and ends with food distribution. In the simplest terms, it involves four steps: production, processing, distribution, and consumer market.

The first step is producing or growing the food — that is, growing plants to feed animals producing meat, and growing grains, fruits, and vegetables for human food. Food production relies on growers, including farmers and ranchers, workers, and critical inputs (soil, sun, natural resources, and water). After harvest, plant or animal products must be stored properly and at proper temperatures, all the way through the process from storage to distribution centers to grocers (usually within only a few days) and then to homes.

When a seed is planted, it can take anywhere from three to six weeks to water and fertilize the crop and ensure that there are no issues with pests. When a fruit or vegetable crop is ready for harvest, it must be picked at the right stage of ripeness and the right time of day. Fruits and vegetables are examined for regularity in size and appearance. Fruits or vegetables that are less than perfect often get used for juices or other foods such as canned soups or fruit. Unfortunately, some imperfect produce will be left in the field too, mostly because consumers expect only "perfect" produce to be on supermarket shelves.

People have strong convictions about food and eating — whether it's discussions about which foods are best to eat, claims about what food can do for you, or how food may harm you.

Over the years, I've heard a lot of misinformation about how food is produced or grown. I've found farmers to be a great resource for learning more about where your food comes from. I've visited many farms across the United States and talked candidly with fruit and vegetable farmers, dairy farmers, and farmers who raise pigs and cattle. Overwhelmingly, I've found them to be good people who care about the land, the environment, their animals, their families, and their communities. They eat the food they grown and harvest, and they're proud to bring safe and nutritious food to the whole country.

Luckily, some farmers have taken to social media to share their stories so those who are removed from the land in which food is grown or produced can better understand the challenges and processes involved in bringing food to our supermarkets.

The following sections cover some common misconceptions.

Organic farming is superior

Farming methods are typically divided into two types: conventional and organic. Around the 1940s, the idea of organic farming began as a "non-chemical" way to farm without synthetic pesticides. According to the United States Department of Agriculture (USDA), *organic farming* is defined as "a production system that is managed to respond to site-specific conditions by integrating cultural, biological, and mechanical practices that foster cycling of resources, promote ecological balance, and conserve biodiversity."

The thing is, conventional farming has a lot of those same goals. Conventional farmers do some of the same practices to maintain soil health by planting cover crops, using natural fertilizers (animal manure), crop rotations, and animal grazing. They also use synthetic fertilizer since natural fertilizer can contribute to run-off issues. Many farms have complex manure management programs to protect water sources, limit runoff, and properly measure fertilizer ingredients for appropriate distribution.

Confusion often arises about pesticide use between the two farming methods. While certified organic is encouraged to control pests, weeds, and disease through physical or mechanical controls (tilling), biological, botanical, or synthetic substances are approved when the latter practices aren't sufficient. "Natural" pesticides are no safer than synthetic ones. The key to safe pesticide application is proper application according to product and industry instructions. In addition, the additional tilling for weed control can lead to loss of moisture, and wind and water erosion.

Technology and agriculture don't mix

Images of a man, clad in overalls and a straw hat, sitting on a green tractor may come to mind when you think "farming," but times have changed. Changes in weather patterns, draughts, land availability, and population growth are just a few reasons it's vital to be able to make the most of our arable land, human resources, and time.

The notion of high-tech tools for farming somehow makes people uneasy. Especially if you bring up bioengineering (see the nearby sidebar "GMOs and you"). Today's farmers are scientists. Almost all of them have bachelor's degrees in agricultural, like plant science, animal science, engineering, or *agronomy* (the science of soil management, crop production, and ecology).

They use technology both to benefit their own efforts and to benefit the planet. Sure, they still use tractors (women and people of all ages and races farm), but they also have a multitude of technological tools available, such as the following, to manage their land and improve crop yields:

>> Seeds that have been modified to tolerate drought or resist pests

>> Drones that fly over fields to check crops

>> Water and soil management systems that use sensors that report soil conditions, pH, and humidity in real time

>> Specialized software that analyzes the sensor data that can then determine whether the soil requires additional nutrients or water

>> Specialized farming equipment, including autonomous tractors and combines that allow farmers to plant and harvest more efficiently using GPS

Many of these tools are managed from a smartphone or tablet that the farmer takes with them on the tractor or as they view their field from their home or barn. They use software to analyze the data and help create crop management strategies. The utilization of technology will likely be an important component of regenerative and sustainable agriculture in years to come. Efforts are in motion to make this technology affordable and available to more farmers across the globe.

Innovations in technology can also enhance sustainability efforts in animal agriculture. I was amazed to see the technology employed when I visited the dairy research barn at Penn State University's animal science department. Each dairy cow is closely monitored with wearable sensors that provide information about their activity (a cow who isn't moving a lot may have an infection or other health issue), body temperature, and milk production so they can more efficiently and accurately monitor their health and welfare.

Eating less meat is better for the planet

Some people believe that eating less meat is the answer to reducing the toll that agriculture, as a whole, takes on the earth. That may sound like a simple solution, but it's not so simple.

A recent movement aims to replace meat with other forms of protein. As of now, it's hard to say what the final answers will be, but it'll likely be a combination of compromises. As previously mentioned, sustainability requires economic viability to be upheld. Critics are quick to point the finger at beef in particular, for producing excess methane (through burps primarily). They believe that ruminant animals like cows are key polluters when it comes to GHG. A lot of sources of data exist but no agreement on how the data is collected and what it means overall.

In contrast, some people believe that grazing animals can play a positive role in changing the climate. Proponents of grazing livestock argue that grazing affects soil carbon so livestock can actually be a potential tool to help reduce atmospheric carbon.

Perhaps this idea that reducing meat consumption can reduce GHG emission is part of the reasons livestock production has come under criticism. Concerns about animal welfare are often part of the discussion as well. If you've ever seen a horrifying video of a farm animal being poorly cared for, I'm here to reassure you that ranchers in the U.S. put animal welfare at the top of their priority list.

According to the Animal Agriculture Alliance, farm families take proper care for their animals very seriously. The Alliance helps support ranchers by providing species-specific animal care guidelines, from beef to poultry to eggs, pork, veal, and lamb. The U.S. meat packing industry is also regulated by the Humane Slaughter Act and is monitored during all operations to ensure compliance. Animal welfare expert Dr. Temple Grandin developed specific guidelines to reduce stress on the animals. In 1997, she partnered with the North American Meat Institute to develop an audit program (the Humane Handling Guidelines and Audit Guide) to ensure that food animals are treated humanely throughout all processes.

REMEMBER

There's a difference between animal welfare and animal rights. Treating livestock humanely isn't the same as treating it as human. Animal rights activists believe that animals shouldn't be used as food, clothing, or experimentation. Animal welfare proponents believe this is acceptable, as long as strict guidelines are in place to treat the animal humanely.

Not only is livestock in the United States raised humanely, but it's also raised with specific nutrition. Animals are fed specific formularies to preserve resources and to reduce unnecessary outputs. For instance, overfeeding can be harmful to both the animal and the environment.

Animals are raised to provide nutritious, affordable protein to your plate. As human science grew to understand that saturated fat in the diet may be linked to disease, animal scientists responded to lower the fat of livestock. By making modifications to animal feed, the final food product is lower in fat.

MEATLESS MONDAY: ENVIRONMENTALLY FRIENDLY OR VIRTUE SIGNALING?

You may have heard about "Meatless Monday." To the uninformed bystander, this movement sounds like a great way to encourage people to add more vegetables and whole grains to their diet while cutting back on meat consumption. However, saving the planet isn't that easy, and neither is healthy eating. In addition, it turns out that the Meatless Monday movement is backed by environmental activists whose goal is to encourage more people to omit animal products from their lifestyle. Around that time, the term *factory farm* was used to describe conventional animal agriculture systems. In fact, farms in the U.S. are family-owned, and while there are larger and smaller ones, they aren't "factories." Just like farmers, ranchers are using sustainable practices to maintain their herds and manage the health of their land.

What you choose to eat is your personal choice. There are many ways to plan out meals that sustain your body and health. In addition, there are social and cultural factors that influence your choices. However, simply omitting all animal products isn't a magic bullet to the complex environmental and social issues we face as a nation. In regard to farming and ranching methods, there's room for both conventional and organic practices. Farmers and ranchers are continually working to improve as they determine what best suits their land and local ecosystem.

With proper management and strategies for storing carbon, some theorize that a balanced use of land for livestock and crops going forward can work and is the most energy-efficient way to produce food.

Bringing It Home: Deciphering Package Icons and Labels

Food labels have never had more information on them, nor been more confusing. Food labels include a standardized Nutrition Facts Panel and list of ingredients that is regulated by the FDA. It also can include a lot of labeling or icons on the front of the package. Most of these front-of-package claims are not regulated and mostly serve as a marketing tactic.

Health claims are regulated, but other claims aren't. For instance, the term *natural* on a food label has no defined meaning nor is it regulated by the FDA. The term *plant-based* sometimes suggests that a product is improved because it's replaced meat with plants. There are too many unregulated and misleading terms to cover here but there are a few I want to highlight.

TECHNICAL STUFF

Green marketing is a form of eco-labeling that states a product is sustainably sourced, developed, or packaged. Companies are usually required to follow guidelines to make these claims, and this comes at a cost. Certification terms such as Sustainably Grown Certified, USDA Organic, and Demeter Biodynamic are well defined and verified by third-party organizations. However, don't be fooled by "greenwashing" label tactics. *Greenwashing* is a form of green marketing that makes false or unsupported claims to make the product appear more sustainable or healthy for the planet. Front of package labeling like "earth-friendly," "natural," or "eco-green" is simply a marketing ploy and has no defined meaning.

USDA Certified Organic

The organic label you see on products at the grocery store is a certification of the USDA Agricultural Marketing Service (see Figure 2-3). Food companies pay to use the label. The label, or seal, indicates that the food was produced through the approved methods as defined by the USDA. In terms of science, all food is organic, as it contains carbon matter. So what's all the fuss about?

The USDA defines organic as crops that haven't used synthetic pesticides, herbicides, or fertilizers and are free from any genetic engineering or ionizing radiation. (Keep in mind that organic crops can still be sprayed with approved natural pesticides. Just because a substance is natural, however, doesn't mean that it still can't be harmful.)

FIGURE 2-3:
USDA Organic seal used to certify food produced organically.

In terms of animals, organic meat is from livestock that is fed organic feed and raised without routine antibiotic use. The USDA Organic label sometimes adds to the costs of farming practices and the packaging of food products. This cost is also passed to the consumer, often resulting in higher prices than conventional products. But are they all-around better for you? Nutritionally, there's no significant difference in organic-certified food versus nonorganic-certified food. Organic farming isn't better or worse than conventional farming; it's simply a method of farming (see the earlier section "Organic farming is superior" for more).

TIP

Like the Certified Organic label, the Non-GMO Project Verified label is a paid labeling verification. This label can be misleading because products are often labeled, even though they wouldn't ever contain any ingredient that has a GM counterpart.

Free-from labeling

There's been a rise in "free-from" labeling on packaged foods over the past decade. This in part may be due to increases in food allergy and sensitivities, but it's often a marketing tactic. As consumers adopt various styles of diets, they may be looking to avoid certain ingredients. For example, a person with celiac disease needs to avoid gluten (although many consumers choose to avoid gluten for no medical reason).

Sometimes the free-from ingredient labeling is useful (such as when someone with an allergy needs to identify certain ingredients in foods). Other times, these labels are misleading. It's confusing when a label includes a free-from claim for an ingredient that wouldn't normally be in the food product anyway — for instance, when orange juice is labeled "dairy-free" or "GMO-free." Orange juice never contained either dairy or any genetically modified ingredients. The simple notion that a product is "free-from" also makes you think that it's somehow better, or that the ingredient it is free from is "bad" or was removed.

Some food labels are free from so many different things that it may make you wonder, what is it actually? With the trend for gluten-free and dairy-free diets, these claims continue to cover packages. Labels may also include GMO-free, vegan, plant-based, egg-free, or nut-free. Some are just ridiculous, such as gluten-free water or GMO-free gin. Most of these labels are added for marketing purposes and don't impact the health and safety of the food. But what do all of these free-from labels really mean?

>> **Gluten-free:** This voluntary labeling regulated by the FDA means that the food bearing the claim doesn't contain gluten or any gluten-containing grain.

>> **Dairy-free:** While the FDA doesn't allow false claims on packages, there's no regulatory definition for the term *dairy-free*. Ideally, a food with this label wouldn't contain any dairy products.

>> **GMO-free:** This is sometimes misleading when there's no GMO counterpart for the ingredient in question. For instance, it's one thing to compare GMO soybean to non-GM soy. But because there's no GM wheat, it makes no sense to label a wheat product "non-GMO."

>> **Egg-free:** Products containing eggs must be labeled "contains eggs," but there's no regulation for the *egg-free* claim.

>> **Nut-free:** This is also an unregulated package claim. While nuts may not be an ingredient in the product, this claim doesn't mean the product doesn't contain the allergen, or was not processed in a factory that processes nuts.

>> **Vegan:** While this term is clearly defined to mean a product doesn't contain any ingredients of animal origin (including honey and gelatin), it isn't regulated by the FDA.

TIP

The FDA requires companies to list ingredients on packaged foods and beverages. Certain foods or substances that cause common allergies have more specific labeling requirements. According to the Food Allergen Labeling and Consumer Protection Act of 2004, products containing any of the nine common food allergens — milk, egg, peanut, tree nuts, wheat, soy, sesame, fish, and shellfish — must be labeled. If you have a food allergy, you need to read labels carefully and avoid that food or ingredient. If in doubt, it's best to read the package ingredient list for the allergens. Consult with an allergen specialist to determine the various names of ingredients related to common allergens.

There are food allergies, and there are also food intolerances.

>> A food allergy occurs when the body's immune system reacts to certain foods by making antibodies (IgE), and this causes typical allergic symptoms (itching, rashes, hives, swollen lips or tongue, stomach pain, vomiting, diarrhea, wheezing, or trouble breathing).

>> A food intolerance can cause similar symptoms with digestion but doesn't cause the immune response. Lactose intolerance (the inability to digest lactose, the sugar in milk), celiac disease (an intolerance to gluten), and Crohn's disease (an inflammatory bowel disorder that often causes diarrhea) are all examples of food intolerance causes.

Unless you've been properly diagnosed by an allergist, there's no health reason to avoid common allergens. According to the Asthma and Allergy Foundation of America, a small fraction of adults and children (almost 10 percent) have a true food allergy.

So-called plant-based products

Unfortunately, science-based guidelines sometimes get skewed in translation. The current U.S. Dietary Guidelines for Americans (DGA) could be described as "plant-based," yet they're sometimes blamed for poor eating habits. These guidelines go through a thorough review process every five years and are science-based. The DGA recommends limiting saturated fat, sugars, and sodium. Beans, lentils, nuts, and seeds are part of the protein foods group. They include dairy and protein foods but emphasize vegetables, fruits, whole grains, and healthy fats.

However, sometimes, small bits of science-based information are used to market foods that may not really be worthy. "Plant-based" is another unregulated front of package label claim. You may see this term used offering the product a "health halo" or suggesting superiority over meat-based foods. For instance, we can say that potato chips and gummy bears are "plant-based," but this doesn't mean we should include them as part of our regular dietary plan. But that won't stop a food company from marketing those types of products to make them appear like a better choice. Read labels closely and think about what the food really is.

The term *plant-based* is sometimes used as a marketing term. In some cases, the term is made synonymous with vegan. When I refer to plant-based *eating*, I'm referring to adding more plant-based whole foods (grains, fruits, vegetables, nuts, legumes, and beans) to your plate, not eliminating all meat products.

Carbon footprint labels

Another up-and-coming trend is carbon footprint labeling and marketing.

Some emerging groups are promoting that you should lower your carbon footprint. But can carbon footprints really be calculated accurately? Supposed food carbon "calculators" and "quizzes" aren't verified or standardized. They're just biased efforts that assign an environmental footprint to foods, based on random assumptions and unproven methods.

At this point in time, there isn't any science-based formula that can accurately estimate the carbon footprint of each item in the food supply. In addition, we really don't know whether measuring the carbon footprint of different foods is going to matter, environmentally speaking.

Beef is estimated to emit the largest amount of GHG when compared to other animal proteins like pork, dairy, chicken, and farmed fish. It's estimated that about half of the emissions from beef are from methane. According to Our World in Data, chocolate and coffee also produce GHG emissions, right behind beef. Still, because beef is often equated with these larger GHG emissions, the beef industry is targeted as a potential way to reduce emissions. It may be a short-sighted solution.

REMEMBER

Every diet has an impact on the environment, as do all our actions. Food, however, also provides nutrition. It's only recently that the field of nutrition and the environment are more often considered together, rather than separately. Some scientists feel that the environmental footprint should be considered in the context of the nutritional footprint, however. It's highly likely that the healthiest diets (calorie moderate, low in saturated fat, high in fiber) are those that are both healthy for the body and the planet.

TECHNICAL STUFF

Carbon footprints are determined by measuring "carbon dioxide equivalents." This unit of measurement was adopted by the Intergovernmental Panel on Climate Change (IPCC). From here, there's some complicated math involved to quantify the GHG emissions of a product. In terms of say, beef, methane is the GHG; however, methane is a short-lived gas, and quantifying the methane produced by ruminant animals is a little bit tricky. Due to the difference in methane's shorter lifetime, carbon footprints of foods such as beef or lamb don't really reflect their long-term impact on temperature.

Chapter **3**

Getting Your Head in the Zero Waste Game

The benefits of zero waste cooking go beyond the obvious (less food wasted). You'll also save money, reduce your garbage at home, and feel better about adding less methane to landfills. You may even experience personal health benefits. You may find yourself eating more vegetables at home and ordering smaller portions when you dine out. In addition, your community can benefit from more food donated or otherwise available. Sounds like a win-win situation to me!

The first step to realizing all these benefits of zero waste cooking is to get your head in the game. This chapter helps you process the idea of zero waste and helps you kick-start your journey with some simple strategies that help you plan to use more and waste less.

You find out more about how to reuse food and ingredients in Part 2 and you can find inspiration from the recipes in Part 3.

Doing Your Homework: Analyzing Your Food Waste Habits

We've all thrown away food. Life gets busy, and sometimes we just go through our daily routine without a second thought. Still, you picked up this book because you're at least a little concerned about wasting food and its toll not only on your budget but also on the environment. It's perfectly okay to start small.

The first step to zero waste cooking is to think about what your current food waste habits look like. The following list helps send you in the right direction.

» Think about what is in your refrigerator and pantry right now — or heck, go look! Are there items shoved to the back that you forgot about? Do you have stockpiles of certain items, more than you're likely to use in the next few weeks?

» Think about how often you dine out. Do you order more than you need? Are you bringing leftovers home? Are you making good use of your leftovers or forgetting that they're in the fridge?

» Think about the types of foods you routinely have on your shopping list and bring home. Do you know what you're going to do with each item you buy? Do you commonly buy specialty items that you use for only one or two recipes? Are there food items that you often buy but don't finish before they expire?

» Think about how you decide what meals and snacks to prepare each week. Do you pick recipes that have ingredients in common so you have fewer items to buy? Do you consider what leftovers certain meals will provide for use later in the week?

» Think about your trips to the grocery store. Do you make a detailed grocery list before you go, or do you wing it when you get there, buying whatever sounds good in the moment?

» Think about how you store food items. Are you storing foods in a manner that preserves them longer? Do you utilize your freezer? Are you using reusable containers, or do you consistently buy, use, and throw away single-use items?

» Think about your cooking habits. Do you find cooking to be a chore? Do you try to save yourself some time and hassle by prepping batches of certain foods in advance?

» Think about how you determine whether a food item is still fresh or good to use. Do you decide whether to keep or pitch something solely by the date on the box, bag, or can? Are you open to eating or cooking with produce that's no longer picture perfect?

>> Think about what you put in your trash can. Does it fill up quickly with food packaging? Do you thrown away all food scraps, or do you compost?

Creating and implementing a plan for how you buy, use, and store food will help reduce what goes into your garbage can and, ultimately, the landfill.

REMEMBER

It's easy to think that the small changes you make aren't impacting the great big earth, but they can! Imagine if 20 percent of U.S. households — that's about 24 million households — adopted just a few of the strategies suggested in this book. I'd say that's impactful!

Keeping the Environment and Your Wallet in Mind

A lot of things may come to mind when you think about the environmental impact of your grocery shopping habits. You may think about how foods are packaged, whether they're grown organically or conventionally, and whether they're local or international. However, throwing away less of the food you buy likely has a greater impact. In addition, shopping only for what you need and wasting less food, saves you money.

Adopting more of a zero waste lifestyle requires you to ask yourself a few questions. For example, how are you going to use the food you buy? Are some of the foods on your list multipurpose items that you can use in multiple ways (such as fresh produce, rice, or canned beans; see Chapter 6)?

When shopping: Will I use this?

To reduce overall kitchen waste, you need to think differently when you shop for groceries. However, the simplest way to zero waste cooking is asking yourself this question when shopping: Will I use this?

Consider what you typically do with food each week. What do you often throw away? What did you buy that you didn't need?

When you put food into your grocery cart, you should know exactly what you plan to do with it. By making a mental note as you shop, you'll be sure to use what you buy. Why do I need this? How and when will I use it? If the answer to the last question is "I don't know" or "Probably not this week," then you may rethink the purchase, unless you intend to freeze it.

Fresh foods are more perishable than canned and frozen foods. Canned or frozen vegetables, fruits, legumes, fish, and meats help reduce food waste.

Become aware of what you've routinely pitched in the past. For instance, if you're always throwing away luncheon meat, maybe you need to buy just half a pound instead of a pound. In general, fresh fruits and vegetables get wasted most, followed by dairy products, breads, and meat.

Also, think about how you grocery shop. Do you go to the store weekly, biweekly, or monthly? Maybe you buy things in bulk and find you never get around to using it all. If so, consider freezing some of it in serving sizes that fit your family. If you buy two loaves of bread or two packs of English muffins, you can pop one in the freezer for the following week. Or maybe you need to reconsider your membership to that warehouse store, or shop with a friend and share the goods.

Check out Chapter 6 to dig deeper into your shopping habits and find some tips for planning and executing zero waste strategies for grocery shopping.

The thing is, you may not know it, but without an organized shopping plan, you'll be wasting food before you even get home. Whether it's wasting your money or food, the best strategy is to have a good plan for what you intend to do with everything you put into your physical or online shopping cart.

RETHINKING SINGLE-USE ITEMS

We are a society of convenience. We're often on the go, which makes single-use items very tempting. Putting sandwiches into plastic bags, packing water bottles for a soccer match, running into the grocery store and coming out with eight more plastic bags to add to your pile. I get it. Using single-use plastic items like these may seem easier, but there's a better way.

Tip: Although sometimes it makes sense to use a plastic sandwich bag, set some goals to use fewer single-use items. You may not be able to completely eliminate them, but it's a start. Whether you reduce them by 20 percent or 70 percent, all reducing has a positive impact. Here are some ideas:

- Instead of regularly using plastic forks and paper plates, consider melamine plates that you can wash, and purchase extra flatware from a secondhand store or reusable cutlery that's made from recyclable materials. Keep a set in your bag and forgo the plastic cutlery when you do takeout lunch with friends. While you're at it, consider replacing paper napkins with a set of cloth napkins that can be reused.

- Forgo the plastic straw and just sip your beverage from the glass. Or try stainless or silicone straws. Keep a set in your bag or car to use on the go.

- Rethink your coffee habits. Coffee on the go comes with a lot of single-use waste — the cup, the lid, the stirrer, the napkin, the cuff. Bring your own reusable cup when you can, or brew your cup at home.

  Note: Although brewing single-use coffee pods at home may be less wasteful than visiting a coffee house for coffee every day, they add waste, too. If your brand has a recycling program, use it. Or simply don't use the pods, or use them less often.

- Buy soda or other beverages in one large 2-liter or gallon and pour into reusable cups. Use refillable water bottles to take ice cold water with you. If you must buy some of those single-use plastic items, do so mindfully (for instance, you may want water bottles to prepare for a natural disaster when water supplies could be limited or unsafe). Otherwise, use your reusables.

- Keep reusable tote bags with you and make a sincere effort to get into the habit of using them when you go grocery shopping. Include an insulated bag so you can put food into if you're delayed. Look for reusable drawstring vegetable/produce bags (they also help keep produce fresh longer) instead of the plastic bags in the grocery store's produce section.

When storing: What's the best way to preserve my food?

Do you sometimes ponder how in the world your kitchen garbage gets so full so quickly? When you're on a zero waste journey, you'll want to rethink what you send into that kitchen can. Proper food storage is a key aspect of a zero waste kitchen. Find out more about how to store fresh produce, what you can freeze, and how to keep a pantry organized for zero waste in Chapters 4 and 5.

REMEMBER

How you store food can impact how quickly it ripens or maintains its overall quality. Because produce is perishable and one of the top wasted categories, it's important to store it properly to get the most from it. Fruits and veggies give off gases as they ripen, and some interact with each other. Simple changes, like keeping things that need to be used quickly on the counter or in the front of a refrigerator shelf, can help.

Because eating a balanced diet is important to health, I don't want to discourage you from keeping fresh produce or dairy products on hand. You just need a plan! And of course, mixing in some canned and frozen fruits and veggies works too.

Think of your refrigerator and freezer as important tools in zero waste cooking. Some appliances today are pretty savvy, so I encourage you to read the appliance manual or instructions (an unknown idea to my husband, but really, there are good tips in there!). Some foods that can be left on the counter or shelf will last longer in the refrigerator. Other foods that are refrigerated can be frozen for up to 6 months or, technically, indefinitely (but I don't recommend it since quality begins to subside after 3 months, and significantly after a year). So even when your best-laid meal plan gets a kink in it, know that you can always rely on your freezer to stash food until you have the time to prepare it.

Food shouldn't sit out for more than two hours without proper refrigeration or cooling.

REMEMBER

When cooking: How can I better use scraps and leftovers?

Once you're home, you need to know when and how you'll cook and store the food you purchased. You'll want to properly store the food you bought right away. (More on how to rethink your food storage habits in the next section.) As you plan for zero waste cooking, think about what you might cook early in the week that creates leftovers to use throughout the rest of the week. Ideally, many cooked leftovers can serve as a time-saving step for a new meal another day. For instance the leftover cooked pork from the Spice Rubbed Pork Tenderloin with Roasted Sliced Grapes can create the quick Pork Pita Pockets with Cucumber Cream later in the week for a quick lunch. Also, plan to use the more perishable fresh fruits and vegetables from your shopping haul first.

You'll find a lot of ideas in this book for using up leftovers and even food scraps. For example, the next time you bring home a rotisserie chicken for dinner, don't throw out the carcass. Instead, bag it up, save it in the fridge, and add any veggie scraps to it over the next few days. Then you can throw it all into a large pot of water and boil it down for stock to be used to flavor new dishes or add to soups and sauces. (Check out the Homemade Stock recipe in Chapter 10.)

Finding new recipes that make the most of your leftovers (see Part 3) is also going to help you reduce waste. You may have noticed that food seems to have gotten, well, bigger, over the years. I'm talking about those muffins as big as your head and half-pound dinner portions of pasta. It's sometimes just too much. When dining out, simply reducing the portions you eat can ultimately help reduce food waste (and bonus — help you maintain your health). Instead of cleaning your plate or sending leftover food back to the kitchen, you may come up with more creative ways to use that doggy bag, beyond just reheating it for lunch the next day.

You can even create cocktail garnishes out of some of your food waste or scraps. Parts from a zested lemon can become Sugared Citrus Peels, and the liquid from a can of chickpeas (aquafaba) can be whipped for a whiskey sour. Celebrating your zero waste goals at the end of the day with a refreshing mocktail or cocktail sounds like a good deal to me!

TIP

While you may not be able to reuse every scrap or spoiled food, some food waste can continue to work for you (feed a houseplant) or the planet (composting). Things that often go into the garbage (citrus peels, leafy greens, vegetable peels) can be turned into compost. (I cover what and how to compost in Chapter 4.) Other common items like coffee grounds can be sprinkled on house plants or over your garden to balance or nourish the soil (they may help repel garden pests, too).

Repeat after Me: Practice, not Perfection

Keep in mind as you work through your zero waste journey that it's about small steps and progress. Despite the title of this book, I don't expect you to be 100 percent waste-free. Zero waste cooking may be 20 percent waste cooking some days and 5 percent waste cooking others. That's okay! Nobody's perfect. Every little effort counts, and the goal is to move in the right direction of reducing, reusing, and recycling more often. Just do your best!

REMEMBER

Like any meaningful change in your behavior, zero waste cooking takes effort. You may sometimes buy food on a whim and not take time to store it properly, or ignore spoiling food in the refrigerator and throw out what smells the worst on garbage night. It may feel easier to do that rather than to perform weekly fridge checks, create a food waste plan for shopping, come up with a food storage plan, compost, and use up leftovers. However, like any positive change you make in your life, the rewards are almost always worth the effort. This book is here to help you establish eco-friendly behaviors even when you're busy.

REDUCE, REUSE, RECYCLE BEYOND YOUR KITCHEN

I'm sure you've heard the jingle — reduce, reuse, recycle. These are considered the "Three Rs of sustainability." Even if you're busy, you can work on a few things to get started on the zero waste journey. The main goal of this book is not only to encourage you to waste less food but also to get you to think about your role in household sustainability.

(continued)

(continued)

I know you can do your best to make a few easy changes in the ways you shop, use, and cook food and ingredients. However, you can also follow a few easy steps to take beyond the kitchen. Start small and begin working on a few ways to reduce all waste in general. Soon you'll find that using fewer single-use and more reusable items allows you to more easily manage a sustainable household.

- Invest in a good reusable water bottle or tumbler to keep your beverages cold or hot. Then use them exclusively. This may seem like a no brainer, but it's a great first step.

- Pack lunches for school or work in a reusable lunch box or bag instead of paper or plastic bags.

- If you use a car daily, keep an insulated bag with you. This can help save leftovers or other items for the trip home.

- Think twice when you wrap birthday or holiday presents. Consider reusing a gift bag or using a more biodegradable butcher paper.

- If possible, look for items that use sustainable packaging.

- Learn about the recycling and composting services in your area so you can recycle as much waste as possible.

- Choose glass or aluminum bottles and cans over plastic since they're more recycle-friendly.

2

Waste Not, Want Not in Your Kitchen

Discover how to take inventory of the food you have and stay organized.

Keep food budgets on track with planning and shopping tips.

Uncover ways to make the most of your food budget with balanced choices.

Streamline your storage and explore reusable options.

Implement zero waste meal planning strategies.

Chapter **4**

Setting Up Your Kitchen for Zero Waste Success

Before taking on any new challenge or establishing new habits, it's a good idea to look at where you are right now. Doing so gives you a way to evaluate the current situation and measure your progress. And moving toward zero waste is, as I've said before, about progress, not perfection.

Looking at how you shop for food, what you buy, how you prep and store it, and when and why you throw some foods out are all important factors when starting your zero waste journey. As you observe your current habits when it comes to tossing food, you'll be more mindful going forward. This won't just be more sustainable for the earth, but it'll save you money, making it more sustainable for your wallet, too.

In this chapter, I walk you through taking inventory of your kitchen pantry, countertop, refrigerator, and freezer with food safety in mind. This will allow you to more easily set up your kitchen workspace to waste less food and move forward in creating more sustainable and money-saving habits.

Taking Inventory of the Food in Your Kitchen

To start organizing your kitchen for zero waste, first note where and how you typically store food — that is, take inventory of what you keep in your kitchen pantry, and refrigerator, and on your countertops — and how much and how often you throw food out when it's gone bad.

Here are some common scenarios resulting in food that ends up unused or thrown away, along with some strategies to change the outcome.

» Dairy foods are often thrown out due to expiration. Keep an eye on the dates on these foods. You can also use sour milk for baking (see Chapter 20).

» Bread products get pitched too often due to their best-by dates, even though they show no sign of mold and aren't yet stale. Either freeze bread products, make bread crumbs, or use them up in another way.

» Instead of buying specialty condiments that you don't think you'll finish up — cocktail sauce, for example — keep the more-often-used ketchup on hand along with horseradish (which has a longer shelf life). Buy fewer bottled salad dressings and make your own vinaigrettes (see Chapter 11 for recipe ideas).

» Households change but shopping habits don't. Any time you have a significant change to your household or schedule, make sure you take inventory and note what you'll actually need before going shopping.

» Grand ideas fall flat. Yes, you truly intended to eat more veggies this week, but . . . It happens to more people than you think. Cooked vegetables last longer than fresh, so if you have fresh veggies that you know you won't be able to use over the next few days, sauté or roast them all up and then store them for later (or use them in one of the recipes in Part 3).

TIP

Consider a regular biweekly check of what's in your refrigerator and pantry. Check expiration dates and general freshness of perishables, and then create a plan to use them quickly. It's also a good idea to take a peek at your freezer once a month, see what may need to be defrosted and used, or perhaps plan some dinners with what you have there. See Chapter 5 for specific ideas about storing food fresh from the grocery or restaurant or after a home-cooked meal.

Finding out what's in your fridge and freezer

Alrighty, put this book down for a few minutes, grab a notepad, and go take a peek in your refrigerator. List what's in your refrigerator by section, as follows, then look to see whether the products have any dates stamped on them and note that, too.

>> Check the food on the door.

>> Inspect the top shelf and each of the other shelves.

>> Look into any drawers you have in your refrigerator (often for meats, cheese, and produce).

Consider further any food that is spoiling. Spoiled foods are items like yogurt or milk that are past the expiration date on the package and have developed mold or bacteria on them, have changed color or texture, or smell unpleasant. Ask yourself some questions: Why did I buy this food, and what did I intend to do with it?

TIP

Save these notes to refer to in Chapter 5, where you find out more about what to store where.

TIP

Your freezer is going to be your new best friend for holding onto items that otherwise won't keep in the refrigerator. Check out Chapter 5 for tips about freezing and storing. It's easy to forget what's in there. For now, open your freezer and do this:

>> When freezing food, always write the date (month, day, year) on the package.

>> If your freezer is jam packed, keep in mind that the appliance won't cool as efficiently if it's over packed. You might want to defrost something for dinner tonight.

>> If it is full, take everything out. Grab a cooler to hold the frozen items as you unload. Then put each item back in one by one, organizing items by category (fruits and veggies in one area, ice cream in another, frozen meats in another, and so on).

>> Consider making a list of the items so you have a general inventory.

Unpacking your pantry

It's easy to allow food to build up in your pantry. As you place new items onto a shelf, other items get pushed to the back. Doing a simple organizational pantry check a couple of times a month can help prevent food waste. Start by cleaning and getting everything reordered. Take everything out of your pantry and wipe the shelves clean. You may even consider using a shelf liner that you can wipe easily. Take a look at the items you pulled out. Are they foods you like? Did you forget you had them? Can you use them up this week?

TIP

Set aside what you won't use in the next two weeks, and then put everything else back on the shelves, keeping the following in mind.

>> Make a list of what you have on hand so you won't buy more of it until you use what's on the shelf.

>> Donate what you don't think you'll use to a local food pantry. Check in with your local facilities to inquire about their donation needs and schedules.

>> Maintain a "first in, first out" system. Check use-by dates and keep items with upcoming dates in the front. (See the later section "Cracking the Code: Deciphering What Product Dates Really Mean" for more on use-by dates).

>> Keep things in categories — for instance, all rice, grain, and pasta in one area; all canned tomato products in another; all canned beans and vegetables in a third area; and so on.

>> Consider using baskets, shelf extenders, or other organizational items that make seeing what you have easier. The more user-friendly your storage is, the more likely you'll maintain order.

>> Label items when needed. If you add dry grains or cookies or nuts to a reusable container, mark them with the date and contents.

TIP

You don't have to buy fancy new containers for kitchen organization. In fact, that just adds to the plastic in your home. Instead, think about things you already have that you can repurpose for pantry shelves — holiday cookie tins, small wire or wicker baskets, packaging containers, small wooden boxes. You can also wash and save plastic takeout containers and use them to store snack bars, herb and spice jars, or other small items. Or wash peanut butter jars and use as an airtight container to store crackers in.

Cruising your countertop

Some food items maintain better quality and freshness when stored at room temperature on your countertop. You may be storing items on your counter that would last even longer if stored elsewhere. On the other hand, you may be storing other items in your refrigerator that belong on your counter. Chapter 5 provides more detail, but here are a few ideas to help you begin to consider what foods you might need to move onto or off of your countertop.

» Bread should be stored at room temperature. If you don't use bread daily, keep an eye on your bread box to be sure there are no signs of mold. It will go stale more quickly if stored in the refrigerator. However, if you don't use it up within about 3 to 4 days, then store the remainder in the freezer.

» Tomatoes belong on the countertop. They ripen and develop more flavor there. Once you slice them, or if they become soft, then put them in the refrigerator.

» Citrus and apples can be left in a bowl on the counter, but they'll last longer in the refrigerator.

» Cucumbers can stay on your countertop, too. After you cut them, store the pieces on an upper refrigerator shelf where you can see them and won't forget about them (plus they won't get too chilled or mushy there).

» Peanut butter can be stored on the counter or a pantry shelf after opening.

» Bananas should be stored on the counter away from any other fruit or vegetable. Hang them on a fruit hanger to reduce bruising.

Cracking the Code: Deciphering What Product Dates Really Mean

When it comes to the kitchen, clean and tidy is the name of the game for best food safety practices. Storing and handling food properly helps avoid cross contamination. Keeping counters clean and washing your hands often is just good common sense — especially in the kitchen.

But what about those dates you see stamped on familiar items like yogurt, bread, rice, eggs, or hot dog buns? You may be surprised to learn that they don't mean what you think they do. Product dates are often confusing to consumers and unfortunately add to food waste. But they don't have to be.

REMEMBER

Food product dating serves two purposes, either to indicate peak quality or mark the production date. Unfortunately these labels add to food waste, since both retailers and consumers misinterpret them as food safety labels.

» An open date is a calendar date referring to when a product will be at peak flavor and quality but for the exception of infant formula, they are voluntary labels, not required by Federal Law. Examples of open dating are as follows:

• **Best if Used By** or **Use Before** labels indicate the best flavor and quality is by that date. Foods with this label are still safe to eat as long as they've been stored properly.

- **Use By** dates are recommendations for when to consume the product for peak quality. However, dates are not an indicator of the product's safety.

» *Closed dating* is a code of letters and/or numbers that manufacturers use to identify the date and time of production. Examples include

- **Sell By** dates are put there by the store to manage inventory. It is not a safety date.

- **Can codes** allow tracking of the products. This helps grocers rotate their stock and makes it easy to identify recalls. These dates refer to the date the product was canned.

Ever wonder what those bar codes mean on produce? These are the Product Look-Up (PLU) code or Universal Product Code (UPC). The PLUs are assigned by the International Federation for Produce Standards. It's a voluntary labeling system, but the same code is assigned all over the world.

Part of the reason packages are marked with dates and numbered codes is for traceability purposes, allowing manufacturers to know the date of production. The best-by labeling you see isn't for the purpose of food safety, nor is it a purchase-by date. The dates on many of these packages are put there by the store or manufacturer to indicate quality, not safety.

It's great to have best-by dates on perishables such as dairy foods. Grocery stores usually do a good job at shelving, but be sure to check the dates when you purchase yogurt, milk, or cheese. Many food experts and environmentalists have challenged this labeling system as a way to reduce food waste.

If using infant formula, you do want to honor the dates. Infant formula is the only product required by law to include use-by product dating. This is to ensure that the vitamins, minerals, and other nutrients aren't less than the quantity described on the label.

Store specials on meat are often marked on sale due to the upcoming expiration date. Supermarkets mark them as less expensive to move these to avoid food waste. However, those specials are money-saving buys that are great to take advantage of when you know you can prepare the meat tonight or tomorrow. In most cases, beef, veal, pork, or lamb is fine three to five days, and poultry within two days, *past* the sell-by date. If you plan on freezing it, the best plan is to freeze it the day you buy it, and use it the day you defrost it.

KEEPING IT CLEAN

It's so simple but so important — clean counters, clean cutting boards, clean knives and utensils, and clean hands! Washing your hands often when handling food — especially after handling raw meat, poultry, or seafood — is the number-one way to prevent food-borne illness. Wash your hands for 20 seconds, being sure to use soap all over (the inside and backs of your hand, your nails, and in between your fingers).

Here are a few other tips for keeping your kitchen clean and safe while prepping and cooking food, based on the CDC Four Steps to Food Safety:

- **Clean.** Germs can cause food poisoning, and they can survive and spread around your kitchen, so it's important to routinely clear and clean. Be sure all your counter-tops and cutting boards stay clean to prevent cross contamination. *Cross contami-nation* is when a food comes into contact with potential bacteria. Also, wash your produce before eating. Consider buying a produce brush for items like potatoes, squash, melons, and mushrooms.

- **Separate.** Use separate knives and cutting boards for produce, raw eggs, and raw meats. Clean knives and boards with hot soapy water in between uses. Never use a knife for one food then use it for another. When you grocery shop, keep raw meat, poultry, and seafood separate from other items, and store them separately in the refrigerator.

- **Cook.** When temperatures get high enough to kill germs, food is safe to eat. Use a thermometer to check.

- **Chill.** Store foods promptly after shopping (within 2 hours, but within 1 hour if the outdoor temperature is above 90 degrees). Your refrigerator should be set at 40 degrees. Thaw foods from the freezer in the refrigerator, never on the countertop.

Check out the USDA FoodKeeper app. It provides additional guidance on the safe handling, preparation, and storage of foods.

WARNING

Don't purchase canned food that is dented or bulging. Bulging indicates bacteria, and dents or damaged cans could be susceptible to bacteria. High acid foods such as canned tomatoes or fruit maintain their peak quality for up to 18 months. Canned meat or vegetables will last on the shelf for up to five years.

Even if a recipe recommends to "freeze up to 3 months," this is mostly for the purpose of flavor and quality. If you have a package of ground beef that you forgot about in your freezer, you can still use it to make Beef Chili (see Chapter 10) or another use. It may not provide the same flavor quality if it isn't sealed properly in the freezer (due to moisture loss), but it's nutritious and still safe to eat (as long as your freezer has held its temperature). When a food is frozen, it maintains the freshness and nutrition of the day it was frozen. So the sooner you freeze it from purchase date (peak quality) the better. Be sure to package tightly to avoid moisture loss and the formation of ice crystals.

Giving Back to the Earth: Creating a Composting Strategy

Sometimes you can't use all of your food scraps, or you have to throw away food because it wasn't refrigerated or stored properly and spoiled. Composting is a great way to make the most of food waste. With a little thought, you can come up with a strategy that works for you and the planet.

Some communities have curbside compost pickup. Others have drop-off services. If this is available in your area, consider signing up. The other option is to create your own compost at home.

Composting turns organic material like food into fertilizer that has a range of benefits. Once the material is decomposed, it can be added to soil to help keep it moist and provide plants with nutrition. The compost also serves as a happy habitat for friendly creatures like worms. And recycling food into compost is another way to reduce greenhouse gas emissions. Composting your food waste is an excellent way to keep it from going to landfills and can also boost your own garden. There are a lot of options.

Composting can be done both indoors and outdoors, and you can start simple or get complex with it. Either way, it requires both green and brown material. Fruit and vegetable scraps and coffee grounds from your kitchen are "green" as are grass clippings. Brown material includes items like eggshells, cardboard, newspaper, twigs, or fall leaves. The way you go about composting will depend on where you live, how much space you have, and how much time you want to invest.

TIP

You'll be more likely to remember to compost if you keep a small bin in your kitchen for scraps. You can place it on the counter near your prep area, under the sink, or near your garbage can. Some people switch their "recycling bin" into two sections — one for compost material, the other for recycling. If using a counter bin, keep a charcoal filter in it to eliminate odor. Or you can keep the bin in the freezer then pull it out and add to it when you're prepping a meal or cleaning out the refrigerator.

Ultimately, you'll need a compost bin outdoors where you can deposit the material and it can decompose further.

It's fine to randomly combine the food waste with other organic matter (leaves, grass clippings). This is called *cold composting.* This type of composting takes the least amount of effort, but requires more time (up to two years) to actually reach "compost" status (be completely decomposed into fertilizer).

Hot composting is a more managed process but produces usable fertilizer in less time. It's done by layering the brown and green material (it's best to alternate layers with a ratio of about four parts brown to one part green materials). You can use a small garbage can or buy a composter that can be easily tumbled. You'll want to turn over and mix the pile (either by hand with a shovel or pitchfork, or a turn of the composting tumbler) about once per week during warm months.

Chickens are natural composters. They'll eat just about any food scrap, fertilize the ground, then lay a quality source of protein! Hens generally lay about one egg a day, or at least four per week. Be sure to always wash eggs well from backyard chickens before using. (If you're interested in raising chickens of your own, check your local farmers supply shop and then pick up a copy of *Raising Chickens For Dummies.*)

» Saving money with environmentally friendly storage

» Making the most of your refrigerator-freezer

» Avoiding impulse buys and using up scraps

Chapter **5**

Storage Strategies to Help Reduce Your Personal Food Waste

In the United States, it's estimated that 31 percent of the food supply is lost or wasted from the retail and consumer levels. This chapter offers you some ideas for reducing food waste by properly storing your food. Whether it's food items in your refrigerator–freezer or on your shelves, proper storage can help your household waste less food.

Packaging is another food waste consideration, so I cover some considerations when choosing some foods based on the type of packaging. You'll also find a primer for reusable food storage options with tips for recycling items that you may already have to use as storage.

Making Smart Decisions for Your Pantry Storage

The number-one way to make it easier to waste less is to buy less. Still, nobody's perfect. We all occasionally forget our list, overbuy, or buy things we already have in the back of the pantry. Keeping your food organized creates less stress when you're looking for an ingredient and makes it easier to take inventory for your shopping list.

Once you're throwing away less food, you can think about how you can recycle some of the food or food scraps you end up with in your kitchen, and how packaging impacts landfills. You'll also start thinking about how to save and recycle common packaging that can then serve as future food storage. Things like pasta or jelly jars, and even plastic takeout containers, can be washed and reused to store leftovers or other food items. See Figure 5-1 for ideas.

ZERO WASTE FOOD STORAGE OPTIONS

FIGURE 5-1:
Reusable storage
options.

Illustration by Elizabeth Kurtzman

Choosing less packaging

Packaging accounts for one-third of municipal waste in the United States, according to the Environmental Protection Agency (EPA). One bonus of buying items in bulk, when possible, is less packaging. It's convenient to have a single-serve item for a lunch box, but all that plastic adds up. If you can, try reusable single-serving bowls with lids to transfer fruit or yogurt from a larger container.

Even if you can use less packaging, it's a win. Consider single-use items as a convenience, but not for everyday use. Once you get into the groove of portioning foods into reusable containers for lunch boxes or snacks, it'll become routine.

REMEMBER

Here are some other ways you can work toward using less packaging in your day-to-day routines:

>> Buy in bulk when possible.

>> Use a reusable water bottle and/or coffee mug.

>> Buy your produce loose or bring your own reusable produce bag to the market.

>> Choose brands that have less packaging or compostable packaging.

>> Don't forget your reusable grocery bags. When you do bring home plastic bags, reuse them to line waste cans or for other garbage.

>> Check out thrift shops to find used items instead of always buying new.

>> Choose a reusable lunch bag or bento box for work or school. Unlike a brown bag, these options easily hold a freezer pack to keep foods safe.

Repurposing containers

Having a variety of containers in a variety of sizes creates less landfill waste and keeps food safely stored. One way you can start accumulating varied containers is to save items that food comes in to use for future storage.

Have you ever had that moment where you remember something that your mom did and find yourself doing it? Well, that's my story with jars. I keep about six repurposed jars in multiple sizes in a kitchen drawer — every size from mini jam jars to larger tomato sauce jars. I use them for all sorts of things. You can store loose herbs in a small one, make overnight oats or a yogurt parfait in a 6-ounce size, or (my personal favorite) use one to shake the flour into gravy. You can also use a jelly jar for your homemade salad dressing, using it to shake or mix it and store it in the refrigerator.

Of course, be sure to wash the jars before you reuse them. You can wash glass jars and lids by hand, or they can go right onto the top rack of your dishwasher.

TIP

It's also useful to repurpose plastic containers. For instance, if you pick up some packaged luncheon meat that came in a lidded plastic container, wash and save the container to put fruit in or use for a sandwich or snacks.

My husband has a soft spot for chocolate-covered raisins from Costco, which come in a large, lidded plastic jar. We save the containers and use them to keep snack bars or cookies airtight, or in the utility room and garage to hold nuts, bolts, or bike tire tubes.

Ditching plastic bags for reusable options

Okay, I'm no hypocrite. Yes, I continue to use some zippered plastic bags for packing a sandwich or a bit of something else to snack on. However, I use much less of them these days thanks to reusable bags. You can find both cloth and silicone zipper bags to replace the plastic ones.

REMEMBER

You can also reuse plastic bags. For example, you can use a plastic food storage bag more than once to cut down on waste. You'll want to be sure the bag is well cleaned with soap and water after use (especially if it held raw meat). If you use a zippered plastic bag to store bakery bread in, you can easily just wipe it down and put it back into the bread box for the next time you need to keep a loaf fresh. Or if you use a snack bag to keep nuts in the car with you, refill the same bag again instead of pitching it.

PLASTIC SAFETY

There's disagreement about the safety of plastics in our food supply, but truly there is very little research about how plastics impact on human health. Across the food chain are all sorts of plastics. These products are made with hundreds, or even thousands, of different chemicals, much of which we know little about the long-term effects. Many products are labeled BPA-free; however, they're replaced with new chemicals (BPS and BPF), and there's disagreement about the health issues with BPA (from a toxicology standpoint, it may not always be the hazard it's perceived to be).

Some reports claim that BPA is a health hazard, while other research studies show that the exposure isn't enough to be hazardous. Like any change in our food supply, when something is removed, something else replaces its function. The important action is to mitigate your exposure (the dose makes the poison). We can't eliminate all risks, but we can limit them. Our bodies can handle the processing of chemicals (food is chemistry!), and in some cases, the "exposure" may be a parts per million situation.

The best strategy is to limit your use of plastic but don't worry about some exposure to it. Use a combination of glass and plastic, and limit single-use plastics. Use glass storage for any food that will be heated. Don't heat any type of plastic in the microwave (or leave a plastic water bottle in the sun) that's not clearly marked "safe for microwave and dishwasher." Remove your food from the takeout containers and reheat in a microwave-safe glass bowl or on a glass plate. Use a metal or glass baking dish for reheating in the oven.

Plastic storage containers are sometimes nice for times when you want to send a friend home with leftovers or give someone a dozen homemade cookies. When possible, switch them out for reusable glass containers. Glass is more sustainable and can be safely used in the microwave and to store hot foods. Scientists don't yet know everything about the long-term health impacts of plastics, but they do know that plastics are unstable by nature. For this reason, it's not recommended that you heat plastics, nor put oily or acidic foods into plastic containers.

REMEMBER

All plastics used in the United States go through rigorous testing and must be approved by the FDA. By the time a product is approved, it's been tested by scientists and toxicologists. While it may not be a perfect system, there is regulation. However, there are also gaps in knowledge about how plastics and food and beverages mix.

Keeping it airtight

Air accelerates how quickly a food can go bad. So your best bet is to store food in reusable containers with covers. This helps keep odors to a minimum and keeps food fresher longer.

Here are some foods that really benefit from an airtight container:

>> **Flour:** Keep flour in an airtight container. You can either put the whole bag into the container or transfer the flour to it.

>> **Sugar:** Sugar attracts moisture and can get clumpy. Keep in a sealed container. This is also useful to avoid attracting pests.

>> **Rice and dried beans:** These should also be sealed. Once you open a bag or box of rice, transfer it to an airtight container or place the whole package into one.

>> **Spices:** Spices will last longer in airtight jars, stored in a dark place. If you notice your garlic powder clumping, transfer it to a well-sealed jar.

>> **Dried fruit:** This will stay softer when sealed.

TIP

Bread that you aren't going to get through will be better off frozen than refrigerated. It will stale more quickly in the refrigerator.

Using reusable food coverings

Plastic wrap, waxed paper, and aluminum foil may be mainstays in a kitchen drawer, but there are several new products on the market that can help you use less of them.

Reusable wrappers made of waxed cotton can serve to take the place of plastic wrap to cover bowls, to wrap a sandwich, or to store a few other food items (refer to Figure 5-1). These sheets come in a variety of sizes and are coated with beeswax. Although they'll break down eventually, you can wash beeswax wrap sheets with soapy water and reuse them for likely up to a year, depending on how often you use them. When they're worn, you can add them to your compost pile, and they'll naturally degrade.

Considering shelf life: The first in, first out system

Keeping canned, boxed, and jarred food on the shelf using a first in, first out system is a great way to reduce waste. I don't know about you, but sometimes I might spend two whole minutes looking for the best-by date on a can! To alleviate that, consider marking the can or box with either the date you bought it or the best-by date, so it's easy to spot at a glance. Then sort things so that the items you bought most recently are in the back, and older items get used first.

REMEMBER Best-by and use-by dates are guideline dates for quality, not food safety. You can still open and use a product past those dates. See Chapter 4 for more information.

TIP Organize foods on your pantry shelves in a way that makes sense for you and your kitchen. You may want to group "like with like" (such as pasta with rice, farro, quinoa, and other grains) and jarred items on one shelf. Or maybe you'd like the peanut butter by the bread drawer and all the tomato products together, separate from other canned or jarred items. It's up to you, how you plan to use things, and your space!

You probably have seen those dream kitchen photos where everything is decanted into lovely clear glass jars. Well, beyond aesthetics, decanting dry items like flour, sugar, beans, rice, small pasta, or cereals can be a good idea to keep foods fresh and safe. Make sure the jars are clean and completely dry before using them. Date the jars when you decant something into them. You may choose a wider jar for items you want to scoop, like rice or flour, and a smaller one for sugar or oats (refer to Figure 5-1).

It's a good idea to transfer items like a bag of flour into its own glass, sealed container. Sometimes, flour and other dried goods can be infested with flour bugs (a small beetle that reproduces in grains). Transfer items like flour or cereal into clear containers so you'll know that they're in good shape and will stay fresher longer in a sealed container. You can upcycle large jars for this purpose or buy a few larger ones to store items like flour.

Consider a monthly pantry check, and if you find you have a few extra items on hand still in their original packaging, gather these to donate to a local food bank. Food insecurity is a federal measure of a household's ability to provide enough food for every person in the household. It's an issue that impacts about 40 million people in the United States, about 13 million of them children. You can help by donating your excess food, volunteering at a food pantry, or donating to your local network. To find a food bank near you, check out Feeding American `www.feedingamerica.org/find-your-local-foodbank`.

Using Your Fridge and Freezer Efficiently

Proper food storage can really help reduce food waste. Using your refrigerator and freezer efficiently helps preserve both the safety and quality of food. Food at room temperature can double the growth of bacteria that causes foodborne illness every 20 minutes! The goal is to store food properly and keep the appliance at the proper temperature.

A 2019 study showed that the average American may not really be using their refrigerator properly. The study showed that while people planned to eat all the meat and vegetables in their refrigerator, they generally finished only about half. The intentions were good, but they didn't meet their own expectations. Overall, the study found that people are concerned about food safety and quality, and this drives the decisions to discard foods. They also found that how often consumers cleaned their refrigerator and how they grocery shopped affected the utilization of their appliance.

Learning how to use your appliance properly helps you meal plan, which can save you money. Do a thermostat check on occasion and check your temperature settings. Put foods that require refrigeration directly into the fridge after shopping or after dinner or prep. Be on the alert every week for spoiled food hidden in a drawer or at the back of your refrigerator.

Like the best-by dates (see Chapter 4), some guidelines for how long you can store a cooked food in your refrigerator is up for debate. Freezing a food keeps it safe indefinitely, although quality will be impacted. Not only will the taste and texture change after a year of being in the freezer, but nutrients may also be lost.

Some brands may recommend refrigeration, but generally, peanut butter can be kept on the pantry shelf for up to 3 months. After it's been open for 3 months, store it in the refrigerator for up to 9 months, but it'll be harder to spread.

Cool rules for you and your appliance

Different parts of your refrigerator and freezer are made to hold things at slightly different temperatures. Appliances also have a "star rating" that lets you know how long a food can be frozen. Check your appliance manual for storage recommendations specific to your make and model, and then also check any instructions on food packages about freezing or refrigerating. Many packages often include storage instructions on the label to help you make the most of them.

Your refrigerator should maintain a temperature of 40 degrees, and the freezer should be at 0. You may consider buying an inexpensive appliance thermometer to check the temperature calibration of your appliance periodically. Various spots within your fridge are going to be slightly different temps. The doors and top shelf are the warmest, and lower shelves and drawers are the coolest. Also, an over-stuffed appliance won't cool properly.

Be sure that foods that require refrigeration don't sit out at room temperature for more than two hours. After two hours, bacteria multiply rapidly and put you at risk for foodborne illness.

Treat your refrigerator like you would a garden. Tend to it daily and do a thorough check weekly. Move things that need to be used to the front of shelves. In the meat and cheese drawer, set cheeses with earlier dates up front to cue you to grab them. Review all the ingredients that you have on hand in the fridge and think about what you can cook over the next day or two to use them up. You may even want to keep a bin in the fridge with the note "use by Thursday" or another cue. Use the ready-to-eat foods like deli meats, cheese, precooked chicken, or precut veggies in your refrigerator quickly. Check those foods regularly for spoilage.

Sometimes you want to meal plan based on "using stuff up" instead of "buying more" food or ingredients. Check what's in your freezer and defrost it for a meal this week instead of buying more food.

Optimizing your fridge's storage zones

To get the most out of your appliance storage, avoid overpacking it. Cold air must be able to circulate around the foods to properly chill. Be sure to keep it clean, wiping down shelves and doors periodically.

Finding containers that stack can help with efficient storage of leftovers or ingredients in your refrigerator and freezer.

Shelves

The top shelf is often the warmest part of the fridge, so it's best for ready-to-eat foods like jarred sauces or salsas or other items that don't require cooking. Cooked meats or leftovers can be stored there, too (or the shelf below), in covered airtight containers.

Milk and dairy products should go on a middle shelf.

The bottom shelf is the best place to store raw meat or fish because it's the coldest. And by placing on the bottom shelf, you're assured any leaks won't contaminate other food.

TIP

Be sure to put refrigerated items away quickly when you return from grocery shopping. Unless you're prepping for a hurricane or blizzard, buy dairy products based on what you know you'll consume.

Door and drawers

The door is a great place for condiments, eggs, butter, or jams and jellies. It's also a nice space for beverages.

Drawers are best used for produce. They often have humidity controls that help keep veggies crisper and help them last longer.

Some vegetables enjoy high humidity, which is what those "humidity drawers" are all about. Most refrigerator models have a lever that controls the humidity from high to low. Stash your veggies that enjoy more moisture (greens, broccoli, cauliflower, carrots, and herbs) into a drawer set at high humidity. Place fruit, mushrooms, zucchini, and peppers into the other drawer set at low humidity.

TIP

To keep potatoes from sprouting, add an apple to the bag. Many fruits give off natural gases as they ripen. If placed near each other, they'll cause other produce to ripen more quickly. Store bananas, apples, and tomatoes by themselves, and don't store potatoes with onions. Potatoes and onions should be stored separately in a cool, dark space. Citrus and apples are hardier and can live in the bin together (they can also be stored on the counter).

However, it's easy to forget what's in the bottom of the drawer, only to later find a mushy mess. To avoid this, don't pack drawers too full, and check it out every couple of days. You can add extra clear bins or drawers to your refrigerator to help keep food organized, and place items in sight that need to be used to help reduce waste. For example, consider keeping the fruit that needs to be eaten more quickly (such as peaches or berries) in plain sight on a shelf.

Tomatoes belong on the counter, not in the refrigerator. They'll last longer in the refrigerator, but they can get mealy. If you aren't going to use them quickly enough, stash them in the fridge.

You can also look for cloth produce bags to store your vegetables in. These reusable bags are washable and allow the vegetables to breath while keeping ethylene out. You can take these bags to the grocery store or farmers' market, too.

Additional tips for storing fruits and veggies

Once you cut into a fruit or vegetable, you need to refrigerate it to slow the growth of bacteria.

Here are a few more tips on how to store fruits and vegetables so they keep longer.

>> Some fruits (like bananas and apples) emit gases that hasten the ripening process. Don't store other fruits with your bananas on the counter.

>> Store fruits and vegetables in separate bins in the refrigerator.

>> Citrus can be left in a bowl on the counter, but it will last longer in the refrigerator. Same goes for apples (but store them in a separate bowl).

>> Salad greens need moisture. Wash your lettuce and dry it after you buy it then store it in the crisper drawer wrapped in a damp paper towel. You can put it directly into a clean drawer, or you can put it into a separate container.

>> Unless you plan to use prewashed bagged lettuce the day you buy it, you should open it and place a paper towel into the bag. Check the paper towel every day to see whether it's soaked, in which case, exchange it for a dry one.

>> You can perk up wilting or drying produce with cold water. If your carrots look dry or your broccoli and asparagus look limp, place them into a bowl of ice water to refresh them before using.

>> Onions, shallots, and garlic should be stored in a cool, dark place. You may want to keep a small basket or bin in your pantry cupboard for these items. Once cut, store onions in the refrigerator in an airtight container.

>> Transfer some items to the freezer if you know you won't be using them quickly enough. You can chop half an onion, place in a small reusable bag or container, and freeze for up to three months. You can also freeze slices of citrus then pop them into your water at a later date.

>> Cucumbers don't like plastic bags. Store them on an upper shelf in the fridge (warmer and less humid). Be sure to dry off after washing, before storing. Once cut, wrap in a paper towel or a reusable produce bag in the refrigerator.

>> Apples naturally create a waxy substance on the skin as a protectant. Some apple processors spray a very thin wax over the fruit so it'll store longer before shipping. This wax is completely safe for human consumption, although you always want to wash all produce.

REMEMBER

Some fruits and vegetables shouldn't be kept in the refrigerator. These include tomatoes, onions, garlic, avocadoes, butternut or acorn squash, and potatoes (store separately).

Knowing what freezes well

The freezer really is a food waste hero. You can freeze a variety of raw or cooked food to preserve it and avoid waste. Essentially, any food can be frozen indefinitely from a food safety standpoint. Wrap foods in an airtight manner and the items will retain quality for up to 3 months, unless noted otherwise.

>> You may not think about freezing things like cooked rice, pasta, or lentils, but you can! Store cooked lentils or grains in the freezer for 3 to 6 months. Leftover cooked pasta dishes in a sauce work best.

>> No time for baking banana muffins? Pop those browning bananas right into the freezer, skin on. You can also mash and freeze them in a reusable airtight bag. These will be suitable for baking or smoothies.

>> Nuts can be frozen to prolong their shelf life. High in fat, nuts can go rancid quickly. Freeze raw nuts you may have on hand for baking or cooking.

>> Butter can be frozen for up to 9 months (or up to 5 months for unsalted butter). Keep sticks in their original wrappers, then wrap tightly in foil or a reusable air-tight freezer bag.

>> Grated cheese can also be frozen, so if you take advantage of a buy-one-get-one sale, slip one into the freezer for later use.

>> Avocados can be pureed or mashed and then frozen. To prevent browning, add 1 tablespoon of lime or lemon juice to them and seal in an airtight container.

» You can even freeze a bag of fresh spinach if you find that you didn't get to it.

» Freeze other vegetables that may be starting to wilt. Even if you simply put them into an airtight container or reusable bag and just pop them into the freezer, they can be used in soups and stews.

» Bacon slices can be cooked and then frozen for up to 6 months to make it easy to pull together a breakfast sandwich that needs only two slices of bacon.

» Did someone pick up an extra half gallon of milk you didn't need? Freeze it. You'll want to open it and pour about a cup out before freezing (or you can transfer the milk to glass jars) since it will expand when frozen. It may get a little too grainy for drinking but will still work well for cooking and baking when defrosted.

» If you opened a can of tomato paste and needed only 2 spoons of it, you can freeze the rest. Transfer it into an airtight reusable silicone bag. Or freeze in an ice tray (each cube is equivalent to about 2 tablespoons) then once frozen, place cube into an airtight bag or container.

REMEMBER

Food will stay safe for a long time in the freezer. Freeze perishable foods like bread, berries, cheese, or meat that you know you won't use in time. Freeze items that you may buy in bulk for future use.

Reusable freezer-safe bags and containers

Silicone bags come in multiple sizes and have an airtight closure and are great for storing leftovers in or to freeze meat or vegetables. Cloth or canvas bags have an actual zipper and are nice for packing a dry snack (like nuts, pretzels, trail mix, or dry cereal) to go. Silicone bags work better for wet snacks, such as fresh fruit slices or moist cookies or muffins.

Knowing how long to keep what

Chapter 4 talks about the limitations of best-by and use-by dates. Shelf life varies in foods that are stored differently. Use your senses to determine whether something is safe to eat. If a food that was stored properly looks and smells good, it probably is.

Perishables, such as dairy, meat, eggs, and produce, obviously have a shorter shelf life than some other processed and packaged foods.

The term "processed" is often met with distain. Items such as plain frozen fruits and vegetables or canned fruits and vegetables are considered "minimally processed food." Essentially any food that isn't raw has been processed in some way.

Consider making one day a week an "empty the refrigerator" day or a "cook from the freezer" day. This is especially helpful after a holiday or special occasion when you may have a lot of leftovers or leftover ingredients that didn't get used.

Don't forget about those leftovers or that doggie bag you brought home from a restaurant. Be sure to refrigerate them right away and keep them upfront in your refrigerator. Consider keeping a special shelf space just for leftovers so you can grab them regularly. Think of leftovers as a night off for cooking or a head start to a meal that you create from something that's already prepped and cooked.

What not to freeze

Some foods aren't a great fit for the freezer. Foods with a high water content like cucumbers, citrus, zucchini, or watermelon don't freeze well. Refrigerate these foods or use them up, and skip the freezer:

- » Eggs or egg whites
- » Cream-based soups
- » Cucumbers, zucchini, celery, cabbage, and lettuce
- » Soft cheese likes cottage cheese, goat cheese, and cream cheese
- » Citrus, watermelon
- » Mayonnaise, yogurt, or sour cream

REGROW YOUR FOOD

Place three toothpicks into the sides of an avocado pit to hold it on top of a glass or jar. Fill a jar with water, and place the pit, bottom side down, on top of the jar. To identify the bottom of the pit, look for a flatter end. The top is sometimes pointier. The water should be just touching the pit. Place it on a warm windowsill and change the water weekly. In about 3 to 4 weeks, you'll see roots start and a plant that springs up from the top. When the plant is 6 to 8 inches tall, you can transfer it into a 12-inch pot of soil, ensuring not to cover the whole pit. Avocado plants grow only in warmer climates and

(continued)

(continued)

need space to grow. They take five or more years to produce fruit, so it may be unlikely that you'll get fruit, but it will be fun to grow a plant!

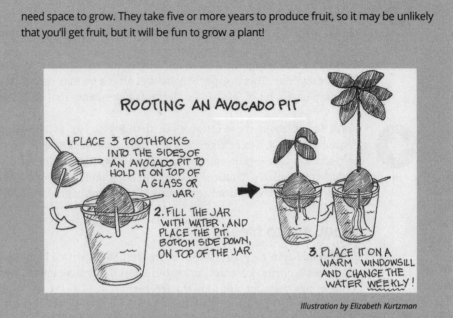

ROOTING AN AVOCADO PIT

1. PLACE 3 TOOTHPICKS INTO THE SIDES OF AN AVOCADO PIT TO HOLD IT ON TOP OF A GLASS OR JAR.

2. FILL THE JAR WITH WATER, AND PLACE THE PIT, BOTTOM SIDE DOWN, ON TOP OF THE JAR.

3. PLACE IT ON A WARM WINDOWSILL AND CHANGE THE WATER WEEKLY!

Illustration by Elizabeth Kurtzman

A sprouted potato can be put into a pot of dirt to grow a potato plant. Or you can grow it avocado-style and place it into a jar of water, eye down. Once you have a lot of roots, transfer to a pot of soil.

Onions, leeks, scallions, and garlic can all be sprouted in water as well. Take a small part of the bulb base with roots attached and place into a glass of water. Change the water every few days until the onion sprouts. Scallions will sprout a clump, while onions will sprout one bulb per bulb.

Celery can also root. Just cut the bottom off a cluster and place into a small shallow bowl with water. Place in a sunny spot and watch leaves sprout in about a week. You can do the same with a fennel bulb.

Carrot, turnip, and beet tops will also regrow. Cut the top off and place into a shallow bowl of water. New greens will sprout from the top. You can use the greens, or you can allow roots to grow then transplant to soil.

If you buy a head of lettuce with some roots intact, you can cut the base off and put that in water to sprout new leaves as well. You can even grow more lettuce or cabbage from a single leaf. Place the leaf in a shallow bowl of water and watch roots grow. Then transplant to soil.

When you buy a bunch of herbs you don't get through, instead of drying them or freezing them, you can root them. Place a stem of mint or basil into a glass of water. Once you have a nice clump of roots, transfer to a small pot of soil and keep it on a sunny windowsill.

Buy Less, Store It Right, and Use It All

This chapter provides some storage strategies, but keep in mind that proper food storage is part of the continuum of food procurement (when and what food you decide to buy) and processing (how you store it when you get it home and after you've cooked it). When you don't overbuy, you'll likely find more ways to consume what you have on hand and you have less to store.

REMEMBER

Repeat after me: Buying less is the number-one way to prevent food waste at home. Storing it properly once it's home helps it last longer and reduces overall waste.

Making the most of what you buy and cook

Chapter 6 provides some examples of how making the most of your grocery list and meal planning can help reduce food waste. Once you have the food you need at home, the next step is to ensure proper storage so you can enjoy the foods when you're ready to eat them.

>> You may simply place some foods in a bowl on the counter, on a pantry or cabinet shelf, or in the refrigerator or freezer.

>> You may place some items (like cheese or lunch meat) into an airtight container to keep them longer. Or you may cut vegetables into ready-to-eat snack sticks or cut a melon and store it so it's easier to eat.

>> You may portion meat or poultry into separate freezer bags in portions that suit your household. Keeping them packaged in an airtight way will prevent "freezer burn" and result in a better product when you defrost them to use.

Proper storage includes some maintenance checks through the week or month to ensure that your containers remain airtight, taking inventory of pantry and freezer shelves to see what needs to be used. Be sure to consider the information in this chapter when refrigerating foods.

Storing the trimmings

You may just throw out your broccoli stems, cucumber peels, or lemon rinds without a second thought, but some of those scraps can be useful. If you don't have time to do anything with scraps when you produce them, that's okay. Store them for later to add to a stir-fry or infuse flavor into plain water, help garnish a cocktail, flavor a soup stock, or even nourish your plants. Every little bit you prevent from going into your garbage can is a little bit less in the landfill.

Here are some tips for storing food scraps:

» Store citrus peels in an airtight bag in the freezer to flavor water, a cocktail, or other beverage or to make the Sugared Citrus Peel Garnish in Chapter 17.

» If your recipe calls for lemon juice, zest the lemon first and save the zest in a freezer bag for future use. A little zest on veggies or in a pasta dish can really elevate the flavor.

» Store pickle juice right in the jar after you've eaten all the pickles. Use the brine from the jar to flavor a sauce or soup. Add it to a bean dip for a little zesty kick. (And some people swear by drinking it as a recovery drink after running a marathon.) Or use the pickle juice as part of a marinade.

» Save leek or green onion tops in an airtight bag or container in the refrigerator for up to a week. Then clean and finely chop them; sauté then add eggs for a delicious onion (or leek) and egg scramble.

» If you're having broccoli but want only the florets for now, slice off the stems and save them in an airtight container. You can slice them within a day or two to enjoy with a favorite dip or you can dice them and freeze to add to soups later.

» When you have no time or can't think of a use for your scraps, compost them (or simply freshen your garbage disposal with citrus rinds and peels).

Chapter **6**

Managing Your Zero Waste Grocery Budget and Staying Healthy

The notion of managing a grocery list and budget may sound overwhelming, but have no fear — it's not the focus of zero waste cooking. Meal planning is simply one strategy that may work for you. You don't have to plan meals weekly or every day of the year. Planning out the food you bring into the home, however, can save you money and help you waste less. Instead of thinking of "planning" as a chore, think of it as a way to save money for those new shoes or that new computer you've been checking out!

REMEMBER

If you want to waste less food, you have to think about it. Any goal in your life works this way. It takes some time in thought, and then those thoughts have to turn into action. Reducing your food waste requires smart grocery shopping and learning how to use the same ingredients in a variety of ways.

This chapter introduces you to the grocery list step in meal planning (see Chapter 7 for more insight into how your weekly groceries turn into meals or snacks that use common ingredients, and it even offers you some sample meal plans). Meal planning begins with knowing what you already have on hand, then deciding what you'll cook or eat through the week, then creating a grocery list to reflect all of that. This chapter also walks you through creating (and sharing, if you want) a weekly, biweekly, or monthly grocery list so you can make sure your kitchen is stocked with just what you need. Finally, to ease any fears or misconceptions you may have about some foods or food groups, this chapter breaks down their nutrition value and provides easy ways to use each one with a zero waste mindset, while you make choices that are right for your health and budget.

Meal Planning Made Easy

Who doesn't love easy? There's no need to be intimidated by the idea of meal planning. That's why I want it to be made easy. Life can be unpredictable at times, and even the best-laid plan isn't going to work some days. I like to plan with open options. Sure, it's a plan, but it's not carved in marble — it's flexible!

Meal planning may be more detailed one week and less detailed another day or week — and that's okay. It has to work around your life, not the other way around.

Key parts of meal planning include deciding on what you want (or like) to eat (and choosing some recipes to help guide you — such as all the delicious options in Part 3), shopping for the ingredients you need, and then prepping and cooking the meals. You don't always have to prep things ahead or batch cook items, but sometimes it may help save you time and lead to less food waste.

Consulting your calendar: Determining when and what to eat at home

Each week may be different, as your schedule changes. Think about how much time you'll have and what activities you have going on each week to determine how many meals you'll actually be home to cook.

Then consider a weekly grocery plan based on the week's schedule. You can shop less often, but if you plan only one week at a time, you may find it easier to buy what you need, use it that week for meals, and then better plan the following week's grocery list. On the other hand, if weekly shopping doesn't fit your schedule, do what does.

Once you know how many meals you'll eat at home in a given week, then you need to create a zero waste grocery list that reflects the ingredients your household will eat! Otherwise, you'll be wasting money on unused or spoiled food. Take a look at the recipes you'd like to cook over the week, and check your pantry before you make the shopping list.

Considering the ingredients already in your kitchen

Maybe you've already begun organizing your zero waste kitchen by examining your pantry and thinking about your shopping habits (or see Chapter 4 for details on how to get started). When shopping for zero waste, it's important to see what you already have before you make your list. For example, maybe you have some frozen chicken you can defrost, some rice, and a can of artichokes — great! You can make Chicken with Rice and Artichokes using the Chicken with Orzo, Artichokes, and Zucchini recipe in Chapter 13.

TIP

Wait, what? How can you make that dish if you don't have orzo or zucchini, you ask? That's the benefit of zero waste cooking and the recipes in this book. You can easily swap things in or out. On the other hand, if you want to make the recipe as is, you'll add orzo and zucchini to your shopping list and won't overbuy other ingredients.

Now that you've checked out what you already have in your kitchen, it's time to make a shopping list of ingredients and food items needed to make the recipes or meals you're planning.

Making a solid grocery list and sticking to it

Making a grocery list isn't brain surgery, but sometimes you may forget to do it. Perhaps you need only a few items and think, "I can remember what I need." Sometimes that works. Sometimes it doesn't, and you either forget an ingredient or end up spending an extra 50 bucks on impulse buys. Not only can impulse buys cost you, but they can also go to waste if you have no plan for them, or you just end up with more food than your family can eat that week or two.

TIP

You may consider keeping a running list posted on your cabinet, adding items to it as you need. If more than one person in your household does the grocery shopping, perhaps you can share a digital list with each other using an app like Mealime or AnyList. Grocery apps can help you keep track of your shopping list, share it with others in the household, and even hold your favorite recipes, making planning for the week easier to track. I find that I sometimes write a list on paper and then forget it, but I always have my phone with me. The apps help you stay organized. Or another idea is to take a photo of your refrigerator or pantry to help you see what you have while you're at the store so you don't buy yet another bottle of mustard or jar of pickles.

TIP

Here are a couple of other tips for making your grocery list:

>> Once you make your list, stick to it. A list helps you reason with yourself when you think about buying something that looks good but you won't have time to make this week.

>> Break up your list into pantry staples, fresh and frozen food, and then things you'll need weekly versus those you need to buy less often. Depending on the size of your household and your budget, the types of ingredients within each group can fluctuate.

Pantry staples: Keeping basic ingredients on hand

Zero waste meal planning is much easier when you routinely keep a few staples on your shelf or in your freezer. These items can help you round out meals with fresh ingredients or create simple zero waste pantry meals.

These basic items are common ingredients for cooking and baking. Most of them will be shelf stable, with some needing refrigeration after opening. Everyone's cooking style and cultural preferences are different; this is just a suggested guide.

>> **Oils and vinegars:** I like to keep a neutral oil (such as soybean or canola) on the shelf for baking and an olive oil for cooking and salads. I like to keep at least two vinegars on hand as well for salad dressings and marinades. There are so many vinegars to choose from — apple cider, red wine, rice wine, balsamic, as well as flavor-infused vinegars.

>> **Canned foods:** Tuna, salmon, chicken, tomato puree, diced tomatoes, an assortment of canned beans, corn, or other vegetable, as well as canned fruit. A container of stock is also a handy item.

>> **Grains:** A variety of pasta and other noodles, rice, farro, barley, quinoa, crackers, bread crumbs or panko, cereal, and oats.

>> **Spices and herbs:** A few staple spices are garlic powder, chili powder, curry powder, cumin, paprika, red pepper, black pepper, and cinnamon. Dried herbs may include basil, oregano, thyme, rosemary, Herbs de Provence, and any other dried herb or spice blends that you prefer. Check out the nearby sidebar "Planting an herb garden to add flavor."

>> **Baking products:** Flour, white sugar, brown sugar, honey, baking powder, baking soda, salt, vanilla extract (and other extracts if desired), dried fruit, and chocolate chips.

>> **Frozen items:** Peas, shrimp, fish, chicken breasts, frozen fruit, vegetables, and pre-cooked grains.

>> **Condiments:** Mustard, ketchup, pickles, olives, capers, soy sauce, Worcestershire sauce, salsa, hot sauce, and other sauces.

>> **Other shelved items:** Peanut butter and other shelf-stable butters, fruit jam, and nuts.

Perishable items: Buying for the week to avoid food waste

Perishable items are things you may need to pick up weekly. Some examples include:

>> Milk, cream, yogurt, and cheese

>> Cuts of meat that you'll either cook that week or freeze

>> Eggs

>> Seasonal fruits and vegetables

PLANTING AN HERB GARDEN TO ADD FLAVOR

Fresh herbs really do make food more appealing to both the eyes and the taste buds. Herbs can be pricey, so planting a few pots of your own will save you money. Snipping just what you need from a plant avoids waste. Plus, they'll be available, right at your fingertips, saving you a trip to the store.

You can grow herbs outdoors during the summer or all year depending on where you live. Or you can keep an indoor garden, as long as you have a sunny window. Parsley and mint are especially hardy and easy to grow. Basil is wonderful, but it can take a little more care.

Rather than start herbs from seed, I recommend getting a head start and buying small plants from your local garden shop. Check the tag on the plant for care instructions. Rosemary and thyme prefer to be in drier soil, while basil and mint need more water.

(continued)

(continued)

Tip: You can even buy an herb garden kit that includes everything you need. Some kits even include self-watering pots.

HERB GARDEN CONTAINERS

Illustration by Elizabeth Kurtzman

Aligning Zero Waste with Budget-Conscious Buying

Wasting less costs less. As Chapter 3 points out, you want to reframe your thoughts about groceries and how you plan to cook them, creating a zero waste mindset. This section looks at when it pays to buy in bulk and when it may not. What and where you buy your groceries is up to you, but keep in mind that one goal of shopping for zero waste cooking is to find out where the best available options are — for your household, budget, and lifestyle. Here are some grocery shopping tips for the budget-conscious:

>> **Shop online.** Shopping online has its pros and cons from a sustainability standpoint. Choosing foods from your smartphone can help eliminate impulse buys or unnecessary purchases.

>> **Avoid grocery shopping on an empty stomach.** When you're hungry, you might cave in to too many treats, or overbuy in general.

>> **Watch out for impulse buys.** Grocery stores put items on the endcap for a reason — they know you may walk by more than once and consider throwing the item into your cart, whether or not you need it. If impulse buys are an issue for you, you may want to plan shopping only twice a month.

Making smarter bulk buys

If you have a large household, bulk buys can save you money and time.

WARNING

Check the pricing! Sometimes larger sizes or bulk packaging isn't less expensive than single items. Look for the "price per unit" on the pricing label. Sometimes sale items aren't the better buy.

Here are a few money-saving items if bought in bulk or larger packages:

>> **Meat:** Buying a package of 12 chicken drumsticks instead of 4 is usually a money saver. The same goes for pork, ground beef, or larger roasts. When you bring a larger package home, split it up into portions you'll use in the next day or two and then freeze the rest in air-tight freezer bags or containers (silicone bags or reusable sealed plastic or glass containers work well; just be sure to tightly wrap meat in freezer or waxed paper before placing in the bag or container). Package the items for the freezer in portions that make sense for your household.

>> **Blocks of cheese:** Shredded cheese is sometimes convenient, but if you use a lot of cheese, you'll save money by buying larger blocks to cut or shred yourself. You can freeze hard cheeses for up to 6 weeks without sacrificing quality. Wrap tightly in waxed paper, then place into a sealed, airtight freezer bag. Defrost in the refrigerator.

>> **Nuts:** Bulk nuts are generally less expensive per pound than the cost of smaller packages (and you'll limit packaging waste), and you can buy the amount you need. You can also store nuts in the freezer for up to 2 years.

>> **Cereal:** If your household includes regular cereal eaters, it may pay to buy double boxes of it.

>> **Paper products:** Toilet paper is a fact of life, and no one wants to be caught without a square to spare. Although you may want to be mindful about how many paper towels you use (or waste), buying these items in bulk results in a lower unit price overall.

Big box stores can have some very tantalizing bulk items for sale, but think carefully about the type of foods you buy there. Buying in bulk can sometimes lead to more food waste, so before you add them to your cart, ask yourself these questions:

>> Will I use this? If yes, when?

>> Do I need this amount right now, or can I store it or freeze it?

>> Is this an actual savings?

Deciding where to shop

Whether you use online ordering options, a big box store, or a local farmers' market, there are more ways than ever to shop for groceries and household staples. Choose the best option for your household and budget.

Specialty stores vs. big box

Specialty stores may have specific items that you prefer to use in your cooking, but they're often pricier. Unless you need a specific ingredient, you'll likely spend less at local chains. In addition, some people seem to assign a status ranking to some of the trendier specialty grocery stores. You may get drawn in, but food from a specialty store isn't any better than food from a typical chain store.

More grocery stores are pledging to reduce food loss and waste. When it comes to zero waste cooking, where you shop may not matter as much as what you know you'll use. For instance, if bagged salads are something you know you'll eat, then that's better than going to the farmers' market and buying a bushel of fresh greens and vegetables that you don't have time to prep and then end up wasting.

Farmers' market strolls

If you have a farmers' market in your town, definitely consider supporting local farmers and your community by visiting each week or a couple of times a month. Buying produce there often ensures that you're getting delicious fruits or vegetables that were locally picked at their peak quality. (Keep in mind, it's not always grown locally, so ask the vendors about produce origin and when it was picked.) To avoid waste, it's best to plan to cook or eat what you buy there within about a week.

Some farmers may also give you a discount if you buy in bulk. For example, if you're making a bunch of pies and need a lot of apples, maybe you can get a discount. They may also give you a deal on "seconds" or less-than-perfect, slightly blemished produce.

Sometimes not having a plan is A-OK! You may find some amazing vegetables or fruits at the market that are either great quality, seasonal, or on sale. Go ahead and grab them. Once you're home, just be sure to come up with a plan to use them that week.

Shopping the specials and BOGOs

As you reduce your food waste, you'll find you may have some extra money left over from your food budget. Still, you want to shop those sales! If you track the sales and buy-one-get-one specials, you can add those items to your shopping list and have a plan for them before you buy them. If you can't use it that week, or don't have time to cook, it's not really savings in the long run.

Compare prices from store to store, looking at local grocer's weekly fliers or website ads, or consider downloading a price comparison app, like Basket, on your smartphone. You may also consider some of the smaller discount grocery stores in your area. Buying off brand can still deliver a quality ingredient at a better price.

Have you ever noticed how hot dogs and condiments are on sale during the summer grilling months and baking supplies are on sale in November and December? All stores have what is called a *sale cycle.* This means they cycle sales of different items through the month. These times of the year may be a good time to save money by stocking up on a few nonperishable items, or stock your freezer. Just don't forget about them!

Enjoying canned and frozen produce

Canned and frozen produce have an undeserved image problem. Sometimes fresh beats out frozen or canned for taste or quality, but not always. Keeping some canned and frozen food on your grocery list not only saves you money but may also help reduce your overall food waste of perishable foods. You can also feel good about fruits and vegetables that are packaged in steel cans, because they can be recycled over and over again.

Sodium is used as a preservative in canned food. Check the labels for sodium in canned vegetables, beans, and soups if you have high blood pressure or a kidney disorder and look for reduced sodium products. Also, rinsing canned vegetables helps reduce sodium.

Fresh produce is great; however, nutritionally, if you're more likely to eat more vegetables and fruits by including some canned and frozen produce, they're a nutrition win as well. Fruits and veggies are picked at peak quality then canned or frozen shortly after harvest, making them just as nutritious as fresh.

Frozen peas are a winner because this delicate veggie is picked at peak ripeness and frozen, so you're always assured quality taste and texture. For a spinach salad, you obviously want fresh, but for soups, dips, or other recipes, frozen spinach is another winner because you get more bang for your buck.

Frozen fruit can come in handy for smoothies or other recipes. Although going blueberry picking is fun in the summer, it's nice to have a bag of blueberries in the freezer when you want to whip up muffins in the dead of winter (see the Basic Muffins recipe in Chapter 16). Don't overlook the convenience factor of frozen, too — no chopping, dicing, or slicing required!

REMEMBER

Frozen foods lose some vitamins C and A if exposed to oxygen, so be sure to seal them up if you use only part of a bag.

TIP

Sometimes you may stock up on meats or vegetables and forget to go back to use it or defrost it. It's a good plan to "cook from your freezer" at least a few days each month. Frozen vegetables lose some nutrition if kept in the freezer for more than a year.

Versatile Foods to Keep You Healthy

Adopting a zero waste cooking strategy doesn't mean you forgo healthy eating. Quite the opposite. All the effort you put into deciding what to cook and planning your grocery shopping and meals will likely lead you to a more balanced plate. A healthy diet is an important component of a healthy lifestyle. It's not nutrition unless you eat it, and it certainly isn't nutrition if it lands in your kitchen garbage can.

What you choose to eat is totally up to you. A lot of things influence our food choices — geographic local, budgets, cultural preferences and eating styles, personal dietary needs, and availability of various foods. The suggestions in this section are just that — suggestions. We all need about the same amount of some nutrients, like vitamins and minerals, so it's a good idea to know which foods provide which nutrients. Also, enjoying a diet that includes a variety of foods is not only good for your health but can also be good for the planet.

Making the most of legumes

Legumes are a type of plant that produce edible seeds. The dry, edible seeds of those plants are called *pulses*. They include many varieties of beans — like kidney, pinto, black, navy, or garbanzo (chickpeas) — lentils, and peas. A pea pod is a legume, but the peas inside it are pulses! Often the seeds, or pulses, end up on your plate. These gems aren't just nutrition powerhouses, but are a sustainable food to add to your zero waste cooking routine. Canned, dried, or frozen, legumes are shelf stable and are good for both you and the planet.

All pulses are legumes, but not all legumes are pulses. A *legume* is any plant from the *Fabaceae family* that includes its leaves, stems, and pods. Legumes include soybeans, peanuts, fresh peas, and fresh beans as well as dried beans, lentils, and dried peas. For more information, check out www.pulses.org.

Beans are magical

Beans are a good source of protein, iron, folate (a B vitamin), and phosphorus. Beans are rich in fiber, making them a smart choice to maintain a healthy gut and manage diabetes or heart disease. Fiber helps maintain blood sugar levels and can lower blood cholesterol. Eating foods high in fiber is satisfying, too, because fiber fills you up. The daily fiber goal is to get about 25 to 38 grams per day. Beans provide about 8 to 10 grams of fiber per ½ cup serving compared to 2 grams per ½ cup brown rice.

Some people shy away from beans because they cause, ahem, gas. Most people find that the more often they include beans into their diet, the less gassy they get. Your digestive system adapts, and you tolerate them better. One way to add some beans into your rotation is to try new recipes that include beans in foods that you already love. For instance, add some black beans to your favorite salsa, or puree them and add them to a baked good. Try the Black Bean Brownie Bites from Chapter 16.

Beans are economical and convenient. Canned beans are quick and easy to use. Rinsing them helps reduce overall sodium and cooking may help you digest them easier. Dried beans take a little more time but are actually easy to cook. *Note:* You don't have to soak dried beans overnight, although it can reduce cooking time by about 30 minutes. Otherwise, just place beans into a pot. Cover them with water and bring to a boil. Simmer for about 1 to 2 hours depending on bean type (check package directions). Discard the water then salt to taste when cooked. You can also cook dried beans in a slow-cooker.

Smart ways to use beans include

>> Adding beans to your tossed green salad (like the Nutty Mixed Salad with Beans, Beets, and Goat Cheese in Chapter 10) or to pasta dishes

>> Pureeing beans to make a dip for crackers or raw veggies or using it for the Layered Bean Dip (Chapter 8)

>> Adding extra beans to your favorite chili or the Bean Soup with Diced Pork recipe (Chapter 10)

Liven up your meals with lentils

Lentils are inexpensive and easy to cook. You can mix cooked lentils into soups and salads or swap them in for other grains. Think of it as adding a scoop of nutrition to familiar dishes.

TIP

Green lentils are the most common, but you can also find yellow, red, black, or French green lentils. They have similar mild flavors. You can sometimes find pre-cooked lentils in shelf-stable pouches or in the refrigerator or freezer sections of the store, which you can quickly reheat in the microwave or use in a recipe. Try the Lentil-stuffed Zucchini in Chapter 13.

Here are some ways to use lentils:

>> Mix cooked lentils to your cooked ground beef or turkey for a taco filling.

>> Add lentils to your favorite soup recipes.

>> Toss lentils into pasta and vegetable salads.

>> Serve a microwave precooked lentil pouch as a simple side dish.

>> Stir red lentils and basil into your pasta sauce and use for lasagna or a pasta topping.

Soy for your health

Soy products such as tofu, tempeh, soy nuts, or edamame are good sources of protein, fiber, folate, and potassium. Edamame beans are typically found in the freezer section. They're easy to add to salads or stir-fries. You'll find tofu and tempeh in the refrigerated produce section. You'll even find some packages seasoned and ready to stir-fry.

Here are some great options for using soy:

>> Add cubed extra-firm tofu to your stir-fry recipes (see the Spicy Tofu Broccoli Bowl in Chapter 13).

>> Crumble firm tofu into your taco filling or chili.

>> Blend silken tofu into salad dressings, dips, or smoothies (see the Tofu Smoothie recipe in Chapter 17).

>> Mix edamame into salads or slaws (try the Black Bean and Edamame Salad in Chapter 12).

SOY FOODS ARE OFTEN MISUNDERSTOOD

Every news headline about nutrition or food as it relates to health doesn't always line up with the actual evidence.

For example, soy contains compounds called *isoflavones*. These compounds are phytoestrogens and can chemically act like a form of estrogen (but they're not estrogen). This has caused concern in regard to risk for certain types of breast cancer; however, no research shows any association for consumption of soy and breast cancer. In fact, postmenopausal women may benefit from regularly including some soy into their diet, because isoflavones can help reduce the frequency of hot flashes.

There's also no scientific evidence that men consuming soy experience lower testosterone or feminizing effects.

Remember: Just because a study is done doesn't make it scientific evidence unless the study was well designed with a large enough sample population.

Getting the most out of grains

Grain foods provide variety to the diet as well as a host of important nutrients, such as B vitamins, magnesium, iron, vitamin E, and fiber. Grains include wheat, corn, rice, oats, rye, barley, and quinoa. You may eat them in their natural form or in the form of pasta, breads, and cereals. Whole grains provide more fiber than processed grains, but both can be included in a healthy diet.

REMEMBER

No food is bad. Food shouldn't be linked to morality. In recent years, many people have found that limiting grain products, such as breads, pasta, rice, or cereals, allows them to maintain their weight or otherwise feel better. Everyone's metabolism varies. While eliminating grains may help one person feel better, it may make another person feel worse. Make the best choice for you. While you work on reducing food waste, remember that food should be enjoyable, too. Grain foods are economical and easy to prepare. Many people have no problem including grains in their diet.

TECHNICAL STUFF

Many industries recycle grain products, ensuring little goes to waste. For instance, some farms pick up leftover or stale bread products from grocery stores to use in their feed formulas. Spent grain is the leftover malt after processing. About 85 percent of the waste from brewing beer is estimated to be spent grain. Many breweries find ways to recycle their leftovers by donating to local farms. Some are using the grain left from the mash to create pizza!

Grains are pretty versatile. Here are some of the many different ways you can use them:

>> Add rice or quinoa to meat dishes like chilis or tacos, or create a stuffing for peppers or squash.

>> Foods like pasta and rice can reduce food waste by being the bed in which leftovers lie. Cook rice or some penne then top with leftover chili or roasted vegetables.

>> When you cook grains, double up so you have one or two extra servings leftover and ready to go for a quick meal. You can also freeze them then defrost and create a quick "power bowl" — mix grains with beans, a vegetable, and cheese or leftover chopped meat. Try the Chickpea Artichoke Grain Bake (Chapter 12).

>> Bread products, pasta, and rice can also serve as a leftovers "canvas." Check out Chapters 14, 15, and 16 for recipe ideas.

Rice to the rescue

Rice comes from a grassy plant and may be short, medium, or long grain. It's an economical and versatile ingredient and creates a strong foundation for nutrition. White rice has a long shelf life (up to 30 years!), making it a food waste hero. White rice starts out brown, but its outer layer is removed, and then it's often polished. Brown rice will last on the shelf for about 6 months (due to its outer bran coating, it can oxidize quickly). To save time, you can keep some quick-cooking varieties on hand.

Rice is a staple food of more than two-thirds of the world's population. It's naturally fat-free and a good source of carbohydrate energy as well as B vitamins (thiamin, niacin, and folic acid) and minerals (phosphorus, iron, and potassium). The vast majority of rice produced today is Asian rice (Oryza sativa).

Common types of rice include

>> **Basmati:** This long-grain rice kernel is slender and has an aromatic scent when cooked. It's popular in Indian cuisine and pairs nicely with masala or curry dishes. You may find a U.S.-grown variety in stores, labeled Texmati. This rice pairs well with the Spiced Chicken over Rice (see Chapter 13).

>> **Jasmine:** These aromatic rice grains are slightly wider than basmati. You may find this type of rice served with Thai dishes or a fried rice. Jasmine rice pairs nicely with the Spicy Tofu Broccoli Bowl (Chapter 13).

- » **Sushi:** This Japanese rice is the kind you find at a sushi restaurant. It's sticky, making it ideal for sushi rolls.

- » **Arborio:** Known for its use in risotto, this is a short-grain rice variety from Italy. It's starchy and sticky, which creates the creaminess of risotto.

- » **Wild:** Although called "rice," it's actually not rice and comes from the grassy Zizania aquatica plant that's grown in the great lakes region of the United States and Canada. Nonetheless, the grocery store labels it as rice, and it can be used in a similar way. It has a chewier texture and is popular for use in dressings for poultry.

REMEMBER

White rice is just as nutritious as brown rice. Brown rice is higher in fiber and phosphorous than white rice, but this doesn't mean you can't enjoy white rice. Most white rice in the United States is enriched and contains more iron and thiamin than brown rice. I say, variety is the spice of life!

Pasta: A food waste hero

Like rice, noodles and macaroni are budget friendly ingredients that can help you use up wilting veggies or cooked leftovers. Pasta is made with a special wheat, durum semolina, and generally considered an Italian food, but according to historians, noodles were likely brought from ancient China. Whether it's rigatoni or linguine, rice noodles or ramen, all types of noodles have a role to play in helping you create meals with less waste. As far as nutrition goes, noodles are rich in carbohydrates and sometimes enriched with B vitamins like folic acid.

Noodles are even better with the company they keep. Veggies add important antioxidant vitamins A and C, along with additional fiber. You can put just about any leftover meat, chili, or stew onto a bed of pasta to avoid wasting leftovers.

REMEMBER

Pasta doesn't make you fat! Often thought of as a comfort food because of its texture and satisfying nature, pasta fits into a healthy diet. A serving is typically one cup.

Ancient grains for modern times

Ancient implies old, and that's just what these grains are all about. Grains like quinoa, amaranth, millet, sorghum, freekeh, farro, and barley have been staples of countries in the Middle East, India, and Africa and have been nourishing people since the beginning of time. Many are more nutritious than other refined grains, and some have become popular in Western countries now as well. They each provide some protein, fiber, and iron.

Since the Dietary Guidelines for Americans recommends that you make half of your grain choices whole grains, adding one or more of these ancient grains may be a good idea. All these grains provide a variety of immune-boosting vitamins and minerals, like zinc, selenium, iron, and vitamins D and C, to keep you healthy.

>> Farro is a wheat grain that can be cooked as a side dish or added to soups. It's a good source of niacin, zinc, magnesium, and iron.

>> Freekeh is young, roasted wheat. Because it's harvested young, it's green. It's a really good sources of fiber and has a slightly smoky flavor and chewy texture.

>> Quinoa is technically not a grain, but it's still considered a whole grain food. Quinoa is a seed that comes from a leafy plant (the same plant family as spinach). These flat oval seeds are a good source of manganese and magnesium and also provides some folate (a B vitamin) and zinc.

>> Barley is likely one of the first crops ever cultivated. Legend has it that Roman gladiators used it for sustained energy! In modern times, we may just want to add it to soups or salads. It's a great source of fiber, magnesium, selenium, and phosphorous and can add texture to a dish.

>> Sorghum is an environmentally friendly grain because it's considered a high-energy, drought-tolerant crop. It's used primarily in agriculture for livestock grazing and ethanol production, but it's becoming more popular in the consumer food market. The petite kernels can be popped like popcorn, or they can be cooked like quinoa or other grains. Like other grains, sorghum is a good source of B vitamins, iron, and zinc.

Modern wheat isn't an ancient grain, but that doesn't mean that it's inferior. Because various grains provide different nutrients, it's a good idea to include a variety. Keep in mind that "pearled" grains have had the outer layer of bran removed, resulting in a grain without dietary fiber.

No bread-bashing allowed

Bread products are traditionally made from wheat or rye flour and are part of the grain food group. There's a wide variety of bread products to choose from — whole grain, Italian, French, potato, rye, multigrain, or sourdough loaves. You can also find pita bread, naan, and other flatbreads available at the supermarket. Tortillas and wraps can add variety to your plate as well.

No matter which bread product you prefer, they'll all work to reduce leftover waste by creating a holder for some delicious toppings, or they can simply accompany a meal. Try to choose a variety of refined and whole grains. If you're concerned about your weight, keep in mind that grain products don't promote weight gain, but it can be a good idea to keep overall portions in mind.

Over the past decade, a lot of misinformation has been shared about bread and grain products in general. Most people have no problem tolerating grains and including them in their diets. However, some people are intolerant or allergic to wheat. People with celiac disease must avoid gluten — a protein found in wheat, barley, rye, and farro. Most commercial bread products are made from wheat and, therefore, contain gluten. Today, many gluten-free bread products are available to choose from. Read labels carefully and talk to a registered dietitian to learn more. You can also find information about celiac disease at www.celiac.org.

Picking produce

Fruits and vegetables provide a lot of important nutrients, including antioxidant vitamins A and C as well as B vitamins (folate, thiamin, niacin, B6, and B12). They're also one of the top perishable foods wasted, so it's important to be mindful as you stroll the produce section.

TIP

Knowing how to choose foods for ripeness and understanding expiration and best-by dates can help you stay healthy and reduce waste. Consider buying a variety of fresh, canned, and frozen produce. And check out Chapter 4 for all you need to know about best-by dates.

Is it ripe?

Shopping for produce when it's at peak ripeness generally ensures better taste and less waste at home (nobody wants a mealy peach, plus most supermarkets have channels in place to repurpose aging produce). I often say that when fruit is on sale (such as a "buy one get one" deal), it tastes best because it's ripe. Those sale items are best purchased when you know you're going to eat it, bake it, or cook with it.

TIP

It may sound a little weird, but you can often determine ripeness by touching and smelling your produce. Here are a few tips for shopping for common items in the fresh produce section:

>> Apples should have good color, be firm, and feel heavy.

>> Apricots, peaches, and nectarines should be fragrant and slightly soft.

>> Asparagus should be firm and bright green.

>> Avocadoes should be slightly soft. If firm, they can ripen on the counter.

>> Green bananas are best if you aren't going to use them right away. Yellow bananas are best for eating now. Bananas with brown spots are best for baking or adding to smoothies.

- » Broccoli should be evenly green (no yellowing) with compact heads. Stalk should be firm and leaves unwilted.

- » Cauliflower should be compact and creamy in color with no browning.

- » Eggplant should be shiny, smooth, and firm but slightly soft to touch.

- » Grapes should be firm and attached to their stems (keeping them on the stem allows them to last longer).

- » Greens like spinach, kale, or salad greens shouldn't have browned edges or be wilted.

- » Melons should be firm and fragrant. Watermelon should sound hollow when thumped, and cantaloupe should be a creamy golden color (not green).

- » Onions should be firm, without soft spots or sprouts.

- » Peppers should be firm and shiny.

- » Pineapples should smell fragrant and have green leaves.

- » Squash should be firm and shiny and without soft spots.

TIP

For more information about selection, nutrition, and storing produce, see `fruitsandveggies.org/fruits-and-veggies`.

REMEMBER

Produce doesn't have to be perfect looking to be safe and delicious. A bruise here or there is normal and won't hurt you. Cut the brown bits off and transfer into compost and use the rest of the fruit or veggie. Find out more about how to use up less-than-perfect produce in Parts 3 and 4.

Relying on seasonal foods

In the United States, we're fortunate to have a safe and abundant food supply. Produce that's picked in California is quickly processed to canned or frozen food or shipped all over the country shortly after picking. In some ways, what you see in your supermarket's produce section is seasonal — somewhere!

We're able to have fresh fruits and vegetables in our markets year-round due to different growing regions in the United States and abroad. Various areas of the country (and world) have different climate conditions at different times during the year, which determines where various fruits and vegetables can be grown. We also rely on greenhouses and imports in the United States.

"Buy local" has become a catchphrase that suggests that to support a healthy environment, you buy only what's local to where you live. While this is great in theory, people live in many different places and don't always have access to locally grown food year-round. In addition, what is "local" may not be enough to sustain your diet. Of course, it's still an excellent idea to support any local farmers' markets you have access to during the growing season. There, you'll find seasonal produce local to your area.

REMEMBER

The current food shipment systems use more natural resources and fossil fuels than if food was shipped only locally. However, making statements such as "buy local" isn't as simple as it sounds. Global food delivery is complex and goes beyond the goal of this book. Focusing on your own shopping and kitchen habits, as well as personal energy use, can have impact, too.

Rather than worry about where you buy your fresh produce, planning how you'll use it or freezing what you don't use are better zero waste solutions.

Making smart meat and dairy selections

While the protein group includes beans, peas, lentils, nuts, seeds, and eggs, it also includes meat like beef, pork, poultry, and seafood. Dairy foods are their own food group and include milk, yogurt, and cheese — all economical protein sources. Because I've discussed the nutritional and budgetary benefits of legumes already, in this section, I focus on making smart meat and dairy choices.

From a nutrition perspective, meat provides protein, iron, and major B vitamins, including thiamin, riboflavin, niacin, vitamin B6, and vitamin B12. Milk also contains riboflavin and B12 plus provides protein, calcium, phosphorous, and potassium and is vitamin-D fortified.

Yes, you can enjoy red meat

Some people feel that the best way to help improve our environment is to transition to a vegetarian lifestyle. Others believe that when animals raised for food are managed properly, they can actually help our environmental woes, by restoring healthy soils. I discuss this topic in detail in Chapter 2. The takeaway is, yes, you can include meat in your diet, while reducing portions and adding more grains, nuts, and legumes to your plate.

Environmentally speaking, while cattle (beef and dairy) and livestock are the number-one agricultural source of greenhouse gas (methane) globally (with about 70 percent lower GHG emissions in the U.S.), doing away with them may not be the solution some think it is. Breeding techniques have allowed ranchers to be more efficient and produce animals that are leaner with more meat.

Beef, veal, and lamb can be included in your zero waste kitchen. Each comes at various price points, depending on the product or cut.

A FEW WORDS ABOUT IRON

Interestingly, iron-deficient anemia has been increasing since 1999. A recent study showed that the American diet had a 15.3 percent reduction in beef and a 21.5 percent increase in chicken meat consumption between 1999 and 2018. According to the study, dietary iron intake decreased by about 6.6 percent and 9.5 percent for male and female adults, respectively.

Heme iron, derived from hemoglobin, is found in animal products and is the most easily absorbed form of iron. Beef in particular is high in heme iron and so are mussels and oysters. Men over 18 need 8 milligrams of iron a day, as do women over 50. Women ages 18 to 50 need 18 milligrams daily. You don't have to eat large portions to get the iron you need.

A 3-ounce serving of beef provides 2 milligrams of iron; 3 ounces of oysters provides 8 milligrams; a 3-ounce serving of pork provides about 1 milligram; while a 3-ounce serving of chicken or fish provides only 0.6 milligrams. You'll get an additional 3 milligrams of nonheme iron from a serving of nuts, beans, and some vegetables. Fortified grains such as breakfast cereal provide a full 18 milligrams per serving.

Smart ways to use beef, veal, or lamb include

>> **Choosing a more expensive cut of beef but doing more with less of it:** For instance, using only 8 ounces of beef to divide among 4 servings then rounding out the plate with grains and vegetables.

>> **Preparing inexpensive cuts like flank steak:** They can also serve multiple purposes for meals. The Grilled Marinated Flank Steak (see Chapter 13) can be used to top the Mixed Produce Salad with Farro (see Chapter 10).

>> **Choosing the budget-friendly choice of ground meat:** This can accommodate many recipes like the Beef Chili (Chapter 10), which can be turned into the Flexible Quesadillas (Chapter 15) the following day.

Getting the most from pork

In addition to the 22 grams of protein per 3-ounce portion, pork provides niacin, phosphorous, thiamin, vitamins B6 and B12, and zinc. It's suggested that pork generally has a lower environmental footprint than beef. Pork has been bred to produce leaner meat than past decades, too. Fresh cuts are low in sodium compared to high-sodium cured or processed pork products. Pork tenderloin and sirloin are the leanest cuts, but as with all meats, you want to eat smaller portions. So even when you enjoy a higher fat cut of pork, the portion will keep things in check.

TIP

To ensure your fresh pork is tender and juicy, cook it to the proper temperature of 145 degrees.

Here are some smart ways to use pork:

>> Pork tenderloins and loin roasts are versatile in recipes and can go a long way. Use leftovers to populate a charcuterie board or for sandwiches like the Pork Pita Pockets with Cucumber Sauce (Chapter 15).

>> Making pork and veggie kabobs is one way to enjoy pork while reducing portions.

>> The best meatballs are made from a combination of ground beef, veal, and pork. You can purchase premade meatballs that are economical and can be frozen for later use.

>> While a boneless pork shoulder is the most popular cut for pulled pork, you can also use leaner cuts like a sirloin roast or loin roast.

Versatile poultry for the win

Poultry is budget-friendly, and some studies suggest it may have a lower carbon footprint compared to other meats. Poultry is so versatile and affordable, it's easy to create nutritious meals with. You'll find a lot of recipes in Chapter 13.

The following explains the different types of chickens and the labels surrounding them.

>> **Farm-raised:** All chickens in the United States are farm-raised. Many are raised in spacious barns equipped with temperature-control systems. Barns helps protect chickens from predators (foxes, raccoons, and birds of prey).

>> **Antibiotic claims:** Technically, all chicken you buy is "antibiotic-free." Farmers do use antibiotics, when necessary, to treat sick animals. However, federal law mandates that the antibiotics must be cleared through the bird's system before they're harvested. Chickens that are raised without the use of any antibiotics may be labeled as "No Antibiotics Ever" or something similar.

>> **Hormones:** It's illegal to use any type of hormone or steroid in raising chickens. Despite the "hormone-free" labeling you may see, no chicken you buy will have ever had added hormones.

>> **Cage-free:** All broiler chickens are raised in large open barns and are technically cage-free.

>> **Pasture-raised:** These chickens are raised primarily outdoors, on pasture.

- » **Free-range:** Chickens that have access to the outdoors are labeled free-range. All USDA Organic chicken is free-range, but not all free-range chicken is organic.

- » **Organic:** This is a USDA seal that means the chicken has been fed only certified organic feed and is free-range. Most of the practices are the same for chickens raised organically and conventionally (see Chapter 2 for more on this). This label defines the agricultural practice and doesn't indicate any higher standard in terms of safety, quality, or nutrition.

- » **Roaster:** A roaster chicken is a larger bird, usually around five to six pounds.

- » **Broilers:** These are young chickens raised for meat and the most common type you'll find at the grocery store.

TIP

Another way to reduce food waste is to adopt a "nose to tail" philosophy. For instance, when you buy a whole chicken, rather than discard the carcass and liver, make soup or pâté. Liver is loaded with iron and can be added to your snack board as a spread for crackers.

TECHNICAL
STUFF

To make Chicken Liver Pâté, simply trim the fat from and cut the liver into chunks. Add it to a sauté pan with a little butter, minced onion (or shallot), and minced garlic. Sauté then add about 2 tablespoons of chicken stock or brandy. Add this to a small food processor along with a tablespoon of cream, pinch of salt, and puree until smooth. Refrigerate and then serve with crackers.

Of course, eggs are another aspect of the poultry industry. Eggs are a nutrition powerhouse with 7 grams of protein per 70-calorie egg. They're also low in saturated fat and an excellent source of choline, selenium, zinc, and B vitamins.

Here's a guide to some labeling lingo:

- » **Cage-free:** Hens are in an open building where they can roam and have roosts or perches and nesting areas. Conventional barns include enclosures for each hen that serves as their nesting space.

- » **Free-range:** These hens have access to outdoors with no enclosures. In addition to their feed, they can forage on grasses and insects.

- » **Certified organic:** Free-range hens raised on organic feed, with access to the outdoors.

- » **Non-GMO:** There are no genetically modified eggs, but some brands may use the term for marketing purposes. Even if genetically modified material is in the hen feed, none of the genetically modified material is passed into the egg.

>> **Omega-3 fortified:** These eggs come from chickens fed a diet high in omega-3 fatty acids. On average one of these eggs can provide 125 milligrams of omega-3s, while a 3-ounce serving of salmon provides over 4,000 milligrams.

>> **Best-by date:** This serves to keep eggs circulated on the shelf and indicates the date at which eggs maintain their quality. Eggs can be safety eaten four to five weeks after this date and can be used in baking after that.

REMEMBER

There's no nutritional difference between brown- and white-shelled eggs. They're simply from different breeds of chickens. Also, keep in mind that cage-free or free-range chicken eggs aren't different nutritionally.

See the options with seafood

Like other types of food, the aquaculture industry is also making improvements to fishing practices so they're environmentally sustainable.

Seafood is packed with nutrition, including protein and heart-healthy omega-3 fatty acids. It provides vitamins A and D, selenium, zinc, B vitamins, and magnesium — all nutrients that support a healthy immune system.

When you think of seafood, you may think about the top three consumed: salmon, shrimp, and tuna. These make up 50 percent of the seafood eaten in America. They're great, but for both nutrition and sustainability, you may want to consider broadening the variety that you eat.

Here are a couple of ways to swap out seafood:

>> Try a different variety. Hake, flounder, rockfish, mackerel, red snapper or hogfish — all fabulous and make good choices for the Fish Tacos (Chapter 15).

>> In addition to using tilapia in the Foil-baked Tilapia with Peppers (Chapter 13), you can substitute mahi-mahi, snapper, or cod.

Using dairy to enhance meals

Dairy products include milk, butter, soft and hard cheeses, cottage cheese, ricotta cheese, sour cream, and yogurt. One 8-ounce cup of unflavored cow's milk has no added sugar and provides 8 grams of protein, 300 milligrams of calcium, about 350 milligrams potassium, and 15 percent of the daily value required for vitamins A and D. The fat content varies in whole, 2%, 1% and nonfat milk. In addition to nutrition, dairy also has unique culinary properties.

DAIRY ALTERNATIVES

There's a plethora of dairy alternatives these days. It may feel a little overwhelming to make the best choice for you. There's really no reason to avoid cow's milk if you tolerate it and aren't vegan. Plant-based beverages have a different nutrition profile and most dairy alternatives are low in protein. Some are fortified with calcium. Here are some facts about a few of the popular alternatives.

- Almond milk is made from ground almonds and filtered water. It usually contains some thickening agents, too. It provides about 50 calories per cup, and although almonds are a good source of protein, almond milk isn't, at only 1 gram of protein per cup.

- Soy milk is made from soybeans and filtered water. It provides about 90 calories per cup and 7 grams of protein. Those fortified with calcium are the most similar, nutritionally, to cow's milk. Flavored varieties have added sugar.

- Oat milk has a creamy texture and is made from oats and filtered water. Compared to other milk beverages, it provides a bit of fiber. One cup provides 120 calories, 3 grams of protein, and 2 grams of fiber. It's often fortified with calcium, potassium, vitamins A and D, riboflavin, and vitamin B12.

- Coconut milk is made from filtered water and coconut cream (unlike canned coconut milk sold in cans for cooking, which is pure cream). It provides no protein and is high in saturated fat.

TIP

If you have high blood pressure, it's important to get enough potassium in the diet. The DASH Diet has been proven to lower blood pressure in people with hypertension (high blood pressure) and recommends a diet low in sodium and saturated fat with eight to ten servings of fruits and vegetables and two to three servings of low-fat dairy daily. You can find out more in *DASH Diet For Dummies*, 2nd Edition.

REMEMBER

Whether you choose a cow's milk product or milk alternatives is up to you. Keep in mind that different types of milk or milk alternatives have unique properties in cooking. The recipes in this book were tested with cow's milk.

Here are some ways to use dairy in your zero waste kitchen:

>> A sprinkling of sharp cheese can take a dish from blah to wow.

>> Adding bit of cream cheese or dollop of sour cream can silken up a sauce.

>> Butter adds flavor, body, and depth to a dish. It's high in saturated fat, so you may want to be mindful of how much you use. Just a teaspoon stirred into a rice or vegetable dish will elevate it.

>> Milk can be used in cooking to create sauces or add liquid. Adding milk to your scrambled eggs will make them lighter and fluffier. Mastering the Basic Cream Sauce (Chapter 11) can enhance your culinary endeavors!

>> Plain yogurt and sour cream are great for making dips, salad dressings, and sauces. You can use them interchangeably. Flavored yogurts are high-protein snacks and a good source of calcium. Greek yogurt provides more protein per cup than regular (about 20 grams per cup versus 14 in regular yogurt).

REMEMBER

Cheese is a good source of calcium and protein. Hard cheese lasts longer than soft cheeses. Once open, use cottage cheese or ricotta cheese within a week. Cream cheese lasts about two or three weeks.

TIP

If you get bloated or have belly pain after you drink milk, you may be lactose intolerant, or intolerant of the protein in milk. You can find lactose-free milk or A2 milk in the dairy section.

TIP

Be sure to check the added sugar on the Nutrition Facts label of plant-based milk products, especially flavored ones. While 8 ounces of unflavored cow's milk contains 12 grams of carbohydrate from milk sugar (lactose), this is a naturally occurring sugar, not added sugar. Milk is also a good source of vitamin D, calcium, and protein — ingredients that support healthy growth in children. Speak with a registered dietitian nutritionist if you have questions about your child consuming plant-based milks.

REMEMBER

Some may feel that dairy milk is harsher on the environment than plant-based milk beverages, but the jury is still out.

What type of diet is best for the planet isn't necessarily an all-or-nothing proposition. Reducing food waste will save you money and reduce GHG in landfills. Still, these reductions are nothing compared to what using less fossil fuel (cars, planes, electricity) can do. One thing is certain: Humans need food to survive. Eating a variety of foods is the easiest way to get essential nutrients.

While there's disagreement about a cow's impact on the environment, the reality is that it'd be challenging to produce food on the type of land that cows and other livestock graze on throughout the world. In addition, not all plant-based meals are superior to animal-based ones, environmentally speaking. For instance, consider the inputs to make the ingredients of a fancy smoothie made with soy milk, avocado, blueberries, cocoa, and a big spoon of almond butter.

Chapter **7**

Sample Meal Plans: Zero Waste Ideas in Action

You may be relieved to know that meal planning for zero waste cooking doesn't require you to turn into a homemaker extraordinaire and plan elaborate meals and snacks for every day of the week.

Instead, the idea of meal planning for zero waste is really about using up what you have, planning what you need to shop for, and creating simple but satisfying meals and snacks.

REMEMBER

This book is really about the day-to-day cooking and eating, not the type of meals you may plan for special occasions or holidays. Eating leftovers is a zero waste strategy, so many of the recipes in this book aim to use leftovers in creative ways.

The four meal plans in this chapter work from my philosophy that you can waste less by planning meals that require similar ingredients. In this chapter, I share a rough grocery list for each meal plan and then provide examples of a week's meals using those ingredients and typical pantry and freezer staples.

Touching on Zero Waste Meal Plan Basics

The meal plans in this chapter are meant to help you get a feel for cooking up nutritious meals that use minimal ingredients and are simple enough for you to count on through your busy week.

REMEMBER

Food is meant to both nourish and provide pleasure. A "healthy diet" doesn't have one rigid definition. Rather, it's the overall balance of your plate over a period of days. Some days, your food and beverage choices aren't going to be as great as others. The same goes for your environmentally conscious shopping and food storage efforts. All you can do is try your best to reduce food waste while eating a diet that supports your personal health goals. Check in with a registered dietitian to learn more about your specific dietary goals.

Using one ingredient in multiple recipes

Meal planning can be creative and flexible, as opposed to boring and rigid. The first grocery list employs a zero waste strategy of using one ingredient in multiple recipes. For example, when you buy bell peppers and roast them, they'll keep in the refrigerator for a week, and you can use them on salads, as a side dish, on pasta, or in the Foil-pack Greek Chicken with Olives, Feta, and Peppers (you can find the recipe in Chapter 13).

In Week 2, you can use the leftover Beef Chili (Chapter 10) to create a beef version of the Chicken-stuffed Baked Potatoes (Chapter 13) for lunch the next day. When you put frozen shrimp into the freezer, you can have shrimp cocktail, or you can make a quick Angel Hair with Shrimp and Spinach dish for dinner (Chapter 14). Speaking of spinach, save some to make a Green Smoothie (Chapter 17). If you have carrots left in the crisper drawer that week, you can steam them, then puree with basil (or carrot tops or any leftover fresh herb), and add the puree to a tomato sauce to top a pasta or to create a soup. You get the idea.

TIP

When you bake the Basic Muffins or Black Bean Brownie Bites (both in Chapter 16), you can stash some in the freezer for quick snacks or breakfasts (yes, permission granted to eat the brownies as part of your breakfast or midmorning snack).

Prepping and cooking extra servings

Another idea that both ensures zero waste and saves you time is batch cooking. Prepping and cooking extra servings of items like grains (orzo, rice, or farro, for instance) can save you time throughout the week. Say you roast vegetables on

Sunday then make extra rice with dinner on Monday, you can enjoy the roasted vegetables with the rice for lunch on Tuesday.

You'll also waste less produce if you consider doing a little bit of prep work. Take an hour on your day off to chop onions and peppers to store in an airtight container or clean carrots and cut them into pieces suitable for roasting or snacking. This way, when you're tired, it'll be easier to make a snack or put a meal together because the washing and chopping is already done.

REMEMBER

Planning is key to wasting less! Don't make a big batch of anything before you leave for vacation or when you know you won't be home during mealtimes for the following few days.

You can also think about "cooking from the freezer" at least three times a month. The freezer is a great tool to use when grocery shopping and storing items you found at a special sale price. However, quality does decline after about three months in some cases, so go ahead and use them.

Another quick and easy idea — create a simple sheet pan dinner with enough for leftovers. Roast a batch of boneless chicken thighs on a sheet pan with potatoes. Mix 1 tablespoon oil, 1 tablespoon Dijon mustard, and 1 teaspoon of honey in a large bowl. Whisk until blended. Add the chicken to the bowl and toss until lightly covered with marinade. Place chicken onto one side of a baking sheet. Add cut potatoes to the other side, season with salt and pepper, and drizzle with olive oil. Bake for 35 to 40 minutes at 400 degrees. Serve for dinner with a side salad and warm up for lunch the next day.

Getting creative with leftovers

With leftovers, whether from your home kitchen or a restaurant, you may have enough for only one sandwich or enough to throw into a salad. The overarching goal is to be creative with leftovers and have a plan for them when you cook a larger meal (like say, the Roast Pork Loin with Apples and Onions in Chapter 13).

Reducing food waste also means planning and handling your restaurant meals. You're still going to eat out, carry out, or have food delivered some nights, and that's totally cool. You'll sometimes work those leftovers into your plan, too (for example, you can eat leftover pizza for breakfast or lunch the next day or incorporate some extra pasta into your leftover restaurant meal to stretch it into two servings). Or you'll pick out a recipe on Wednesday to use the leftovers from that rotisserie chicken you picked up on Monday. You don't even need a recipe in some cases. For instance, you can throw together a bowl of cooked chicken, stir-fried veggies, and rice — a quick and easy meal!

REMEMBER

Do what works for you. Being mindful as you shop for groceries can make a big difference in food waste. And heck, sometimes you don't even have to create a meal — wasting less can be as easy as topping a sandwich with leftover roasted vegetables.

Sample Meal Plans: Ready-Made with Flexibility

This section shows you examples of four weeks of meals. The suggested meals include recipes from this book in **bold** as well as other ideas that are either typical, no-cook, or easy to pull together from your shopping list (produce, dairy, protein) and on-hand staples from your refrigerator-freezer or pantry shelf.

These planning ideas mostly assume breakfast and lunch for one and then dinner according to your needs. You can adjust the serving sizes (and grocery list portions) to suit your household. (Most of the bold recipes from the book are for two to four servings. I find it easier to double a recipe rather than cut it in half.) Check the recipes for the week, check your pantry, and create your grocery list (which will also include breakfast or lunch items that you normally enjoy during the week).

REMEMBER

The meal ideas presented here are just examples. I want you to get the feel for how planning your grocery list leads to zero waste cooking. The grocery list includes kitchen staples (foods or ingredients kept on the shelf or in the refrigerator or freezer) and then a list of fresh groceries you'll need for each week's plan. Side dishes can be any starch or vegetable (check out delicious and easy options in Chapter 12). Keep in mind that you may not need to purchase items in the staples category every week, but amounts are given as a guide.

In addition to trying some of the recipes in this book, your actual grocery list will include all the foods and flavors that you enjoy so you can also create a meal planning strategy that works for your preferences and favorite dishes. And if you prefer shopping less often, no worries. You can adjust your meal planning to suit your household.

TIP

It can be helpful to come up with a theme for the week, so you'll use ingredients in multiple dishes. Or build some one-dish meals into your repertoire that you can use at the end of the week. For instance, you may have a few ounces of roast pork left, some cooked veggies, and maybe some leftover rice. Create a "power bowl" by adding all the ingredients into a single-serving bowl of rice then add extra canned beans, shredded cheese, sour cream, or some hot sauce to it and reheat for lunch.

Week 1 sample meal plan

See Table 7-1.

See Table 7-1.

TABLE 7-1   ## Week 1 Meal Plan

	Breakfast	Lunch	Dinner	Snacks
SUNDAY	**Basic Frittata (Ch. 9)**	Sandwich with banana	**Vegetable Lasagna (Ch. 14)**	Popcorn
MONDAY	**Tofu Smoothie (Ch. 17)** Banana	Leftover Basic Frittata Grapes	**Mushroom Turkey Burgers (Ch. 15)** with **Roasted Bell Peppers (Ch. 12)**	Canned peaches
TUESDAY	Eggs with toast	Leftover Vegetable Lasagna	**Foil-pack Greek Chicken with Olives, Feta, and Peppers (Ch. 13)**	Grapes, nuts
WEDNESDAY	Toast topped with ricotta cheese, cinnamon, and sliced bananas	**Tuna "a la Niçoise" Salad (Ch. 10)**	Power Bowl with leftover ground turkey (cooked), plus canned beans, salsa, and rice	Yogurt parfait (yogurt, fruit, and granola or other cereal)
THURSDAY	Cereal with milk and berries or sliced peaches	Leftover Foil-pack Greek Chicken (chopped) with farro and green beans	**Teriyaki Chicken Tenders (Ch. 13)** with rice and **Garlic Broccoli (Ch. 12)**	**Berry Smoothie (Ch. 17)**
FRIDAY	Oatmeal with bananas and maple syrup	**Mixed Produce Salad with Farro (Ch. 10)**	**Spicy Tofu Broccoli Bowl (Ch. 13)** with rice	**Creamy Veggie Dip (Ch. 8)** with raw veggies or crackers
SATURDAY	**Basic Muffins (Ch. 16)** — freeze some! **Basic Egg Strata (Ch. 9)**	Leftover Creamy Veggie Dip with pretzels or fruit	**Penne Bake with Veggies (Ch. 14)**	**Greek Stuffed Bread (Ch. 8)**

Grocery list

Produce: 8 ounces mushrooms | 3-4 large bell peppers (or 1-pound bag of mini bell peppers) | 2 zucchini | 2 heads or crowns of broccoli | 10-16 ounces mixed salad greens | 12-16 ounces green beans (fresh, canned, or frozen) | 4 bananas | 1 pound other fresh or frozen fruit (berries, peaches, apples) | 1 bag of grapes |

Dairy: 8 ounces ricotta or cottage cheese | 16 ounces plain yogurt | 8-ounce block feta cheese | 8 ounces cream cheese | 8 ounces shredded mozzarella cheese

Protein: 6 boneless chicken breasts or thighs | 1 pound chicken tenders | 12- or 14-ounce firm or extra-firm tofu | 1 ½ pounds ground turkey | 1 dozen eggs |

Staples: 1 loaf whole grain bread | 5 pounds flour | 3 pounds sugar | baking powder | salt | black pepper | garlic powder | burger seasoning blend | 1 jar salsa | 6- to 8-ounce can olives | 15-ounce can black beans | 15-ounce can peaches | 24-ounce jar tomato sauce or 28-ounce canned tomato puree | 5-ounce can tuna | 8- to 14-ounce package farro | 1 package quick-cooking rice | dried parsley | 4 garlic cloves | 1 pound penne pasta | popcorn

Week 2 sample meal plan

See Table 7-2.

TABLE 7-2   ## Week 2 Meal Plan

	Breakfast	Lunch	Dinner	Snack
SUNDAY	**High-Fiber Waffles (Ch 16)** with fruit and yogurt	**Roasted Veggie Trio (Ch. 12)** with rice	**Spice-rubbed Pork Tenderloin with Roasted Sliced Grapes (Ch. 13)**	Popcorn
MONDAY	Basic Muffins leftover from Week 1	**Pork Pita Pockets with Cucumber Sauce (Ch. 15)**	Baked sheet pan chicken with potatoes and a canned veggie	Fruit
TUESDAY	Cereal with milk	Leftover Roasted Veggie Trio with crackers	**Veggie-roast Pasta Primavera (Ch. 14)**	Hummus with veggies
WEDNESDAY	**Green Smoothie (Ch. 17)**	Sandwich with **Black Bean and Edamame Salad (Ch. 12)**	**Beef Chili (Ch. 10)** with cornbread and a salad	Apple slices with **Peanut Butter Yogurt Fruit Dip (Ch. 16)**
THURSDAY	Bagel or toast with peanut butter and fruit	Sandwich with fruit	**Chicken with Orzo, Artichokes, and Zucchini (Ch. 13)**	Hummus with crackers, sliced apple
FRIDAY	Oatmeal with fruit	**Chicken-Stuffed Baked Potatoes (Ch. 13)**	Grilled pork with **Roasted Carrots with Honey Glaze (Ch. 12)**	**Black Bean Brownie Bites (Ch. 16)**
SATURDAY	Egg sandwich on bagel	Sandwich Fruit Leftover Black Bean Brownie Bites	**Lentil-stuffed Zucchini (Ch. 13)** with **Fruit Cobbler (Ch. 16)**	Yogurt parfait

Grocery list

Produce: 1 medium eggplant | mushrooms (left over from Week 1) | bell peppers (left over from Week 1) | 2 zucchini | 1 large, sweet onion 1 pound potatoes | 3 to 4 baking potatoes | 4 apples

Dairy: grated parmesan cheese | Plain yogurt (leftover from Week 1 or new 16-oz)

Protein: 2-pound pork tenderloin | 1 pound ground beef | 1 pound boneless chicken | 14 to 16 ounces lentils (canned or dry)

Staples: ketchup | horseradish | fettucine pasta | 15-ounce can black beans | 15-ounce can garbanzo beans | 16-ounce can green beans | 12 to 14 ounces artichoke hearts | high fiber cereal | oats | 10 ounces frozen snap peas | 12 ounces frozen edamame | 6 pita pockets | 6 bagels | loaf of bread | peanut butter | flour | sugar | 1 pound bag brown sugar | honey | baking powder | salt | cinnamon | garlic powder | chili powder | paprika | cumin

Week 3 sample meal plan

See Table 7-3.

TABLE 7-3   ## Week 3 Meal Plan

	Breakfast	Lunch	Dinner	Snack
SUNDAY	**Omelet (Ch. 9)** with toast	Sandwich and fruit	**Whole Roast Chicken (Ch. 13)**, roasted carrots, and mashed potatoes	Leftover Fruit Cobbler from Week 2
MONDAY	**Green Smoothie (Ch. 17)**	Leftover Chicken from Whole Roast Chicken, leftover roasted carrots	**Chicken Parmesan Stuffed Mushrooms (Ch. 8)** **Angel Hair with Shrimp and Spinach (Ch. 14)**	**Baked Apples (Ch. 12)**
TUESDAY	Cereal with sliced banana and milk	**Protein-packed Waldorf Salad (Ch. 10)**	**Roast Pork Loin with Apples and Onions (Ch. 13)**	**High-Fiber Waffles (Ch. 16)** with yogurt and sliced banana

(continued)

TABLE 7-3 *(continued)*

	Breakfast	Lunch	Dinner	Snack
WEDNESDAY	Yogurt with berries and granola	**Pork Tacos with Peppers, Onions, and Lime Crema (Ch. 15)**	**Chickpea Artichoke Grain Bake (Ch. 12)**	Leftover Black Bean Brownie Bites from Week 2 or freezer
THURSDAY	**Egg Muffin Cups (Ch. 9)**	Leftover Chickpea Artichoke Grain Bake	**Bean Soup with Diced Pork (Ch. 10)**	Leftover Protein-packed Waldorf Salad
FRIDAY	Oatmeal with peanut butter and banana	Egg burrito with leftover Egg Muffin Cup wrapped in tortilla with cheese and salsa	**Broiled Salmon Fillet** (Ch. 13; make extra salmon for tomorrow's salad) with rice and a vegetable	Cheese and crackers with fruit
SATURDAY	**Cheesy Veggie Crustless Quiche (Ch. 9)** **Add Anything Scones (Ch. 16)** — freeze some!	**Salmon Spinach Salad with Sliced Grapes (Ch. 10)**	**Spiced Chicken over Rice (Ch. 13)**	**Peanut Butter Yogurt Fruit Dip (Ch. 16)** with apples

Grocery list

Produce: 1 pound carrots | 8 ounces mushrooms | 1 pound celery | 10 to 16 ounces fresh spinach | 5 apples | 5 bananas

Dairy: 16-ounce container plain yogurt

Protein: Roaster chicken | 3-pound pork loin | 3 salmon filets | 2 pounds frozen shrimp | 1 dozen eggs

Staples: 1 pound angel hair pasta | 2 onions | 10 ounces frozen peas | 14-20 ounce bag frozen bell pepper and onion mix | 10-ounce can chickpeas | 15-ounce can black beans | 14-ounce box brown rice | 12 to 16 ounces quinoa | 12-ounce can chicken | 15 ounces coconut milk | 15-ounce can tomatoes | 10 taco shells or tortillas | flour | sugar | baking powder | salt | cinnamon | garlic powder | tarragon | oregano | curry powder | turmeric | cumin

Week 4 sample meal plan

See Table 7-4.

See Table 7-4.

TABLE 7-4 ## Week 4 Meal Plan

	Breakfast	Lunch	Dinner	Snack
SUNDAY	**Bagels with Smoked Salmon and Cream Cheese (Ch. 15)**	Leftover Spiced Chicken (from Week 3) Cole slaw	**Garlic Linguine with Clams (Ch. 14)**	**Pizza Rolls (Ch. 8)**
MONDAY	Avocado toast with sliced tomatoes	Leftover Cheesy Veggie Crustless Quiche (from Week 3), fruit or salad	**Smoked Salmon Pasta with Asparagus (Ch. 14)**	Leftover Pizza Rolls, grapes
TUESDAY	Oats with fruit	**Seafood Salad Sandwich (Ch. 15)**	**Grilled Marinated Flank Steak (Ch. 13)** Leftover cole slaw	Yogurt parfait
WEDNESDAY	Breakfast burrito	Sandwich with fruit	**Fajitas with Avocado Cream (Ch. 15)**	**Layered Bean Dip (Ch. 8)** with chips
THURSDAY	**Fajita Eggs (Ch. 9)**	**Protein-packed Waldorf Salad (Ch. 10)**	**Moroccan Veggie Skillet (Ch. 13)**	Nuts
FRIDAY	Cereal with milk	Leftover Moroccan Veggie Skillet	**Baked Fish with Herbed Bread Crumbs (Ch. 13)**	Leftover Protein-packed Waldorf Salad
SATURDAY	**Potluck Egg Bake (Ch. 9)**	**Flexible Quesadillas (Ch. 15)**	**Skillet Meatballs (Ch. 13)**	**Add Anything Scones (Ch. 16)**

Grocery list

Produce: 4 bananas | 4 apples | 12 ounces Romaine lettuce | 2 tomatoes | 16-ounce bag cabbage slaw | 1 bunch asparagus | 1 avocado

Dairy: 8 ounces mozzarella cheese | 8 ounces Colby Jack cheese | 16 ounces plain yogurt

Protein: 8 ounces smoked salmon | 1 pound ground beef | 2 pounds beef flank steak | 5-ounce can tuna | 10 to 12 ounces canned clams | 12 to 16 ounces frozen fish (tilapia, mahi-mahi, perch) fillets (plain, not breaded)

Staples: 4 bagels | 1 loaf of bread or 6 rolls | 1 pound linguine | 10-ounce can chickpeas |15-ounce can black beans | 1 pound frozen bread dough | 1 pound frozen shrimp | 6 flour tortillas | flour | sugar | baking powder | salt | garlic powder | steak seasoning blend | Worcestershire sauce

3 Zero Waste Recipes

Discover how to create tantalizing appetizers and egg dishes while reducing waste.

Try your hand at homemade stock, warming soups, and scrumptious salads.

Master homemade marinades, salad dressings, sauces, and toppings.

Save time and money on simple side dishes.

Get more from your meat, fish, and poultry — or try meatless mains if you prefer.

Discover how to cook pasta to perfection.

Find out how to up your sandwich game.

Create zero waste snacks, smoothies, and desserts.

Upcycle scraps into smoothies, mocktails, and cocktails.

Chapter **8**

Guest-Pleasing Starters

RECIPES IN THIS CHAPTER

Chicken Parmesan Stuffed Mushrooms

Lemony Salmon Patties

Ham Fritters

🖑 Layered Bean Dip

🖑 Creamy Veggie Dip

🖑 Basic Cream Cheese Dip

🖑 Roasted Grape Tomatoes with Feta

🖑 Texas Caviar

🖑 Pizza Rolls

🖑 Greek Stuffed Bread

S ometimes you may have a little bit of a roast, a piece of chicken, or a small serving of veggies leftover and you wonder, "Should I save that?" The answer is yes! You can add that piece of chicken, leftover tomato or carrots, or the salsa left in the bottom of the jar to other ingredients to create appetizers, snacks, or dips so delicious, even your guests won't mind that you made them using some leftovers.

Sharing Small Plates to Make a Meal

The recipes in this chapter can serve as an appetizer or snack, or they can be enjoyed together as a meal, as a variety of smaller plates, or *tapas* — a small snack in Spanish cuisine that's often served before a meal and enjoyed with a cocktail. When you have cooked leftovers in the refrigerator, instead of reheating them as is for another meal, think about creating small snacks with them. For example, your leftover roast may make only two sandwiches, but if you slice it thinly, you can create six or eight sliders or mini sandwiches for friends. Add one or two of the dips in this chapter, and you just planned your first tapas party!

Here are a few more ideas: The Chicken Parmesan Stuffed Mushrooms pair well with the Roasted Grape Tomatoes with Feta dip. And the Lemony Salmon Patties pair nicely with the Texas Caviar. You can make a meal with the Greek Stuffed Bread by adding a large green salad.

Don't forget that just about every recipe in this book can be modified by using the ingredients you have on hand.

Chicken Parmesan Stuffed Mushrooms

PREP TIME: 25 MIN	COOK TIME: 15 MIN	YIELD: 18 MUSHROOMS

INGREDIENTS

One 14-ounce can diced tomatoes, or 1 cup tomato sauce

1 teaspoon dried basil

¼ teaspoon garlic powder

18 small white button or baby Bella mushrooms

1 cup chopped cooked chicken

2 tablespoons bread crumbs

½ cup shredded or grated Italian cheese, divided

¼ cup chopped parsley

1 egg, beaten

DIRECTIONS

1 Preheat the oven to 425 degrees. Line a baking sheet with parchment paper.

2 If using canned tomatoes, place the tomatoes in a small saucepan. Add the basil and garlic powder and cook over low heat while preparing the mushrooms.

3 Scrub mushrooms. Remove stems and finely dice them. Place the mushroom caps, bottoms up, on one side of the parchment-lined baking sheet. On the other side of the baking sheet, place the diced mushroom stem pieces. Roast for 10 minutes. Turn the caps over to pour out liquid, return them to the pan, bottoms up, and stir mushroom stems. Roast another 5 minutes. Remove the roasted stems from the baking sheet and set aside for use in another dish; refrigerate once cooled.

4 While mushrooms roast, add chicken, bread crumbs, ⅓ cup of the cheese, and parsley to a medium bowl. Add beaten egg, and mix thoroughly.

5 Scoop up about a tablespoon of the chicken mixture and mound onto the top of each mushroom cap. Gently press the mixture into the cap, flattening it evenly (it's okay if the mixture mounds the mushroom).

(continued)

6 Move the mushroom caps so they're close together (touching) on the baking sheet. Generously spoon the tomato mixture onto each mushroom cap. Sprinkle with the remaining cheese.

7 Bake for 15 minutes until cheese is lightly browned. Transfer to a serving platter and enjoy while warm.

NOTE: The recipe calls for 18 mushrooms, but you may use 15 or 20, depending on the size. Just be sure to have zero waste! You can use the cooked diced mushroom stems to top salads, include in a stuffing, or add to a burger or tomato sauce. Or, instead of saving the cooked stems, you can chop the stems and use them in the stuffing as well.

TIP: Cooking the mushrooms prior to stuffing ensures that the stuffing isn't soggy and the mushrooms are tender. Also, these mushrooms can be baked ahead and then reheated for 10 minutes at 325 degrees.

VARY IT! You can use any leftover cooked meat or seafood, or a leftover vegetarian chili, to stuff mushrooms with. It's a great way to use up a small amount of leftover protein.

Lemony Salmon Patties

PREP TIME: 20 MIN | COOK TIME: 10 MIN | YIELD: 2 PATTIES

INGREDIENTS

6 ounces salmon, cooked or canned

½ cup bread crumbs, divided

1 teaspoon dried dill

1 egg, beaten

1 teaspoon Dijon mustard

1 lemon, halved

Black pepper to taste

Pinch of salt

2 tablespoons vegetable oil

DIRECTIONS

1 Mix the salmon, ¼ cup bread crumbs, dill, egg, mustard, 1 teaspoon juice from half a lemon, 1 teaspoon lemon zest, pepper, and salt in a medium bowl until well combined. Form into two patties. Pour the remaining ¼ cup bread crumbs onto a small plate. Dredge each patty into the plate of bread crumbs until each side is lightly coated.

2 Heat oil in a 10-inch skillet over medium heat. When the oil is hot, gently place patties into skillet and cook until lightly browned on each side, about 3 minutes per side, turning once.

3 Transfer patties to a platter lined with a paper towel, then serve with lemon wedges from remaining lemon half.

NOTE: If using cooked salmon, crumble it before mixing into bowl.

TIP: Serve on top a salad, as an entree, or in a sandwich.

VARY IT! Spice it up with some chopped hot peppers or add a teaspoon of hot sauce.

Ham Fritters

PREP TIME: 15 MIN | COOK TIME: 15 MIN | YIELD: ABOUT 10 FRITTERS

INGREDIENTS

1 cup flour

1 teaspoon baking powder

1 teaspoon sugar

2 eggs

¼ cup milk

1 cup finely chopped, cooked ham

¼ cup minced sweet onion

3 tablespoons pickle relish

1 teaspoon garlic powder

1 teaspoon oregano

⅓ cup vegetable oil

Honey (optional)

DIRECTIONS

1 Mix the flour, baking powder, and sugar in a medium bowl.

2 Make a well in the center of the flour mixture and add the eggs and milk. Beat until well blended into a batter.

3 Fold in the ham, onion, relish, garlic powder, and oregano. Stir until just mixed.

4 Heat a large skillet over medium–high heat. Add enough oil to cover about ¼ inch of the bottom of the pan and heat.

5 Once the oil is 350 degrees (see Tip), drop ¼ cup of the ham batter into the hot oil. Carefully flip to cook the other side after about 2 to 3 minutes, or until lightly browned. Adjust heat as needed.

6 As fritters finish cooking, gently remove them using a metal slotted spoon and transfer to a plate lined with a paper towel or a drip rack. Serve these ham fritters with a small dipping bowl of honey (if desired).

TIP: If you don't have an instant-read thermometer, the easiest way to tell whether the oil is ready is to stick the end of a wooden spoon into the oil. If you see many bubbles form around the wood and they start to float up, your oil is ready for frying. If it's bubbling hard, the oil is too hot; let it cool a bit and check the temperature again.

VARY IT! If you have leftover corn or frozen corn kernels, add ½ cup to the batter before frying. You can also garnish these fritters with a squirt of hot sauce or chipotle sauce or a dollop of plain yogurt or sour cream.

Layered Bean Dip

PREP TIME: 20 MIN | COOK TIME: NONE | YIELD: 8 SERVINGS

INGREDIENTS

One 15-ounce can refried beans

1 cup plain yogurt

2 tablespoons taco seasoning

3 small avocados

1–2 tablespoons lime juice, or juice from 1–2 limes

½ cup shredded Cheddar cheese, or a shredded Mexican blend

1 cup bell pepper, chopped

½ cup finely chopped tomatoes

One 2.25-ounce can sliced black olives, drained and rinsed

2 tablespoons chopped cilantro (optional)

DIRECTIONS

1 Open can of refried beans and put into a medium-sized microwave-safe glass cup or bowl. Microwave on high for 1 to 2 minutes, checking and stirring at 1 minute, until mixture is smooth.

2 Spread beans evenly onto a medium to large platter.

3 Mix the yogurt with the taco seasoning in a small bowl until completely blended. Dollop the yogurt onto the bean mixture, and gently spread over the beans, almost to the edge.

4 Rinse or wipe out the bowl to mash the avocados. Halve each avocado, remove the pit, and scoop flesh into bowl. Using a fork, mash the avocado pieces (some small chunks are fine). Add the lime juice and stir to blend. Gently spread avocado mixture onto the middle of the yogurt layer.

5 Sprinkle the shredded cheese on top of the avocado.

(continued)

6 Combine the bell peppers, tomatoes, and olives in a small bowl. Sprinkle evenly over the top of the bean and cheese layers.

7 Serve immediately or refrigerate 2 hours or overnight. Garnish with fresh cilantro (if desired).

NOTE: This is an easy dip to put together and allows you to mix and match toppings and dippers. Use any leftover tomatoes, chopped lettuce, or peppers that you have on hand. You can also use canned diced tomatoes (drained) if fresh aren't available. Serve with tortilla chips, raw celery, carrot or pepper strips, or pita chips for dipping. Better yet, use up leftover chips from a restaurant or those last few hard shells left over from taco night.

TIP: To make ahead, stop at Step 3 then finish up the steps before serving.

TIP: Modify the recipe to suit your health needs by using a low sodium taco seasoning, low fat or nonfat plain yogurt, or any variety of baked beans you choose. You can also make your own seasoning — simply combine 1 tablespoon chili powder, ½ teaspoon paprika, ¼ teaspoon cumin, ¼ teaspoon garlic powder, ¼ teaspoon salt.

VARY IT! You can add some heat with jalapeño pepper slices or add a few drops of hot sauce over the top. You can also add corn or black beans to the top layer. Or if you happen to have leftover cooked black beans or pinto beans, mash them and make a smaller version.

DIPPING IN TO LEFTOVERS

One of my favorite uses for leftovers is dips, because they are forgiving when it comes to add-ins. Here are some great tips for items almost everyone has on hand. Also check out the *Vary it!* options included with most recipes in this chapter.

- Keep a block of cream cheese in your refrigerator to create a quick dip using the Basic Cream Cheese Dip recipe any time you have a few leftover veggies or herbs to use up. (*Tip:* That recipe calls for an 8-ounce block, but you can make it with a smaller amount.)

- Swap out different veggies to layer your Layered Bean Dip with.

- Slice up any stale bread you have — French baguette or otherwise — to make crostini or to toast and serve with dips.

Creamy Veggie Dip

PREP TIME: 20 MIN PLUS TIME TO REFRIGERATE	COOK TIME: NONE	YIELD: 4 SERVINGS

INGREDIENTS

1½ cups chopped carrots

2 tablespoons water

One 7.7-ounce can chickpeas, drained

1 teaspoon cumin

2 tablespoons olive oil

Pinch of salt

1 garlic clove, or 1 teaspoon minced garlic

¼ cup water or stock

2 tablespoons peanut butter

1 tablespoon lemon juice, or juice from ¼ lemon

Any fresh or dried herb (optional)

1 teaspoon honey or oil (optional)

DIRECTIONS

1 Place carrots in a microwave-safe bowl. Add 2 tablespoons of water and cook on high for 3 minutes in the microwave to soften.

2 Add carrots and remaining ingredients to a food processor or high-speed blender. Blend until smooth and all ingredients are incorporated.

3 Transfer into a bowl and chill for one hour or overnight. When ready to serve, garnish with a favorite herb or a drizzle of honey or oil (if desired).

TIP: This dip is great served with crudités or crackers — but use whatever you have on hand!

TIP: Pureeing your leftover or dried-out carrots is a great way to use them up. Simply peel or cut off any dry parts of roots and put into a processor with a few spoons of water to blend. You can store in the refrigerator for up to 3 days.

VARY IT! You can substitute almost any leftover cooked vegetable for the carrots and make it into a dip. If you like a little heat, add a chipotle pepper with adobe sauce or 1 teaspoon of hot sauce.

Basic Cream Cheese Dip

PREP TIME: 10 MIN	COOK TIME: NONE	YIELD: 8 SERVINGS

INGREDIENTS

8 ounces cream cheese

2 tablespoons of your favorite fresh herb blend, or 1 tablespoon dried

⅓ cup plain yogurt or sour cream

DIRECTIONS

1 Blend all ingredients in a food processor.

2 Place in a bowl, cover, and refrigerate for an hour or more before serving.

TIP: Serve this basic dip with raw vegetables, chips, or whole grain crackers.

NOTE: The options are endless, and this dip is a great way to use up canned tuna, smoked salmon, or bits of leftover chicken or veggies, like green onions, tomatoes, or peppers, or condiments like cocktail sauce or pepper jelly. Simply fold in to the blended mixture and serve with whole grain crackers.

TIP: You can also make a hot dip — just bake at 350 degrees for 20 to 30 minutes until bubbly. For a hot artichoke dip, add a can of chopped artichoke hearts, 2 minced garlic cloves, and bake. Serve with crackers, corn chips, or pumpernickel bread pieces.

VARY IT! Add ½ cup of shredded cheese and some salsa for a Tex-Mex-style dip to serve with tortilla chips. Add ½ cup of chopped chicken, 2 tablespoons hot sauce, and ½ cup of chopped celery for a Buffalo chicken dip, great served with celery sticks and tortilla chips. For a shrimp dip, add 2 tablespoons of cocktail sauce to the cream cheese then fold in chopped shrimp and serve with whole grain crackers.

Roasted Grape Tomatoes with Feta

PREP TIME: 10 MIN | COOK TIME: 15 MIN | YIELD: 2 SERVINGS

INGREDIENTS

4 ounces feta cheese

1 cup grape or cherry tomatoes

2 teaspoons oregano or a favorite herb blend

2 teaspoons olive oil

DIRECTIONS

1 Preheat the oven to 400 degrees.

2 Place the feta into a small baking dish.

3 Add the tomatoes around the feta. Sprinkle with the oregano or herb blend. Drizzle the tomatoes with the olive oil.

4 Bake for 15 minutes, or until tomatoes bubble. Remove from oven and soften the cheese with a spoon and blend in the tomatoes before serving.

TIP: Serve this yummy tomato-cheese dip with crostini, crackers, or pita chips.

NOTE: You can use an herbed feta and skip the herb blend.

VARY IT! You can easily double this recipe and top pasta with it for a side dish or meal.

Texas Caviar

PREP TIME: 20 MIN	COOK TIME: 16–18 MIN	YIELD: 8 SERVINGS

INGREDIENTS

¼ cup rice vinegar or white balsamic vinegar

3 tablespoons olive oil

1 tablespoon lime juice, or juice from ⅓ lime

1 teaspoon ground cumin

1 tablespoon honey

One 14-ounce can black beans, drained and rinsed

One 14-ounce can pinto beans, drained and rinsed

1 cup frozen corn, or drained canned corn

1 cup bell pepper, diced

1 jalapeño pepper, seeded, minced

½ onion, finely chopped

2 tablespoons fresh cilantro chopped, or 1 teaspoon dried

DIRECTIONS

1 Whisk the vinegar, oil, lime juice, cumin, and honey in a small bowl. Set aside.

2 Mix beans, corn, peppers, and onion in a large bowl. Toss to combine.

3 Pour the vinegar dressing over the bean mixture and stir to combine. Refrigerate for at least 1 hour before serving. Garnish with the cilantro.

TIP: Serve with tortilla chips. You can also add this to a salad or top a taco, burrito, or wrap with it.

TIP: Allowing this dip to marinate in the refrigerator longer improves the flavor. If you can, marinate it for 3 hours or up to a day ahead.

NOTE: The beauty of this sort of recipe is that the measurements don't have to be spot on. Whether it's a cup of corn, or a bit more or less, it's fine. Just be sure to dice or mince ingredients uniformly for the best end product.

VARY IT! Use black-eyed peas in place of either bean. If you have leftover tomatoes, you can chop and add them in, too. You can also add chopped cooked shrimp to this dip.

Pizza Rolls

PREP TIME: 15 MIN   COOK TIME: 15 MIN   YIELD: 12 ROLLS

INGREDIENTS

1 8-ounce can crescent roll dough

½ cup tomato sauce

½ cup shredded Mozzarella cheese

1 tablespoon dried Italian seasoning (optional)

DIRECTIONS

1 Preheat the oven to 375 degrees. Line a baking sheet with parchment paper or a silicone mat.

2 Roll the dough into an 8-x-12-inch rectangle.

3 Spread the tomato sauce onto the dough, leaving 1½ inch bare on one long end. Top with cheese.

4 Roll up lengthwise, jelly-roll style. Pinch the end into the roll to seal.

5 Cut the roll into twelve 1-inch slices. Arrange on prepared baking sheet, sprinkle with Italian seasoning (if desired), and bake for 15 minutes until lightly golden. Transfer to a plate to serve.

NOTE: You can make these into heart shapes for a festive treat. Simply pinch the top and bottom of each cut roll into a heart shape before baking.

TIP: You can use 8-ounce crescent dough sheets instead of the rolls.

VARY IT! Have leftover fresh baby spinach leaves beginning to wilt? Add them onto the sauce before rolling.

STORING OR REUSING FRYING OIL

When you use oil to deep-fry, you may be concerned with the amount of oil used. In the Ham Fritters recipe, you use only ⅓ cup of oil in a pan. If you use a deep fryer and want to save the oil to reuse again, keep these tips in mind:

- It's not recommended to use oil more than twice. The oil will take on some of the flavor profile of the food. So if you fry potatoes in the same oil you fried seafood or a ham fritter in, the potatoes will taste like fish or ham.

- Store oil properly to avoid rancidity. Cool the oil completely. Strain it through a fine strainer or cheesecloth to remove any fried bits. Transfer the oil to a clean container, using a funnel. Cover and store in a cool, dark place. Also, when oil is exposed to oxygen, it can develop "free radicals." These rascals are hard on the body and can have a negative impact on health.

- Don't pour oil down the drain. Put it in a sealed container and find out how to recycle it by checking your zip code at www.Earth911.com.

Stuffed Greek Bread

| PREP TIME: 20 MIN | COOK TIME: 35 MIN | YIELD: 12 SERVINGS |

INGREDIENTS

1 pound frozen bread dough, thawed

1 teaspoon vegetable oil

½ cup chopped mushrooms

2 cups chopped tomatoes

10 ounces baby spinach

½ cup black or kalamata olives, chopped

1 cup crumbled feta cheese

1 egg

2 tablespoons Parmesan cheese (optional)

1 tablespoon dried herbs (optional)

DIRECTIONS

1 Thaw bread dough according to package directions. Preheat the oven to 375 degrees.

2 Roll out the dough into a 12-x-16-inch rectangle. Transfer to a baking sheet lined with parchment paper or a pizza stone and allow to rest for 10 minutes while you sauté the veggies.

3 Heat oil in a large sauté pan over medium heat. Add the mushrooms. Sauté until tender, about 3 minutes. Add the tomatoes and sauté another 3 minutes. Add the spinach leaves, stir, then cover. Steam for 1 to 2 minutes. Remove from heat and set aside.

4 Spoon the tomato-spinach mixture and olives evenly down the center length of the dough. Top evenly with the feta.

5 Starting about 3 inches from the top of your rectangular dough, make four to six 1½-inch to 2-inch cuts at the edges of the dough, on a diagonal (see Figure 8-1). Beginning at the top, braid the bread by taking one cut strip, gently twisting it, and pulling it over to the other side of the bread, left over right, right over left. Alternate sides from top to bottom, pinching each end onto the side.

6 Beat the egg and brush it onto the entire loaf to create a shiny, golden crust. Sprinkle with the herbs and Parmesan cheese (if desired).

(continued)

7 Bake for 25 to 35 minutes until golden brown.

8 Cool for 10 minutes and slice using a bread knife and then transfer to a serving dish.

NOTE: You can also use 12 frozen dinner rolls. Thaw, combine into one ball, then proceed with Step 1.

TIP: Spread ½ cup tomato sauce onto the dough if you don't have tomatoes.

VARY IT! You can use just about any leftovers you have as a filling. How about a Thanksgiving bread with turkey, stuffing, and chopped green beans? Or leftover pulled pork and pickles? Or any veggies you need to use up that are in the crisper drawer.

FOLDING STUFFED BREAD

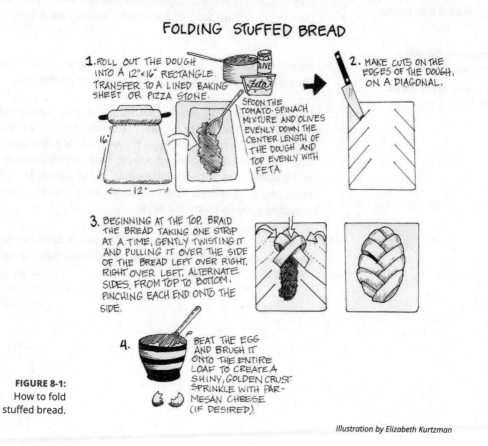

1. ROLL OUT THE DOUGH INTO A 12"×16" RECTANGLE. TRANSFER TO A LINED BAKING SHEET OR PIZZA STONE.

SPOON THE TOMATO-SPINACH MIXTURE AND OLIVES EVENLY DOWN THE CENTER LENGTH OF THE DOUGH AND TOP EVENLY WITH FETA.

2. MAKE CUTS ON THE EDGES OF THE DOUGH, ON A DIAGONAL.

3. BEGINNING AT THE TOP, BRAID THE BREAD TAKING ONE STRIP AT A TIME, GENTLY TWISTING IT AND PULLING IT OVER THE SIDE OF THE BREAD LEFT OVER RIGHT, RIGHT OVER LEFT, ALTERNATE SIDES, FROM TOP TO BOTTOM, PINCHING EACH END ONTO THE SIDE.

4. BEAT THE EGG AND BRUSH IT ONTO THE ENTIRE LOAF TO CREATE A SHINY, GOLDEN CRUST. SPRINKLE WITH PARMESAN CHEESE (IF DESIRED).

FIGURE 8-1:
How to fold stuffed bread.

Illustration by Elizabeth Kurtzman

Chapter 9

Anytime Egg Dishes for All

RECIPES IN THIS CHAPTER

☺ Egg Muffin Cups

Fajita Eggs

Leftover Steak and Eggs

☺ Cheesy Veggie Crustless Quiche

Basic Egg Strata

☺ Basic Frittata

Potluck Egg Bake

Easy Cheese Soufflé

Eggs truly are food waste saviors and an economical protein that you can enjoy at any meal. Scrambled eggs were one of the first meals I taught my children to cook for themselves (and part of my college son's survival plan). A vegetable omelet is the perfect solution to using the extra vegetable that's about to go limp in your crisper drawer or that one ounce of cheese left from the block. You can use up leftover meat, cheese, and vegetables to make a frittata for dinner. That little bit of leftover fajita filling you didn't use last night? Try my delicious Fajita Eggs another morning this week. Having weekend company? The Basic Egg Strata is a launchpad for a make-ahead breakfast that'll be sure to satisfy your guests.

AN EGG A DAY . . .

Want to improve your memory, mood, muscle control, and other brain and nervous system functions? Eat eggs! Eggs are an excellent source — one egg provides 147 milligrams — of the important B vitamin choline, which is needed to produce acetylcholine, an important neurotransmitter. Adults need 425 to 550 milligrams of choline, teens aged 14 to 18 need 400 to 550 milligrams, and children from infant to 13 years need varying amounts daily from 125 to 375 milligrams (check with your doctor or pediatrician).

On the other hand, if you think "cholesterol" when you think about eggs, stay calm and read on. Dietary cholesterol in eggs isn't anything to worry too much about. All animal products contain cholesterol, and meats are the primary contributor to the diet, contributing about 42 percent, while eggs contribute 25 percent. One whole egg provides about 185 milligrams of cholesterol. The overall recommendation is to limit cholesterol to less than 300 milligrams per day. For those with a diagnosis of high blood cholesterol, reducing saturated fat and increasing fiber in the diet are key goals, along with limiting cholesterol to less than 200 milligrams daily, although some studies showed no adverse effects in including one egg a day in the diet.

How to Tell Your Quiche from Your Frittata

You can prepare eggs in many different ways, beyond just frying or boiling. You can bake them or make a strata, scramble them into a full meal as a quiche or frittata, or impress your friends with a soufflé.

>> **Bake:** If you have more than two people to feed, or you're short on time, baking eggs is an easy option Scramble up a big batch or drop eggs onto a pan to bake them sunny side up:

- To make a batch of scrambled eggs for a crowd, crack a dozen eggs into a bowl. Add 8 to 10 ounces of milk and salt and pepper to taste. Beat the eggs until well combined. Pour into a 3-quart oven-safe dish that's been sprayed with vegetable oil spray. Bake at 350 degrees for 15 to 20 minutes, stirring halfway through.

- To bake sunny side up eggs, crack eggs without breaking the yolks into a bowl. Spray a nonstick baking sheet liberally with cooking oil spray. Gently pour the whole eggs onto the pan. Bake at 350 for 5 minutes if you want runny yolks and 8 to 10 minutes for harder yolks.

>> **Strata:** A strata typically includes bread, eggs, cheese, and diced meat or vegetables. It's a great dish to make to use up leftover bits. You can prepare a strata ahead of time and bake when ready to serve. It makes a nice meal for breakfast, brunch, or dinner. Check out the Basic Egg Strata recipe in this chapter.

>> **Frittata:** A frittata is a fried scrambled egg dish that originated in Italy. Some call it the Italian version of the French omelet, but unlike an omelet, the frittata add-ins are mixed *into* the eggs. To make a frittata, scramble eggs and then add any number of chopped meats, vegetables, and cheese to them. Pour the mixture into an oiled pan and fry until brown on the bottom then either flip or place into a hot oven to finish baking the top. See the Basic Frittata recipe in this chapter.

>> **Omelet:** The omelet is made on the stove top and can also include a multitude of fillings (cheeses, diced meats, and vegetables). Unlike the frittata, strata, and baked eggs, omelets are made one at a time, so they're best when you're cooking for just one or two people. It takes a bit of practice to master the omelet, so no worries if your first few attempts aren't snapshot worthy. Once you master this classic dish, you may use your skill to impress a special someone for a dinner date at home (yep, omelets are great for dinner!). To make an omelet, read the details in the next section.

>> **Quiche:** A quiche is another French egg dish. Like the frittata, it adds ingredients to scrambled eggs. It differs from the frittata in that it has a bottom crust. A classic quiche includes fried bacon, onions, and Swiss cheese. I tend to prefer a vegetable-cheese quiche, but you can really add whatever you want. The basic formula is one pie crust (you can use store-bought or homemade), 4 eggs, 1½ cups milk, 1½ cups shredded cheese, and 2 cups of mix-ins. Some delicious combinations include asparagus, chives, and goat cheese; and broccoli and Cheddar cheese. You can also make a crustless quiche, like the Cheesy Veggie Crustless Quiche in this chapter.

>> **Soufflé:** Making an egg soufflé can seem intimidating, but it results in a beautiful, delicious culinary delight. If you find yourself with leftover egg whites, that may be the perfect time to get adventurous and make a cheese soufflé. The Easy Cheese Soufflé in this chapter is a mini version for two, so it's less intimidating.

Easing into Egg Recipes with an Omelet

Making an omelet is a culinary skill that can transform scrambled eggs to elegance. This classic dish is worthy of a little practice. An omelet can be served at any mealtime, and you can fill it with any sort of leftover vegetables, chopped cooked meat, or even fruit preserves and chopped nuts. If using a filling, consider about ⅓ cup for add-ins.

It helps to have an omelet pan. Omelet pans are small and have shallow curved sides. But you can make an omelet in any small pan. Nonstick pans make omelets super easy, but if you don't have nonstick, be sure to butter the pan well or spray with nonstick cooking spray before adding the egg mixture.

Here are the basic steps to an easy, breezy, delicious omelet.

1. **Beat 2 eggs and a pinch of salt and black pepper with a whisk in a small bowl until well blended.**

2. **Heat nonstick pan over medium heat.**

3. **Add a teaspoon of butter, allowing it to melt, and move pan around until the bottom and part of the sides are fully coated with the butter.**

4. **Add the egg mixture to the pan.**

    Allow egg mixture to set for a few seconds then gently place a spatula under the edges, allowing liquid to pour under the edges. Continue doing this until most of the egg liquid is set.

5. **Add the filling to the top of omelet, keeping it all toward one side.**

6. **Flip the empty side over the filling.**

    Allow to cook another minute if needed, then slide onto a plate. Enjoy!

USES FOR YOUR EGGSHELLS

When you're done cracking all those eggs, you may wonder how you can reuse the shells. Rinse them with water when you finish cracking them and save for later use, such as the following ideas:

- Remove stains from coffee mugs or pots. Add eggshells and then add a little bit of water to the mug or pot. Let sit overnight then clean in the morning.

- Make sidewalk chalk. Wash four to six eggshells and let dry. Crush them in a food processor (you can also use a mortar and pestle or a coffee grinder if you have one). Mix 1 teaspoon of flour with 1 teaspoon of water in a small bowl until it's paste-like. Add a tablespoon of the crushed eggshells along with a drop of food coloring. Mix until combined and you can shape into a log (you may need another spoon of water). Wrap the log in paper towels and let dry for a week.

- Feed the birds. Collect eggshells and spread them onto a baking sheet. Bake in a 300-degree oven for 20 to 30 minutes. Once cooled, crush them and transfer to a sealed container. You can then spread this on the bottom of a bird feeder or on the ground in your yard for the birds.

Check out Chapter 18 for a few more uses for eggshells.

Egg Muffin Cups

INGREDIENTS

5 eggs

3 tablespoons milk

Pinch of salt

Black pepper to taste

Nonstick cooking spray

½ cup spinach, chopped

3 tablespoons minced sweet onion

¼ cup shredded Swiss cheese

DIRECTIONS

1 Preheat the oven to 350 degrees. Crack eggs into a medium bowl and whisk with the milk. Add the salt and pepper and mix well with a fork or whisk. Set aside.

2 Spray a 6-cup muffin pan with cooking spray. Divide the vegetables and cheese evenly into 6 muffin cups.

3 Pour egg mixture into each muffin cup, filling about two-thirds full.

4 Bake for 12–15 minutes, until firm, but not overly browned. Let cool for 5 minutes then remove from muffin pan and serve warm.

NOTE: Most silicone muffin pans don't require spraying with cooking spray, but products can vary.

TIP: Wrap leftovers in plastic wrap and store in the refrigerator for 2 days. Or you can freeze in an airtight container, silicone freezer bag, or wrapped in plastic wrap for up to a month. When ready to eat, transfer to microwave safe plate and reheat in microwave or warm 300-degree oven or toaster oven. Put together a sandwich by adding the egg cup to an English muffin, tortilla, or your bread of choice.

VARY IT! You can add any chopped vegetable or type of cheese you like in place of the spinach, onions, and Swiss cheese. Great combinations include goat cheese with asparagus; bell peppers and Colby Jack cheese; or onions and mushrooms with a sharp Cheddar.

Fajita Eggs

INGREDIENTS

1 cup fajita filling (see fajita recipe in Chapter 15)

4 eggs

2 tablespoons milk

Pinch of salt

Black pepper to taste

⅛ teaspoon chili powder

DIRECTIONS

1 If using leftover fajita filling, heat it in the microwave for 1–2 minutes until hot.

2 Heat a nonstick pan over medium heat. Beat eggs and milk in a small bowl. Add salt, pepper, and chili powder. Pour into pan and scramble until set, about 1–2 minutes.

3 Add the fajita mixture to the eggs and stir until combined and eggs are cooked through, another 1–2 minutes.

TIP: You can enjoy these eggs on their own, or fill a flour tortilla with this mixture and enjoy it as a classic fajita. Warm 2 flour tortillas on a microwave safe plate, under a damp paper towel, microwaving on high for 20 to 30 seconds. Divide egg mixture between tortillas, and garnish with cheese, salsa, or sour cream if desired.

NOTE: You can also make this into an omelet, using the fajita filling and adding 2 tablespoons of Monterey Jack cheese. (See the section "Easing into Egg Recipes with an Omelet" for steps to making an omelet.)

Leftover Steak and Eggs

PREP TIME: 15 MIN	COOK TIME: 10 MIN	YIELD: 2 SERVINGS

INGREDIENTS

4 eggs

2 tablespoons milk

Pinch of salt

Black pepper to taste

1 teaspoon vegetable oil

⅓ cup thinly sliced onion

3 ounces cooked steak, thinly sliced

DIRECTIONS

1 In a medium bowl, beat eggs with milk until well blended. Add salt and pepper. Set aside.

2 Heat oil in a medium-size skillet over medium heat.

3 Add onions and sauté for 3–4 minutes. Add steak to heat through. Remove steak and onions from pan and cover with foil to keep warm, or keep in a 200-degree oven.

4 Pour the eggs into the hot pan and allow to set for 1 minute. To scramble, move the eggs around the pan with a spatula. Cook until eggs are just set (most liquid is firm) or to desired doneness. Remove from pan.

5 Serve eggs along with the steak and onions.

NOTE: Whether for breakfast or dinner, this dish pairs well with whole grain toast and sliced tomato, avocado, or fresh fruit.

VARY IT! You can cook the eggs over easy or any way you like and serve the steak and onions on the side. You can also cook other vegetables, such as sliced zucchini, spinach, mushrooms, or chopped broccoli — or whatever you have on hand — with the onions. Sliced green onions are also delicious with scrambled eggs.

Cheesy Veggie Crustless Quiche

PREP TIME: 10 MIN | COOK TIME: 35 MIN | YIELD: 6 SERVINGS

INGREDIENTS

Nonstick cooking spray

½ cup flour

½ teaspoon baking powder

7 eggs

½ cup milk

Pinch of salt

Black pepper to taste

½ teaspoon dried dill

¼ cup diced onions

½ cup shredded Swiss cheese

1 small zucchini, thinly sliced

DIRECTIONS

1 Preheat the oven to 375 degrees. Spray a 9-inch glass pie dish with cooking spray.

2 Evenly place sliced zucchini into the pie dish, starting on the outside and working your way into the middle, creating a circular pattern. Set aside.

3 Mix flour and baking powder together in a small bowl and set aside.

4 Whisk eggs and milk in a medium bowl. Stir in salt, pepper, dill, onions, and Swiss cheese.

5 Add the flour mixture to the egg mixture and mix well.

6 Slowly pour onto zucchini in the pie dish.

7 Carefully place the pie dish in the oven and bake for 35 minutes or until lightly golden.

8 Cut into wedges and serve.

NOTE: This crustless quiche has the "crust" built into it. You can also prepare this in an 8-x-8-inch glass baking dish. It makes a lovely brunch served with a side of fruit.

VARY IT! The zucchini gives this an elegant look, but you can also use cut asparagus or mix spinach into the egg mixture in Step 3 and simply pour into the dish and bake.

Basic Egg Strata

INGREDIENTS

Nonstick cooking spray

6 eggs

1 cup milk

Pinch of salt

1 teaspoon Dijon mustard

Black pepper to taste

5 slices stale bread, cut into 1-inch cubes

½ cup shredded cheese

½ cup chopped ham

1 cup chopped spinach

½ cup chopped onions

DIRECTIONS

1 Spray a 9-x-11-inch baking dish with cooking spray.

2 Whisk eggs, milk, salt, mustard, and pepper until well blended.

3 Fold in the bread cubes and cheese. Stir in the ham, spinach, and onions.

4 Pour mixture into the prepared baking dish, cover, and refrigerate for at least 4 hours or overnight.

5 When ready to bake, preheat the oven to 350 degrees and bake strata for 45 minutes until top is slightly puffy and golden and eggs are set.

6 Let cool for 10 minutes then cut into 6 rectangular servings.

NOTE: Strata is an excellent way to use stale bread; however, if you don't have stale bread, no worries. You can use any type of bread — sliced, white, wheat, buns, or gluten free. Stale or dried out bread will soak in more of the eggs when left overnight. If you're feeding a crowd, double the recipe and pour into a 11-x-13-inch baking dish. Increase baking time by 10–20 minutes.

TIP: This is a great dish to make the night before then refrigerate and pop into the oven in the morning.

VARY IT! Add cooked sausage, cut cooked asparagus, chopped bell pepper, or any favorite vegetable to this dish at Step 3.

Basic Frittata

INGREDIENTS

Nonstick cooking spray

1 teaspoon olive oil

½ cup diced sweet onion

1 cup grape tomatoes, halved

Pinch of salt plus ½ teaspoon

8 eggs

½ cup milk

1 teaspoon dried thyme

½ cup ricotta cheese

½ cup shredded Asiago or other sharp cheese

Black pepper to taste

DIRECTIONS

1 Heat the oven to 400 degrees and spray an oven-safe fry pan with cooking spray.

2 Heat oil in the pan over medium-low heat. Add the onions and sauté for 2 minutes. Add the grape tomatoes and the pinch of salt and cook for another 3–4 minutes over medium-low heat.

3 While tomatoes are cooking, whisk the eggs, milk, ½ teaspoon salt, thyme, and ricotta cheese in a medium bowl. Blend well then fold in the shredded cheese.

4 Pour the egg mixture into the pan with the onions and tomatoes. Add black pepper onto the top. Cook on the stove top for about 5 minutes then carefully transfer pan to oven.

5 Bake for 10–15 minutes or until eggs are set (dip a knife into the middle, and if it's too soft, keep in the oven for a few more minutes).

6 Allow to cool for 5 minutes before serving. Cut into wedges.

TIP: Serve right in the pan or invert onto a serving platter.

VARY IT! You can add another ½ cup vegetables or ½ cup meat (or up to a full cup total) at Step 3.

Potluck Egg Bake

INGREDIENTS

Nonstick cooking spray

½ cup cooked pulled pork

½ cup roasted bell peppers, chopped

2 teaspoons dried thyme or tarragon

5 eggs

¼ cup milk

½ teaspoon Dijon mustard

½ cup shredded Cheddar cheese

Pinch of salt

Black pepper to taste

DIRECTIONS

1 Preheat the oven to 350 degrees. Spray an 8-x-8-inch glass baking dish with cooking spray.

2 Add the cooked pork and peppers to the baking dish. (This is a great way to use any leftover meat or veggies!) Sprinkle with thyme or your favorite herbs (use up any that may be wilting).

3 Whisk eggs, milk, mustard, cheese, salt, and pepper in a medium bowl until well blended.

4 Pour egg mixture into prepared baking dish and bake for 35–40 minutes until set.

5 Cut into squares and serve.

NOTE: A side salad makes a nice accompaniment to this meal. An egg bake is perfect for a weekend breakfast or main dish.

TIP: You can also bake this dish in 6 small ramekins, making individual egg bakes for each person with custom fillings. Spray ramekins with cooking spray then pour egg mixture into them at Step 4 and bake for 20–25 minutes until set.

VARY IT! Use leftover cooked turkey (great during Thanksgiving season) or use a cup of chopped raw broccoli florets and stems in place of the pulled pork and peppers. You can use any scraps of raw veggies about to expire that you have in the refrigerator. Vary the cheese and herbs as well. Try smoked salmon with asparagus and goat cheese. Or try these cheese-herb combos: Swiss and dill, American and parsley, Fontina and rosemary, or Colby and cilantro.

Easy Cheese Soufflé

PREP TIME: 25 MIN   COOK TIME: 15 MIN   YIELD: 4 SERVINGS

INGREDIENTS

1 tablespoon butter, softened

2 tablespoons flour, divided

4 eggs, separated

4 ounces shredded Cheddar cheese, divided

Salt and pepper to taste

½ cup milk

DIRECTIONS

1 Preheat the oven to 375 degrees. Butter four 3-inch ramekins then dust with 1 tablespoon of flour. Place them onto a baking sheet and set aside.

2 Place the egg whites into a small mixing bowl and set aside.

3 Fill just the bottom of a double boiler with water and heat to low boil. (If you don't have a double boiler, use a medium saucepan and a metal bowl that will fit over it.)

4 In the top of the boiler or bowl, toss together the cheese, remaining flour, and a pinch of salt and pepper. Stir in the milk and heat over the water pot until steamy and the cheese melts, about 5 minutes.

5 Beat two egg yolks in a small bowl then slowly drizzle it into the hot milk-cheese mixture, stirring constantly with a whisk until blended. Remove the bowl from heat and set aside.

6 Mix the egg whites with an electric mixer, using the whisk attachment, until stiff peaks form. Fold a third of them into the cheese mixture, and then gently mix in the rest.

7 Evenly divide this mixture into the prepared ramekins and bake for 12–15 minutes, or until puffy. Serve immediately.

NOTE: Don't open the oven until the egg is puffed.

TIP: Refrigerate the leftover 2 egg yolks for another use, like a key lime pie, lemon bars, or a hollandaise sauce.

Chapter 10

Leveraging Leftovers for Nutritious Soups and Salads

RECIPES IN THIS CHAPTER

Homemade Stock

Empty-the-fridge Chicken Vegetable Soup with Egg Noodles

Beef Stew with Potatoes, Carrots, and Peas

Beef Chili

Kitchen Sink Chicken Chili

Wedding Soup with Spinach

Bean Soup with Diced Pork

🖲 Mixed Produce Salad with Farro

Protein-packed Waldorf Salad

Salmon Spinach Salad with Sliced Grapes

🖲 Chopped Salad with Lemon Vinaigrette

Tuna "a la Niçoise" Salad

🖲 Nutty Mixed Salad with Beans, Beets, and Goat Cheese

Homemade soups and salads are great ways to waste less. Less-than-perky veggies do just fine when chopped into a stew, chili, or soup (you can even freeze them for another meal on another day). A bonus is that adding vegetables into soups and stews ensures that you get all the nutrients those veggies offer.

A bed of lettuce is a perfect landscape for high-quality protein, other fruits and vegetables, and healthy fats. And making your own dressing saves time and money — the bonus here is that you can use whatever you have on hand (see Chapter 11 for my Everyday Vinaigrette Dressing and Citrus-mustard Salad Dressing).

Gone are the days of skimping on salad dressing! Fats help your body absorb important fat-soluble vitamins (vitamins A, D, E, and K) that are found in many vegetables. You don't have to drown your salad in dressing, but the oils and other healthy fats you top salads with, like nuts and seeds, add overall nutrition and definitely make the salad more enjoyable.

REMEMBER

Zero waste cooking isn't just about saving money and being kind to the environment; it's also about taking better care of yourself. When you switch your mindset to preparing food from whole ingredients and utilizing as much of it as possible, you're also making it your mission to make the most of the food you have. In the end, you'll be providing better nourishment for your family.

Putting Stock in the Benefits of Homemade Stock

Making stock involves cooking down meat or vegetables in water, resulting in a nutritious liquid. The longer it simmers, the more nutritious it gets.

Stock is an excellent way to use up food scraps. You can turn whole veggies or scraps (like boiled-down onion skins) as well as leftover chicken or beef bones into delicious homemade stock. Although it may seem time-consuming, once you get into the groove of throwing a pot of water on to make stock, you'll find it's so worth it.

REMEMBER

Stock isn't just for soups; it's also a great ingredient that adds flavor to recipes. Use stock instead of water for both added flavor and nutrition in rice dishes or casseroles; simply substitute the same amount of stock for the water in the recipe. Vegetables can also be cooked in stock for added flavor. For example, cook carrots in chicken stock. You can also use stock in pasta dishes such as the Vegetable Lasagna recipe (see Chapter 14) and the Basic Cream Sauce recipe (see Chapter 11); substitute stock for half of the milk or cream in those recipes.

TIP

If you don't have time to make the stock as you generate bones or scraps, save them in an airtight container and store in the refrigerator for up to five days. You can also make stock using an instant pot, if you have one. Use the same ingredients, but pressure cook for 40 minutes, then strain once cooled.

Homemade Stock

| PREP TIME: 15 MIN | COOK TIME: 2 HRS | YIELD: 1½ QUARTS |

INGREDIENTS

1 pound leftover bones of a whole chicken or beef bones, with some meat bits

1 cup chopped carrots

½ cup onion, roughly chopped

1 cup celery, roughly chopped (including tops)

2 tablespoons or sprigs of fresh thyme or rosemary

½ teaspoon salt, optional

8 cups water

DIRECTIONS

1 Place all ingredients into a large stockpot.

2 Add the water and bring to a simmer over medium-low heat. Reduce heat and allow to simmer for 2 hours. The longer you simmer, the more flavor you'll get.

3 Allow stock to cool (you can skim off fat if desired). Strain the stock into another pot or large bowl. Ladle into pint-size freezer-safe containers to freeze for up to 3 months or store in the refrigerator and use within a week.

VARY IT! To make a vegetarian stock, simply omit the chicken or beef bones and use a variety of vegetables such as mushrooms, spinach, onions, carrots, and celery.

TIP: Stock is generally not seasoned since it's meant to be used as an ingredient, so the salt is optional. If making beef stock, adding 1 tablespoon apple cider vinegar can help dissolve the collogen from bones.

NOTE: You can be flexible when you make stock. If you have 4 stalks of celery to use up, use them. If you have less carrots, it's okay. You can use a whole onion if you have it, but if you have part of one left over, use it. You can use steak bones or rib bones for beef stock, or a chicken or turkey carcass (the bones left from the whole bird) or the bones of poultry parts for chicken stock.

Empty-the-fridge Chicken Vegetable Soup with Egg Noodles

PREP TIME: 40 MIN	COOK TIME: 20 MIN	YIELD: 6 SERVINGS

INGREDIENTS

½ teaspoon olive oil

1 cup diced carrots

2 stalks of celery, chopped

6 cups chicken stock (see Homemade Stock recipe earlier in this chapter)

4 boneless, skinless chicken thighs

Salt and black pepper to taste

2 cups egg noodles

1 cup spinach leaves, chopped

3 tablespoons grated Parmesan cheese

DIRECTIONS

1 In a small stockpot, heat oil and sauté carrots and celery for about 2 to 3 minutes. Add stock and bring to a low boil. Reduce heat to simmer and add the chicken thighs. Simmer on low for 20 to 25 minutes. Remove the chicken and shred or cut finely.

2 While cutting chicken, bring the stock back to boil then add the egg noodles and cook for 7 to 8 minutes.

3 Reduce heat and return chicken to the pot. Season with salt and pepper. Add the spinach and simmer for another 3 to 5 minutes.

4 Ladle the soup into 6 bowls. Garnish with Parmesan cheese.

NOTE: You can also use 1 or 2 cups of leftover cooked chicken.

VARY IT! Use up whatever vegetables you have in the fridge at Step 3 — chopped broccoli or cauliflower, peas, cut green beans, or sliced zucchini all work well. You can also use 2 split chicken breasts instead of thighs.

Beef Chili (Chapter 10)

Tuna "a la Niçoise" Salad (Chapter 10)

Roasted Bell Peppers (Chapter 12)

Stuffed Baked Potatoes (Chapter 13)

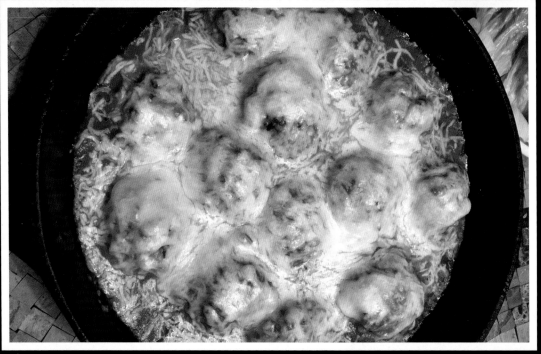

Skillet Meatballs (Chapter 13)

Foil-baked Tilapia with Peppers (Chapter 13)

Moroccan Veggie Skillet (Chapter 13)

Flexible Quesadillas (Chapter 15)

Black Bean Brownie Bites (Chapter 16)

Fruit Cobbler (Chapter 16)

Green Smoothie (Chapter 17)

Mocktails and Cocktails (Chapter 17)
Special Whiskey Sour Cocktail (Chapter 17) with Aquafaba Fluff (Chapter 11)

Beef Stew with Potatoes, Carrots, and Peas

PREP TIME: 20 MIN	COOK TIME: 2 HR	YIELD: 6 SERVINGS

INGREDIENTS

1 pound round steak, cut into small cubes

¼ cup flour

¼ teaspoon salt

1 teaspoon black pepper

1 teaspoon canola oil

½ cup chopped onion

1 cup sliced carrots

1 clove garlic, crushed, or 1 teaspoon jarred minced garlic

1 cup dry red wine

3 cups beef stock (see the Homemade Stock recipe earlier in this chapter)

1 8-ounce can tomato sauce

1 tablespoon tomato paste

2 tablespoons balsamic vinegar

1 teaspoon fresh thyme, or ¼ teaspoon dried

2 cups cubed potatoes, with skin (wash well before cutting)

½ cup fresh or frozen peas

DIRECTIONS

1 Place beef cubes into a bowl, and sprinkle with flour. Add salt and pepper and toss to coat evenly.

2 Heat oil in 4-quart saucepan over medium heat. In batches (adding enough to cover bottom of pan), brown beef on all sides then remove to a clean bowl. Continue batches until all the beef is browned. Remove from pan and set aside.

3 In the same pot, sauté the onion and carrots over medium-low heat until tender, about 3 minutes. Watch the heat and lower if onion is browning. Add the garlic and cook for another minute. Deglaze the pan by gradually pouring the wine into it, stirring to remove brown bits from the bottom of the pan.

4 Add the beef stock, tomato sauce, tomato paste, and balsamic vinegar. Stir to combine. Add the beef back to the pot, along with the thyme then simmer for 60 to 90 minutes on low heat.

5 After the meat has simmered, add the potatoes and peas. Bring back to a boil then reduce heat to simmer and cook for an additional 30 to 45 minutes.

6 Season with additional salt and pepper to taste. Serve in bowls.

NOTE: If you don't have wine, you can use 4 cups of stock instead. You also can substitute chuck roast or boneless short ribs for the round steak.

VARY IT! Substitute ½ cup sun-dried tomatoes for the tomato sauce. I love flavored balsamic vinegars, and an espresso balsamic works beautifully for any beef dish.

Beef Chili

PREP TIME: 15 MIN   COOK TIME: 60 MIN   YIELD: 8 SERVINGS

INGREDIENTS

1 pound ground beef

½ cup diced onion

2 cloves garlic crushed, or 2 teaspoons jarred minced garlic

1 cup diced bell pepper

2 tablespoons chili powder, divided

1 teaspoon cumin

1 teaspoon salt

Two 15-ounce cans pinto (chili) beans in sauce

Two 14.5-ounce cans diced tomatoes with green chilies

1 teaspoon smoked paprika

¼ cup shredded sharp Cheddar cheese

DIRECTIONS

1 Brown beef in a 3- to 5-quart stockpot or Dutch oven. (If using higher fat beef, drain off excess fat.) Add the onions, garlic, peppers, 1 tablespoon of the chili powder, cumin, and salt. Stir to blend, and cook another 2 minutes.

2 Add the beans and tomatoes to the beef mixture. Stir in remaining chili powder and paprika. Bring to a boil then reduce heat.

3 Simmer, covered, for an hour over low heat. Add up to a cup of stock if desired.

4 Spoon chili into bowls. Garnish with cheese.

TIP: Pair this chili with cornbread and a tossed salad for a complete meal.

NOTE: If you prefer leaner ground beef, you may need to add a teaspoon of oil when browning in Step 1.

VARY IT! Substitute black beans or kidney beans for all or part of the pinto beans. Use any cheese blend that you like for garnish. You can also make this a vegetarian chili and substitute another can of beans or 2 cups of plant-based meat crumbles for the beef.

Kitchen Sink Chicken Chili

PREP TIME: 10 MIN	COOK TIME: 30 MIN	YIELD: 6 SERVINGS

INGREDIENTS

Two 14-ounce cans cannellini beans, drained and rinsed, divided

1 teaspoon canola oil

1 pound boneless, skinless chicken breasts

½ teaspoon salt

Black pepper to taste

⅔ cup diced sweet onion

3 cups chicken stock (see the Homemade Stock recipe earlier in this chapter)

1 tablespoon chili powder

1 teaspoon paprika

1 teaspoon cumin

1 teaspoon garlic powder

1 4-ounce can chopped green chilies

1 bell pepper, seeded and diced

Shredded Monterey Jack cheese, plain yogurt, and fresh cilantro for garnishing (optional)

DIRECTIONS

1 Mash ½ cup of the beans in a small bowl and set aside. Cut chicken into small ½-inch chunks.

2 Heat oil in a large Dutch oven or stockpot. Add the chicken, salt, pepper, and onions. Cook, stirring often, until chicken is no longer pink and onion is translucent.

3 Add the stock, spices, green chilies, bell pepper, and mashed beans. Stir to combine.

4 Bring to a boil then reduce heat to simmer. Add the remaining beans, cover and simmer for 30 minutes.

5 Ladle soup into bowls and garnish with shredded cheese, a dollop of yogurt, and chopped cilantro (if desired).

VARY IT! You can virtually add any bean or vegetable to this chili. You can also substitute 2 cups of leftover chopped chicken for the chicken breasts and add it with the stock at Step 3.

Wedding Soup with Spinach

PREP TIME: 15 MIN | COOK TIME: 30 MIN | YIELD: 4 SERVINGS

INGREDIENTS

1 teaspoon olive oil

½ cup diced onion

½ cup diced carrots

2 stalks celery, diced

½ teaspoon red pepper flakes (optional)

6 cups chicken stock (see the Homemade Stock recipe earlier in this chapter)

½ teaspoon salt

Black pepper to taste

1 cup shredded cooked chicken

1 cup ditalini, or other small pasta

2 cups chopped spinach

¼ cup grated Romano cheese

DIRECTIONS

1 Heat the oil in a stockpot or Dutch oven.

2 Add the onion, carrots, celery, and pepper flakes (if desired), and sauté over medium heat for about 5 minutes, stirring often.

3 Add the stock, bring to a boil, and then reduce heat. Season with salt and pepper.

4 Add the chicken and simmer for 20 minutes.

5 Add the pasta and simmer another 8 minutes. Stir in the spinach until it's wilted.

6 Ladle soup into bowls, garnish with cheese, and serve.

TIP: Serve with a side salad and fresh bread.

NOTE: Traditional wedding soup often includes homemade miniature meatballs, but this version is quick and uses up leftover chicken.

Bean Soup with Diced Pork

PREP TIME: 5 MIN	COOK TIME: 30 MIN	YIELD: 6 SERVINGS

INGREDIENTS

1 teaspoon olive oil

½ cup diced onion

½ cup celery, finely chopped

1 cup diced carrots

2 tablespoons tomato paste

1 cup diced cooked pork
or ham

Two 15-ounce cans great
northern beans, drained,
rinsed, and divided

5 cups chicken stock (see the
Homemade Stock recipe earlier
in this chapter)

½ teaspoon salt

DIRECTIONS

1 Heat the oil in a stockpot or small Dutch oven. Sauté the onion, celery, and carrots for about 4 minutes, or until onion is translucent.

2 Stir in the tomato paste. Add the diced pork and heat through.

3 Mash about ½ cup of the beans in a small bowl. Add the stock, salt, and mashed beans to the pot and stir. Bring to a boil, add the rest of the beans, and then reduce heat to simmer. Simmer for 20 to 30 minutes.

4 Ladle soup into bowls and serve.

NOTE: This soup freezes well. Allow to cool then pour into a freezer-safe bowl with secure lid. Defrost and reheat within 2 months.

VARY IT! Omit the pork and use a vegetable stock to make this a vegan soup.

Mixed Produce Salad with Farro

PREP TIME: 15 MIN	COOK TIME: N/A	YIELD: 2 SERVINGS

INGREDIENTS

3 cups washed mixed greens

½ cup sliced cucumber

½ cup chopped broccoli

½ cup grape tomatoes, halved

1 cup cooked farro (follow package directions), or any leftover cooked grain

2 tablespoons chopped fresh parsley or 2 teaspoons dried

3 tablespoons prepared salad dressing

DIRECTIONS

1 Add all ingredients to a large bowl and toss well. Add 3 tablespoons of your favorite salad dressing and toss until evenly coated.

2 Divide between two plates and serve.

TIP: Top this salad with 3 ounces of fish or chicken for a main dish.

NOTE: The Everyday Vinaigrette Dressing in Chapter 11 works well for this salad.

VARY IT! You can chop any vegetable you have into this salad bowl. Try leftover corn on the cob or any type of pepper. Swap out any favorite herb for the parsley.

Protein-packed Waldorf Salad

INGREDIENTS

¼ cup plain yogurt

1 tablespoon mayonnaise

Pinch of salt

2 tablespoon lemon juice, or juice from half a lemon

1 cup cooked chopped chicken

1 large apple, cored and cut into ½-inch pieces

½ cup chopped walnuts

½ cup celery, sliced

½ cup halved seedless grapes

DIRECTIONS

1 Whisk the yogurt, mayonnaise, salt, and lemon juice in a medium bowl.

2 Fold in the chicken, apples, walnuts, celery, and grapes. Toss until dressing coats ingredients and then serve.

TIP: You can serve this salad on top of lettuce or as a side dish to your entrée.

NOTE: You can add various quantities of apples and grapes to your liking for this recipe.

VARY IT! Use leftover cooked salmon or canned tuna in place of the cooked chicken.

Salmon Spinach Salad with Sliced Grapes

PREP TIME: 20 MIN | COOK TIME: 10 MIN | YIELD: 2 SERVINGS

INGREDIENTS

Dressing

2 tablespoons olive oil

1 tablespoon apple cider vinegar

1 tablespoon honey

½ teaspoon Dijon mustard

Salt to taste

Salad

8 ounces salmon filet, divided

2 teaspoons cooking oil

Salt and black pepper to taste

4 cups baby spinach

⅔ cup halved seedless grapes

½ cup chopped pecans

2 ounces goat cheese or feta cheese, crumbled

DIRECTIONS

1   Add all dressing ingredients into a small bowl and whisk until well combined. Set aside.

2   Heat a small skillet over medium-high heat. Add the pecans and toast in the pan, stirring constantly for 1 to 2 minutes, carefully watching not to burn. Remove from heat and transfer to a small bowl.

3   Season the salmon with salt and pepper. Using the same pan you used for the nuts, return to medium-high heat. Heat the oil for a minute then place the salmon filet in the pan, skin-side up. Sear each side for 4 to 5 minutes, turning only once. Remove from heat and set aside while you prep the salad.

4   Toss the spinach, pecans, and goat cheese into a large bowl. Pour dressing over the salad and toss to combine and coat.

5   Divide salad evenly between two plates. Top each with salmon filet.

VARY IT! You can use walnuts in place of pecans. You can also use a diced apple or pear or ¼ cup dried cranberries in place of the grapes.

Chopped Salad with Lemon Vinaigrette

PREP TIME: 20 MIN	COOK TIME: N/A	YIELD: 2 SERVINGS

INGREDIENTS

Lemon Vinaigrette

2 tablespoons olive oil

1½ tablespoons lemon juice, or juice from 1 lemon

1 teaspoon Dijon mustard

Pinch of salt

2 teaspoons honey

Salad

3½ cups romaine lettuce, chopped

¼ cup chopped celery

2 plum tomatoes, sliced then halved (or 1 medium tomato, any variety)

3 tablespoons diced red onion

⅔ cup chopped carrots

DIRECTIONS

1 Add all vinaigrette ingredients into a small bowl and mix until well combined. Set aside.

2 Place salad ingredients into a medium bowl and toss well.

3 Drizzle the vinaigrette over the salad and toss gently. Divide evenly onto two salad plates to serve.

TIP: Chop all ingredients in a mostly uniform size.

VARY IT! Add ½ cup crumbled feta or shredded cheese to the salad. You can also add a hard-boiled egg, chickpeas, bell peppers, cucumbers, or any veggies you have on hand.

Tuna "a la Niçoise" Salad

PREP TIME: 20 MIN | COOK TIME: 30 MIN | YIELD: 2 SERVINGS

INGREDIENTS

1½ cups baby or fingerling potatoes, or 1 large russet or red potato sliced

1 tablespoon olive oil

1 clove garlic, crushed, or 1 teaspoon jarred minced garlic

Pinch of salt

Black pepper to taste

4 cups spring mix salad

1 cup cooked green beans

2 soft-boiled eggs, shelled, sliced

1 5-ounce can oil-packed tuna fish, drained

Go-to Honey Dijon Salad Dressing (see recipe in Chapter 11)

DIRECTIONS

1 Preheat the oven to 425 degrees.

2 Place potatoes onto a baking sheet lined with parchment paper. Drizzle the oil over the potatoes. Add the garlic then toss to mix in garlic and coat potatoes with the oil.

3 Bake for 25 minutes, or until fork tender. Set aside to cool, then slice into ¼-inch slices.

4 Divide the spring mix evenly onto two plates. Place one sliced egg onto each plate. Arrange the green beans next to the egg. Next, add the tuna.

5 Place the potatoes onto the salad plate.

6 Drizzle the Go-to Honey Dijon Salad Dressing evenly onto each salad and serve.

NOTE: A classic Niçoise salad includes green beans, potatoes, a cooked egg, and tuna, making it a great platform for zero waste. You can put this type of salad together with really whatever leftover cooked veggies you have. Also, there are so many delicious varieties of potatoes. You can use any baking potato, golden, or red potato.

TIP: For slightly soft-boiled eggs, cook for 8 minutes in boiling water, drain, and add cold water back to pot until ready to peel.

VARY IT! Add olives or chopped cucumber to the plate as well. Or substitute leftover broccoli for the green beans.

Nutty Mixed Salad with Beans, Beets, and Goat Cheese

PREP TIME: 20 MIN	COOK TIME: N/A	YIELD: 2 SERVINGS

INGREDIENTS

3 cups arugula

½ cup chickpeas

⅔ cup sliced beets (canned, roasted, or pickled)

⅓ cup pistachios, chopped

3 ounces goat cheese, crumbled

Go-to Honey Dijon Salad Dressing (see recipe in Chapter 11)

DIRECTIONS

1 Place arugula, chickpeas, beets, and pistachios in a medium bowl and toss gently.

2 Divide the salad between two plates. Top each with half of the goat cheese.

3 Add the Go-to Honey Dijon Salad Dressing and serve.

NOTE: Substitute toasted walnuts for the pistachios.

VARY IT! You can use spring mix or any mixed greens in place of or in addition to arugula.

Chapter **11**

Wasting No Time or Money on Dressings, Sauces, and Toppings

RECIPES IN THIS CHAPTER

- Citrus-mustard Salad Dressing
- Everyday Vinaigrette Dressing
- Go-to Honey Dijon Salad Dressing
- Easy Basic Marinade
- Basic Cream Sauce
- Quick Canned Tomato Pasta Sauce
- Versatile Pesto
- Aquafaba Fluff
- Apple-Ginger Chutney

How many half-used bottles of salad dressing do you have in your refrigerator? More than two? That's what I thought. I love a good, bottled salad dressing, too, but I generally don't always use up the entire bottle before it passes its prime. In addition, bottled dressings can have a lot more added salt and sugar than you need.

To maintain your zero waste kitchen, having a couple of quick salad dressing recipes in your back pocket is a great idea. You can vary the dressings in this chapter with whatever fresh herbs you have on hand. You can also play around with the ingredient portions and create a favorite dressing of your own! When you whip up your own dressing, you not only make your salads taste delicious, but you can also make just the right amount — no waste!

Keep a small jar on hand to mix, shake, and store salad dressings in. This is good use of any old, clean jelly jar.

Knowing how to make a few basic sauces helps reduce waste and use up common ingredients you have in the kitchen, too. Once you master the basic white cream sauce, you can create a kid-pleasing cheese sauce for broccoli or pasta. It can also serve as the base for a cream soup or a casserole (goodbye canned mushroom soup). Just add various seasonings or cheese to modify the flavor. You'll feel like an accomplished home chef as you return to this white sauce recipe again and again!

Flavorize and Tenderize

A marinade or salad dressing is something you add to a food before cooking, while a sauce is used after the food is cooked. You may be wondering what the difference is between a salad dressing and a marinade? Well, sometimes they can be interchangeable. A marinade is part acid, part fat, and part flavor. It serves a couple of roles: It infuses flavor, and when you marinate meat, it can also tenderize. The acid in the marinade is what serves as the tenderizer; the oil in the marinade helps seal in moisture as well. Then you can season it with herbs and spices that pair with the food you're making.

You can use a vinegar, citrus juice, or wine for the acid. The acid could be any variety of vinegar or citrus juice. There are so many varieties of balsamic and flavored vinegars on the market. Choose a new flavor that inspires you. I love lemon infused white balsamic for salads. Apple cider vinegar and rice wine vinegars are also useful to have on hand and make good dressings. The beauty of vinegar is that it essentially has an eternal shelf life. So you can go ahead and keep a few on hand for variety without worrying about waste.

Salad dressings don't just make salads and vegetables taste better, but they also help your body absorb the nutrients in the vegetables. To make a basic vinaigrette, you'll generally be mixing 3 parts oil to 1 part acid.

There are options for oils, too. I regularly use olive oil in both my salad dressings and cooking. I also enjoy avocado oil. Unlike vinegars, however, oils have a short shelf life. If unopened, a bottle of oil can last about 2 years on the shelf, but once opened, it should be used within a year; otherwise it can go rancid.

Always discard marinade after you've soaked raw meat, fish, or poultry in it. If you want to use it to baste the meat or poultry, either set some aside or cook it — bring any marinade that raw meat soaked in to a full boil.

Citrus-mustard Salad Dressing

PREP TIME: 10 MIN	COOK TIME: N/A	YIELD: 4 SERVINGS

INGREDIENTS

3 tablespoons olive oil

1 tablespoon apple cider vinegar

2 tablespoons orange juice

2 teaspoons Dijon mustard

Pinch of salt

1 teaspoon honey

1 teaspoon lemon or orange zest

DIRECTIONS

1 Whisk all ingredients in a small bowl or jar. Blend well.

TIP: You can use this dressing immediately or make ahead and store in the refrigerator for several days.

Everyday Vinaigrette Dressing

PREP TIME: 5 MIN	COOK TIME: N/A	YIELD: 4 SERVINGS

INGREDIENTS

2 tablespoons vinegar

Salt and black pepper to taste

1 teaspoon sugar (white or brown)

¼ cup olive oil

DIRECTIONS

1 Mix vinegar, salt, pepper, and sugar with a whisk. Gradually whisk in the olive oil to blend.

NOTE: A basic vinaigrette is generally 3 parts oil to 1 part acid (vinegar or lemon juice, for instance). I use about a 2 to1 ratio (so 2 parts oil to 1 part acid), and I enjoy a pinch of sugar. You can modify to suit your taste and use any vinegar or oil you have on hand. Apple cider vinegar, rice wine vinegar, or a white balsamic vinegar are my favorites, along with olive or avocado oil. I enjoy a little sweetness from sugar (either white or brown will do) to balance the acidic vinegar, but the sugar is always optional; you can use maple syrup or honey instead.

TIP: This vinaigrette can be stored in a jar right on the counter for a few days or in the refrigerator for up to two weeks.

VARY IT! To make this a raspberry vinaigrette, simply add ¼ cup of fresh or frozen raspberries. Use a small food processor or emulsion blender to blend all the ingredients together. If you don't have one, you can muddle the berries in the bottom of the jar, and then add the ingredients and shake well to blend.

VARY IT! Add a teaspoon of minced garlic, a tablespoon of mayonnaise, and a teaspoon of lemon juice to this basic vinaigrette, and you'll have a Caesar-style dressing.

Go-to Honey Dijon Salad Dressing

PREP TIME: 10 MIN	COOK TIME: N/A	YIELD: 2–3 SERVINGS

INGREDIENTS

2 tablespoons olive oil

1 tablespoon white balsamic vinegar

1 teaspoon Dijon mustard

Pinch of salt

2 teaspoons honey

DIRECTIONS

1 Pour all ingredients into a small bowl or jar and mix until well blended.

TIP: Use this dressing immediately or refrigerate in a jar for up to a week.

TIP: I call this my go-to dressing because the flavors work well with lots of vegetables and other poultry, pork, and seafood dishes. It's also a delicious way to dress steamed green beans or grilled asparagus. Simply drizzle it over your cooked vegetables before serving.

VARY IT! This dressing is delicious as is, but you can add fresh or dried herbs of your choice if you like. A teaspoon of dried tarragon, thyme, or parsley works well.

Easy Basic Marinade

PREP TIME: 15 MIN	COOK TIME: N/A	YIELD: 11 OUNCES

INGREDIENTS

¼ cup vinegar

3 tablespoons olive oil

¼ cup water or stock (see the Homemade Stock recipe in Chapter 10)

½ teaspoon salt (¼ teaspoon if using stock)

2 cloves garlic, minced, or 1 teaspoon jarred minced garlic

1 teaspoon honey or brown sugar

1 tablespoon of your favorite dried herb (optional)

DIRECTIONS

1 Whisk together all ingredients in a shallow bowl or dish, or put all ingredients in a large, zippered bag (such as a reusable silicone bag) and use your fingers to move ingredients around to combine. Squeeze or shake bag until sugar and salt are dissolved and blended.

NOTE: When you're ready to use the marinade, place a pound of meat, such as chicken or pork, into it, move the pieces around until well coated, and then cover the dish and refrigerate for 2 hours or overnight. You can make the marinade ahead and store in the refrigerator for up to three days. This recipe covers one pound of meat and can easily be doubled.

TIP: Since zero waste cooking is about using what's on hand, you can use any type of flavored vinegar for the acid or substitute wine or citrus juice. A white balsamic works nicely for poultry, and a dark balsamic is great for beef. For pork, you might try a red wine vinegar or orange juice.

TIP: If you mix ingredients right into a zippered bag, you can then place chicken or pork directly into it, seal it up, and put the bag in the fridge without dirtying a dish.

VARY IT! You can use pre-blended herbs for steak or poultry, or make your own. Sage, thyme, oregano, and parsley pair well with pork and poultry. Rosemary, sage, thyme, and parsley are great for a beef marinade. If you can find an espresso balsamic, it's fabulous for marinating beef, too.

Basic Cream Sauce

PREP TIME: 5 MIN	COOK TIME: 15 MIN	YIELD: 4 SERVINGS

INGREDIENTS

1 tablespoon butter

1 tablespoon flour

1 cup milk

2 tablespoons cream cheese

¼ teaspoon salt

Black pepper to taste

DIRECTIONS

1 Melt the butter in a nonstick saucepan over medium-low heat.

2 Add the flour and whisk constantly to blend. Cook for 1 to 2 minutes. Reduce heat if needed to prevent browning too quickly (1 minute may be enough).

3 Reduce heat to low and gradually pour the milk into the mixture, while stirring constantly with the whisk as you add it.

4 Stir the sauce continuously with your whisk for 1 to 2 minutes, and then stir in the cream cheese. Continue stirring until cream cheese has melted and sauce is slightly thickened, about 5 to 8 more minutes. Add salt and pepper and stir.

TIP: I always use low-fat milk for this sauce. This sauce is a perfect base for macaroni and cheese (just add ¼ cup shredded American, Colby, or Cheddar cheese) or an alfredo pasta sauce (just add ¼ cup shredded Parmesan or Romano cheese). Add ½ cup Swiss cheese to this sauce to top baked fish filets. It can also be a substitute for any recipe that uses canned cream of mushroom soup.

NOTE: Every basic white cream sauce begins with a *roux*. This is a French term for a butter and flour mixture that serves as the thickening base of the sauce (see Step 2). Cream cheese also helps thicken the sauce while keeping it light. If you use whole milk, use only 1 tablespoon cream cheese.

TIP: Step 3 is key to a lump-free white sauce. Be sure to stir constantly and watch the heat.

Quick Canned Tomato Pasta Sauce

PREP TIME: 10 MIN	COOK TIME: 45 MIN	YIELD: 6 SERVINGS

INGREDIENTS

1 teaspoon olive oil

2 cloves garlic, crushed, or 2 teaspoons jarred minced garlic

One 28-ounce can tomato purée

1 tablespoon Italian spice blend

1 teaspoon salt

Black pepper to taste

DIRECTIONS

1 Heat a stockpot or small Dutch oven over medium heat. Add the oil and heat until hot, about 1 minute. Add the garlic and cook for 1 to 2 minutes until garlic is tender and slightly colored.

2 Add the tomato purée, Italian spice blend, salt, and pepper. Bring to a slow bubble then reduce heat.

3 Simmer over low heat for 45 minutes (or 1 hour if you want a richer, thicker sauce).

NOTE: You can add meat or vegetables to this sauce. During Step 1, add a pound of ground meat or boneless pork ribs; brown the meat until cooked through. Or add up to a cup of finely chopped vegetables (like carrots, celery, onions, or mushrooms) to the hot oil before adding garlic. Then proceed to Step 2 and continue simmering.

TIP: Serve this sauce over pasta. Store leftovers in the refrigerator for up to a week, or freeze in an airtight container for up to 6 months.

VARY IT! You can make your own Italian spice blend using 1 teaspoon each of oregano (or basil), parsley, and thyme. You can also add some red pepper flakes for a hot kick. And use crushed tomatoes if you prefer in place of tomato puree.

Versatile Pesto

INGREDIENTS

½ cup pine nuts, walnuts, or pistachios

1 clove garlic, or 1 teaspoon jarred minced garlic

1 large bunch of fresh basil (about 4 cups leaves)

½ cup olive oil

½ teaspoon salt

¼ cup grated Parmesan cheese

DIRECTIONS

1 Place the nuts and garlic into a food processor and pulse for 1 minute.

2 Add the basil and pulse for 30 seconds.

3 Gradually add the oil and blend until combined.

4 Add the salt and cheese and pulse until blended, about 30 to 60 seconds.

NOTE: Pesto can be used on pasta, fish, and poultry; as a spread for sandwiches; or as a dip with veggies and crackers or bread. Store in the refrigerator for up to a week or freeze for up to 3 months. Consider freezing in ice cube trays or in small, two-serving containers or freezer bags to make it easier to defrost.

TIP: In addition to this Versatile Pesto, you can try a Chimichurri. Like pesto, you simply chop up any fresh herbs on hand, add vinegar, olive oil, minced garlic, and seasoning. Boom! You have a delicious topping for meat or vegetables.

VARY IT! Use whatever extra herbs you have — parsley works well. You can even throw in green carrot tops if you have any of those around.

Aquafaba Fluff

PREP TIME: 10 MIN	COOK TIME: N/A	YIELD: 1½ TO 2 CUPS

INGREDIENTS

½ cup liquid from one 15-ounce can of chickpeas

⅓ cup powdered sugar (or equivalent sweetener)

DIRECTIONS

1 Add chickpea liquid and sugar to a medium mixing bowl.

2 Beat for 10 to 12 minutes or until thickened.

TIP: For best result, use immediately. You can refrigerate the drained, canned bean liquid for up to a week and make the aquafaba another time.

TIP: It's best (and easiest) to use the wire whisk attachment on a stand mixer for this fluff, but if you have a hand mixer, that'll work too. Some hand mixers come with a whisk attachment, but if yours didn't, a regular beater will work fine.

NOTE: You can omit the sugar and simply whip the bean liquid. This is a great way to reduce waste when you open a can of beans for another recipe (you can use liquid from cannellini or great northern beans as well). If you refrigerate the fluff, you'll need to rebeat it when ready to use.

TIP: Try using this as a food-safe egg white substitute for cocktail recipes that call for egg white, like the Special Whiskey Sour in Chapter 17.

VARY IT! You can bake this into vegan meringues. Heat the oven to 300 degrees. Line a baking sheet with parchment paper or a silicone mat. Add 1 teaspoon of cream of tartar to the liquid and whip until white and glossy. Then add the sugar and beat until it forms stiff peaks. Drop by large tablespoons onto the prepared baking sheet. Bake for 45 minutes or until lightly golden and firm to touch. Turn off the oven. Allow them to dry out in the oven overnight.

Apple-Ginger Chutney

PREP TIME: 10 MIN | COOK TIME: 45–60 MIN | YIELD: 6 SERVINGS

INGREDIENTS

3 large apples, peeled, cored, and diced

1 clove garlic, minced, or 1 teaspoon jarred minced garlic

1 cup diced onion

¼ teaspoon ground ginger

¼ cup raisins

1½ cups apple cider vinegar

¾ cup sugar

½ teaspoon salt

DIRECTIONS

1 Place all ingredients into a medium saucepan.

2 Heat on medium heat and stir until sugar is dissolved and just starting to bubble.

3 Reduce heat and stir until thickened. Simmer for 30 minutes. Keep an eye on it and stir occasionally, ensuring that it doesn't burn or stick. Cool chutney completely before storing in a glass jar or container.

TIP: Use this chutney as a condiment to top crackers or cheese or as a side garnish for roasted pork, poultry, or beef. You can also use a spoon of it to sweeten a soy sauce stir-fry or as a dipping sauce for egg rolls or pot stickers.

NOTE: Baking apples like Granny Smith, Jonagold, Braeburn, or Rome work best for this recipe. You can make chutney with pears, peaches, or other dried fruit like currents, cranberries, or apricots. You can also throw in a chopped tomato or celery. For each additional cup of fruits or veggies, add about ½ cup vinegar. This chutney is a good way to use scraps of fruits and veggies and older onions that are less than good quality.

TIP: If you plan to keep this chutney for a while, pour into a clean jar while hot then seal tightly with a clean lid. You can then store it on the shelf in a cool, dry place for up to a year.

VARY IT! You can make chutney with pears, peaches, or other dried fruit like currents, cranberries, or apricots. You can also throw in a chopped tomato or celery. For each additional cup of fruits or veggies, add about ½ cup vinegar. Try using 3 cups of cut mango and 2 tablespoons chopped, crystallized ginger in place of the apples and ground ginger.

Chapter **12**

Simple Sides for Busy Times

RECIPES IN THIS CHAPTER

- ♻ **Roasted Veggie Trio**
- ♻ **Garlic Broccoli**
- ♻ **Roasted Bell Peppers**
- ♻ **Zucchini with Caramelized Onions**
- ♻ **Chickpea Artichoke Grain Bake**
- ♻ **Roasted Carrots with Honey Glaze**
- ♻ **Cheesy Herbed Rice**
- ♻ **Kicked-Up Cannellini Bean Salad**
- ♻ **Black Bean and Edamame Salad**
- ♻ **Beans and Rice**
- ♻ **Baked Apples**

When cooking at home, side dishes may seem like an afterthought. Or maybe you're in a side dish rut, with frozen potatoes and boxed rice dishes on repeat. This may result in your produce bin looking a bit limp. The recipes in this chapter are all about making mealtime easier, with a dose of good nutrition. Roasting up a big batch of vegetables is quick, requires little effort, and results in delicious veggies that can be used in lots of ways. They can serve as a simple side with any leftovers being used as a pasta topping or even a sandwich filler later in the week. Once you roast your first bell pepper, you'll wonder what you've been waiting for. Easy and delicious!

Caramelizing an onion here or adding a touch of honey there can really make veggies taste better. Mixing up different combinations or adding a sprinkle of cheese also makes them more inviting. Finally, a side dish chapter can't exist in my world without beans. I encourage you to try a variety of them, and then use the ones you like. Fun fact: Research about the diet and lifestyle of Centurions (people who live to 100 years old) around the world (known as Blue Zones) all have one dietary component in common: beans.

Getting Creative Sides to the Table

One barrier to being more creative with vegetables is the time it takes to prep and cook them. A simple solution is to do some prep and batch cooking. So the next time you bring home a load of veggies, consider roasting them in a big batch (using a method like the Roasted Veggie Trio recipe in this chapter). When they're already prepped and cooked, you likely will eat them since you can bring them right to the table both now and at another meal later in the week, saving you time. For example, you can use the roasted veggies for the Pasta with Roast Vegetables and Salmon or the Veggie-Roast Pasta Primavera, both in Chapter 14. You can prep and cook spinach ahead as well. Cook the whole bag, enjoy half right away, and then store the other half for another meal. This way, it will last in the fridge for a couple of days, and you have cooked spinach ready to make a dip or stir into a soup or pasta.

In addition, batch cooking can help reduce food waste. It essentially takes the same amount of time to cook 8 servings of vegetables as it does 2 or 4. When you cook a bigger batch, the vegetables can last for up to a week, instead of raw, forgotten veggies rotting in the refrigerator drawer.

Employing a variety of ingredients, such as the following, can really bring boring vegetables up a notch.

>> Simple sauces, like the one used for Garlic Broccoli in this chapter, amp up the flavor and are versatile enough to be used for a variety of veggies (like a mixed stir-fry or with carrot coins).

>> The 30 or so minutes it takes to caramelize onions in the simple Zucchini with Caramelized Onions recipe in this chapter (most of it hands-off cooking) is so worth it.

>> Beans are an economical way to boost texture, flavor, and nutrition (protein, fiber, B-vitamins) in just about any side dish. They're as easy as opening a can.

>> Herbs, seasonings, and butter or olive oil bring out the joy in vegetables. (**Bonus:** Fat helps you absorb the vitamins that veggies provide.)

REMEMBER

Like many recipes in this book, you'll find that you can substitute a variety of vegetable and herbs in the ingredients. For instance, the Chickpea Artichoke Grain Bake recipe in this chapter can be super versatile, helping you use up whatever veggie you have on hand in place of the artichokes. That's how reducing food waste in your kitchen works — having flexibility and the knowledge to know how to sub in something else.

Roasted Veggie Trio

PREP TIME: 20 MIN   COOK TIME: 35 MIN   YIELD: 6 SERVINGS

INGREDIENTS

1 medium eggplant, cubed

8 ounces mushrooms, quartered

2 bell peppers, chopped into 1-inch pieces

½ cup chopped onions

2 cloves garlic, crushed, or 2 teaspoons jarred minced garlic

2 tablespoons olive oil

Pinch of salt

Black pepper to taste

DIRECTIONS

1 Preheat the oven to 425 degrees. Line a baking sheet with parchment paper or a silicone mat.

2 Place prepared vegetables onto the baking sheet, mixing them to combine. Sprinkle evenly with the garlic.

3 Drizzle the olive oil all over the vegetables and then toss to coat. Be sure they are evenly distributed on the pan. Add salt and pepper.

4 Roast for 35 minutes, turning after 20 minutes. Serve immediately or store in the fridge for up to one week.

NOTE: Make a smaller batch and use less olive oil. You may need to shorten baking to 25 to 30 minutes.

TIP: This versatile dish pairs well with Baked Fish with Herbed Breadcrumbs or Grilled Marinated Flank Steak (see Chapter 13). It's delicious to mix into rice or to use in a Power Bowl (see Chapter 21 for tips about creating Power Bowls).

VARY IT! You can add or substitute any vegetable to this pan, including carrots, cut asparagus, broccoli, or cauliflower florets.

Garlic Broccoli

PREP TIME: 10 MIN | COOK TIME: 15 MIN | YIELD: 4 SERVINGS

INGREDIENTS

½ cup chicken or vegetable stock (see the Homemade Stock recipe in Chapter 10)

2 tablespoons soy sauce

2 teaspoons corn starch

1 teaspoon honey

1 teaspoon olive oil

1 large head broccoli, cut into florets and stems sliced thinly (about 2 cups total)

3 cloves garlic, crushed, or 3 teaspoons jarred minced garlic

DIRECTIONS

1 Mix the stock, soy sauce, corn starch, and honey in a small bowl and set aside.

2 Heat oil over medium-high heat in a wok or large frying pan.

3 Add the cut broccoli stems and *stir-fry* by constantly moving it around the hot pan for 2 minutes. Add the florets and continue to stir-fry 3 to 4 minutes until crisp-tender. Add the garlic and stir-fry another minute.

4 Reduce heat to medium and pour the sauce over the broccoli. Mix well to coat and then stir-fry for another 2 minutes until sauce is slightly thickened. Enjoy!

NOTE: This dish can be refrigerated for up to seven days.

TIP: Serve this sauce along with the Teriyaki Chicken Tenders or Broiled Salmon Fillet recipes (see Chapter 13). Or you can use the sauce with mixed vegetables. Add a protein like cubed extra firm tofu or chicken to turn this side into a meal.

VARY IT! In place of the homemade stock, you can use low-sodium prepared stock.

Roasted Bell Peppers

PREP TIME: 10 MIN	COOK TIME: 40 MIN	YIELD: 4 TO 6 SERVINGS

INGREDIENTS

4 large bell peppers, washed

1 tablespoon olive oil

DIRECTIONS

1 Heat the oven to 450 degrees.

2 Place whole peppers directly onto oven grate (for easy clean up, place a baking sheet on the rack under the peppers to catch any drippings). Roast for 35 to 40 minutes, turning after 15 minutes. The peppers' skin should be mildly bubbled and slightly charred. Carefully remove them from the oven using tongs.

3 Place peppers into a small paper bag, top folded to close, or in a bowl covered with foil or reusable beeswax wrap. Allow to steam for about 20 minutes, or until they're cool enough to handle. Remove and peel off the skins.

4 Remove stems and then cut peppers in half and remove all seeds. Cut each pepper into 6 to 10 slices. Place pepper slices into a glass bowl and drizzle with olive oil. Use immediately or cover and refrigerate for up to two weeks.

NOTE: You can make as many peppers as you like. Adjust the olive oil based on number of peppers.

TIP: To avoid wasting any part of the pepper, carefully run your knife around the top of the roasted pepper in Step 4 to slice around the stem. Then pull out the stem and seeds. You can compost the seeds and inside ribs.

GRAIN-STUFFED VEGETABLES

Rice and ancient grains like farro or quinoa work well in stuffing. An easy way to use up the peppers, mushrooms, or squash in your refrigerator is to stuff them. Try this simple technique using any grain and a variety of vegetables. Prepare the grains according to package directions.

Preheat the oven to 375 degrees. Cut two bell peppers in half, from the stem down. Remove the seeds. Brush the peppers with oil and place into a baking dish, cut-side up. Mix 1 cup cooked rice, farro, or quinoa with ½ cup tomato sauce (or ½ cup of coconut milk). Sauté ¼ cup onion, the top of the pepper (diced), and garlic (add leftover cooked, chopped meat to the mixture if you have it), then add the onion-garlic to the grain mixture and stir it all together. Spoon the grain mixture into each pepper. Place the peppers into a shallow baking dish. Sprinkle with Parmesan cheese (if using tomato sauce) or chopped cilantro (if using coconut milk). Season with salt and pepper. Cover with foil or a lid. Bake for 30 to 45 minutes until pepper is soft.

Tip: Instead of bell peppers, you can use a medium zucchini or spaghetti squash, cut in half. Scoop out seeds then stuff with the grain mixture. If you have a few mushrooms or spinach left in the fridge, sauté that and add to the stuffing. Get creative!

Zucchini with Caramelized Onions

PREP TIME: 10 MIN | COOK TIME: 30 MIN | YIELD: 2 SERVINGS

INGREDIENTS

1 teaspoon olive oil

½ cup thinly sliced Vidalia onion

2 small zucchinis, cut into ¼-inch rounds

Splash of white wine (about 2 tablespoons), optional

⅛ teaspoon salt

DIRECTIONS

1 Place a medium nonstick pan over medium heat. Add oil and heat.

2 Add onions to the pan. Sauté until golden and tender and begin to brown, about 15 minutes, stirring often. Reduce heat to low and continue cooking for another 10 to 15 minutes until they begin to darken in color.

3 Add zucchini and cook for about 5 to 7 minutes, until zucchini is tender. Deglaze the pan with the wine (or water) if needed, and then stir and cook for 1 more minute. Serve immediately.

4 Serve immediately.

NOTE: If using a larger zucchini, slice then cut slices in half.

TIP: Onions may take less or more time to caramelize depending on the pan. Watch carefully and reduce heat if they're browning too quickly.

TIP: Try it with Skillet Meatballs or Baked Fish with Herbed Bread Crumbs (see Chapter 13).

Chickpea Artichoke Grain Bake

PREP TIME: 15 MIN | COOK TIME: 40 MIN | YIELD: 6 SERVINGS

INGREDIENTS

Cooking spray

½ cup bread crumbs

1 teaspoon olive oil

1 teaspoon dried basil, or 2 teaspoons fresh

1 egg, beaten

½ cup cottage cheese or ricotta, optional

1½ cups cooked grain (barley, quinoa, pasta, or rice)

One 15-ounce can chickpeas (garbanzos), drained

One 12-ounce jar marinated artichokes, drained, chopped

1 cup frozen peas

2 teaspoons lemon zest

1 clove garlic, crushed, or 1 teaspoon jarred minced garlic

Black pepper to taste

DIRECTIONS

1 Preheat the oven to 375 degrees. Spray a 9-x-11-inch (or deep 8-x-8-inch) baking dish with cooking spray.

2 In a small bowl, mix the breadcrumbs with the olive oil and basil and set aside.

3 Add egg to a large mixing bowl. Whisk in the cheese until blended. Add the grain, chickpeas, artichokes, peas, lemon zest, and garlic to the bowl. Fold all ingredients together until well combined.

4 Transfer the mixture into the prepared baking dish. Top evenly with bread crumb mixture. Add black pepper to taste.

5 Bake for 40 minutes until golden on top and then serve.

NOTE: Make this dish vegan by substituting ½ cup of whipped chickpea liquid (aquafaba) for the cottage cheese and egg. I prefer using frozen peas for this pantry meal, but you can use fresh or canned peas as well.

TIP: Try this side dish with any simple main, like grilled chicken or fish. This can serve as a meatless main dish as well.

TIP: Saved liquid from the chickpeas (aquafaba) can be used to make a meringue or a mixed drink. See Chapter 11 for Aquafaba Fluff.

VARY IT! Use equal amounts of any vegetable you like in place of the artichokes and peas. You can use frozen, drained spinach in place of artichokes, another pickled vegetable, or omit them. You can also add chopped green olives. The artichokes add enough sodium for me, but feel free to add a pinch of salt in Step 4. You can also use sunflower seeds in place of the bread crumb mixture.

Roasted Carrots with Honey Glaze

| PREP TIME: 10 MIN | COOK TIME: 25 MIN | YIELD: 2 SERVINGS |

INGREDIENTS

2 teaspoons honey

1 tablespoon citrus juice
(orange, lemon, or lime)

1 cup water

Pinch of salt

1½ cups carrots, chopped

2 teaspoons butter, melted

¼ cup chopped pistachios

DIRECTIONS

1 Stir honey and citrus juice together in a small dish. Set aside.

2 In a small saucepan, bring water to a boil. Add salt and carrots, reduce to simmer, and cover loosely.

3 Cook carrots for 5 minutes. Drain, transfer to serving dish, and set aside.

4 Add butter to the pan and stir until melted. Add the pistachios and cook over medium heat for 2 to 4 minutes until lightly browned. Return the carrots to the pan. Stir in the honey mixture and cook for another 2 to 3 minutes. Then serve.

NOTE: You can also add chopped parsley or cilantro to garnish.

TIP: Serve with the Whole Roast Chicken, Slow Cooker Pulled Pork, or Baked Fish with Herbed Bread Crumbs mains (see Chapter 13).

Cheesy Herbed Rice

PREP TIME: 5 MIN	COOK TIME: 5 MIN	YIELD: 2–3 SERVINGS

INGREDIENTS

2 cups cooked rice

¼ cup water or stock (see the Homemade Stock recipe in Chapter 10)

½ cup shredded sharp Cheddar cheese

¼ cup chopped parsley, or 1 tablespoon dried

½ teaspoon turmeric or cumin

DIRECTIONS

1 Put rice in a microwave safe dish. Add liquid and stir.

2 Mix in cheese, parsley, and turmeric.

3 Microwave on high for 1 to 2 minutes until evenly warm. Then serve.

NOTE: You can add any herb or spices that you prefer!

TIP: Serve as a side dish with baked chicken or the Roast Pork Loin with Apples and Onions recipe in Chapter 13.

VARY IT! Add leftover protein like tofu chunks, chopped chicken, or ground beef or meat alternative crumbles. You can also substitute any sharp cheese for the Cheddar.

Kicked-Up Cannellini Bean Salad

PREP TIME: 20 MIN PLUS REFRIGERATION TIME	COOK TIME: N/A	YIELD: 6 SERVINGS

INGREDIENTS

Bean Mixture

One 15-ounce can cannellini beans, drained and rinsed

3 tablespoons minced onion, any variety

2 tablespoons minced celery

2 tablespoons fresh hot pepper, seeded, minced (see Note)

3 tablespoons chopped fresh parsley or basil, or 1 tablespoon dried

Dressing

1 clove garlic, crushed, or 1 teaspoon jarred minced garlic

3 tablespoons olive oil

2 tablespoons wine vinegar

1 teaspoon honey or sugar

Pinch of salt

Black pepper to taste

DIRECTIONS

1 In a medium bowl, add the beans, onion, celery, hot pepper, and parsley.

2 In a small bowl, mix the dressing ingredients.

3 Pour the dressing over the bean mixture and toss to coat evenly. Add the salt and pepper and toss once more.

4 Refrigerate for at least an hour or overnight before serving. This salad will keep for up to a week in the refrigerator.

NOTE: You can choose any hot pepper you like, from a milder pepper to a spicier variety — banana pepper, jalapeño, chili pepper or habanero. You can also substitute a pickled hot pepper as well. Use diced red bell pepper if you prefer no heat.

TIP: You can use 1 tablespoon of the bean liquid in the dressing and save remaining for Aquafaba Fluff (see Chapter 11). This dish pairs well with any pasta or fish dish like Foil-baked Tilapia with Peppers (see Chapter 13).

VARY IT! Add ¼ cup sliced black olives and ½ teaspoon of red pepper flakes. Make this a main dish by adding leftover or canned tuna or salmon, drained. Or make it into a pasta salad by adding 2 cups of cooked pasta and doubling the dressing.

Black Bean and Edamame Salad

PREP TIME: 25 MIN	COOK TIME: N/A	YIELD: 4–5 SERVINGS

INGREDIENTS

Salad

One 15-ounce can black beans, drained and rinsed

⅓ cup chopped sweet onion

½ cup diced red bell pepper (or any color)

1 cup corn

1 cup edamame

2 tablespoons chopped cilantro, or 2 teaspoons dried

Dressing

1 clove garlic, crushed, or 1 teaspoon jarred minced garlic

3 tablespoons olive or avocado oil

1 tablespoon red wine vinegar

½ teaspoon cumin

1 teaspoon honey

2 tablespoons lime juice, or juice from one lime

⅛ teaspoon salt

Black pepper to taste

DIRECTIONS

1 In a medium bowl, mix the beans, onion, pepper, corn, and edamame. Sprinkle the cilantro in. Toss to combine.

2 Make the dressing by combining all ingredients in a small bowl and whisking until combined. Pour the dressing over the bean mixture, season with salt and pepper to taste, and toss to combine. Serve as a delicious side.

NOTE: You can use apple cider or a wine or balsamic vinegar.

TIP: Refrigerate overnight to meld flavors. Also, this side pairs well with a sandwich or the Mushroom Turkey Burgers or Fish Tacos (both in Chapter 15).

VARY IT! Add cooked shrimp to this salad for a main meal.

Beans and Rice

INGREDIENTS

1 teaspoon canola oil

¼ cup minced onion

½ cup chopped celery

½ cup diced yellow bell pepper (or any color)

1 clove garlic, crushed, or 1 teaspoon jarred minced garlic

1 teaspoon chili powder (or cumin)

2 cups cooked rice, white or brown (cooked according to package directions)

4 cups chicken stock (see the Homemade Stock recipe in Chapter 10)

1 teaspoon Worcestershire sauce

One 15-ounce can black beans, drained and rinsed

1 lime, cut into wedges, or 2 tablespoons lime juice

¼ teaspoon salt

½ cup sour cream or plain yogurt, optional

2 tablespoons chopped fresh cilantro, or 2 teaspoons dried, optional

DIRECTIONS

1 Heat oil in a large saucepan. Add onion, celery, and peppers, and sauté until onion is translucent. Add the garlic and chili powder and stir another minute. Add the rice and combine, toasting until lightly brown, for about 1 minute in the pan before adding the stock.

2 Stir in the stock and Worcestershire sauce and bring to a boil. Once boiling, reduce heat to low, stir in the beans, cover, and cook for about 20 minutes, until liquid is absorbed, and rice is tender.

3 To serve, squeeze the lime juice over the rice. Season with salt if needed.

4 Garnish with a dollop of sour cream or plain yogurt, a sprinkling of cilantro, and extra lime wedges (if desired).

TIP: Serve as a meatless meal or pair with Slow Cooker Pulled Pork (see Chapter 13) or Pork Tacos with Peppers, Onion, and Lime Crema (see Chapter 15).

VARY IT! Add chopped tomatoes or a can of diced tomatoes during the last 10 minutes of cooking in Step 2. Mix up the spice by using cumin or paprika instead of chili powder.

Baked Apples

PREP TIME: 15 MIN	COOK TIME: 45 MIN	YIELD: 4 SERVINGS

INGREDIENTS

4 large apples, such as Honey Crisp or Fuji, cored

1 cup of your favorite granola

2 teaspoons ground cinnamon

¼ teaspoon nutmeg

2 tablespoons brown sugar

2 tablespoons butter, melted

1 cup water

DIRECTIONS

1 Preheat the oven to 350 degrees. Place the apples into a 9-x-9-inch baking dish (or one large enough to give them some space).

2 In a small bowl, mix the granola, spices, and brown sugar. Add the melted butter, and mix to combine.

3 Fill each apple with the granola mixture, dividing evenly.

4 Pour the water around the bottom of the pan, surrounding each apple. Cover loosely with foil. Bake for 30 minutes then remove foil and baste the apples with the liquid. Check the apples after another 10 to 15 minutes and baste again during the last 5 minutes. Serve as a sweet, spiced side.

TIP: For a little added flavor, you can use apple juice or cider in place of the water.

TIP: These apples pair well with pork chops, a roast, or the Whole Roast Chicken in Chapter 13. They're also nice to serve along with egg dishes for brunch.

VARY IT! Substitute maple syrup for the brown sugar. In place of granola, use ½ cup of chopped almonds, walnuts, or pecans.

Chapter **13**

Barnyard, Seaside, and Vegetarian Main Dishes

RECIPES IN THIS CHAPTER

Whole Roast Chicken

Chicken with Orzo, Artichokes, and Zucchini

Foil-pack Greek Chicken with Olives, Feta, and Peppers

Teriyaki Chicken Tenders

Spiced Chicken over Rice

Chicken-Stuffed Baked Potatoes

Grilled Marinated Flank Steak

Skillet Meatballs

Spice-rubbed Pork Tenderloin with Roasted Sliced Grapes

Slow Cooker Pulled Pork

Roast Pork Loin with Apples and Onions

Broiled Salmon Fillet

Baked Fish with Herbed Bread Crumbs

Foil-baked Tilapia with Peppers

🍎 Moroccan Veggie Skillet

🍎 Spicy Tofu Broccoli Bowl

🍎 Lentil-stuffed Zucchini

This chapter (the whole book really) aims to help you cook easy weeknight meals with ingredients that can be used in multiple ways, thereby reducing your food waste. Several recipes in this chapter will leave you with leftovers that can be used in other recipes in the book. Others, like Foil-baked Greek Chicken with Olives, Feta, and Peppers or Foil-baked Tilapia with Peppers, are quick cooking methods to make it easier to use what you have on hand and are versatile enough to make ingredient substitutions.

REMEMBER

You can always omit an ingredient you don't like, or substitute something else. For example, if you don't like peppers, skip them, or add another vegetable you enjoy. Don't like cumin? Substitute another spice. Be sure to check the Tips at the end of most recipes throughout Part 3.

Or go meatless! You'll be happy to know that creating a meatless meal can be delicious, satisfying, and a great opportunity to add nutritious ingredients, like beans, soy, or lentils, into your diet. Most people don't eat enough vegetables, so planning a meatless meal or two through the week can help with that goal. The

Moroccan Veggie Skillet is loaded with flavor and is quick to put together on a weeknight. Although the Skillet Meatballs use a beef mixture, you can certainly experiment with a veggie crumble instead.

Adopting the adage "cook once; eat thrice" is a good zero waste cooking strategy to keep in your back pocket. Batch cooking is one way to do this. While some people set aside one day to batch cook for the whole week, you can also simply cook extra servings of an item any day of the week to use the following days. Rather than viewing batch cooking as cooking a whole bunch of complete meals, think of it as simply cooking larger batches of one or more ingredients that you can utilize for new meals during the week. For example, use leftovers from the Roast Pork Loin with Grapes for a sandwich like the Pork Pita Pockets with Cucumber Sauce in Chapter 15.

This chapter also gives you the lowdown for cooking a whole roaster chicken. It's not difficult, but this classic dish is always impressive because it makes for a delicious meal that looks great on the table for either a regular weeknight or a special occasion with family and friends. It's great for zero waste cooking too, because if you're just cooking for two to four people, you'll have enough left over to utilize it for other recipes like the Chicken Parmesan Stuffed Mushrooms in Chapter 8 or the Spiced Chicken over Rice in this chapter, later in the week. Or you can just top your salad with some cooked chicken, making it a meal. This saves time, hassle, and money. If you're cooking for a family of four to six, a roast chicken feeds everyone, and you can make a delicious stock with the carcass (see the Homemade Stock recipe in Chapter 10).

Prepping and Carving a Whole Chicken

Chicken and turkey are economical options for the budget-minded family. Buying a whole chicken is often less expensive than separate parts. Plus, it's easy yet elegant and delicious and versatile.

These prep tips work for any poultry, including turkey, duck, or Cornish hens. When you buy a frozen bird, always defrost it in the refrigerator. This can take up to three days for a 14-pound turkey.

TIP

Don't forget to remove the bag of giblets, heart, and neck from the cavity of the bird! Yep, we all know someone — no judgment here — who roasted the bird with those inside it.

Trussing the bird will keep the legs and wings tucked close to the body. This helps the chicken cook evenly without drying out. See Figure 13-1.

1. **Loosen the skin from the breast by running your fingers under the skin and pulling skin from breast meat.**

2. **Cut out the wishbone from the neck cavity to help make the breast meat easier to carve later.**

3. **Tuck the wings under the bird.**

4. **Tie the legs together with butcher string.**

5. **Tie another string around the bird and its wings to keep bird compact so it stays juicy and cooks evenly.**

TRUSSING A CHICKEN

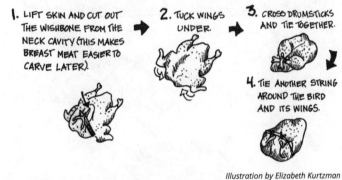

1. LIFT SKIN AND CUT OUT THE WISHBONE FROM THE NECK CAVITY (THIS MAKES BREAST MEAT EASIER TO CARVE LATER).

2. TUCK WINGS UNDER.

3. CROSS DRUMSTICKS AND TIE TOGETHER.

4. TIE ANOTHER STRING AROUND THE BIRD AND ITS WINGS.

FIGURE 13-1: Trussing a chicken for roasting.

Illustration by Elizabeth Kurtzman

To carve a chicken, you'll need a large carving board, large fork, and sharp knife. (If possible, use a meat carving board that has a well around it to collect juices.) Don't forget to save the carcass for soup! See Chapter 10 for a Homemade Stock recipe.

Allow the bird to rest for 15 minutes after removing from the oven. This allows the juices to set and keeps the meat moister. See Figure 13-2.

1. **Transfer the chicken to a cutting board large enough to allow for juices to flow.**

2. **Slice the chicken at the joints.**

   Start with the legs. Position the bird so that the wings are facing away from you, at the top of the board, so the legs are closest to you. Use a fork at the breast to stabilize the bird as you cut. Insert your knife at the joint and cut through to remove the drumstick and thigh in one piece.

3. **If desired, slice the meat off the leg into slices, or just separate the drumstick and thigh, and place on a platter.**

4. **Cut the wings at the joint in a similar fashion.**

5. **Now that the legs and wings are removed, remove each breast.**

   Stabilize it with your fork then slice from the bottom, making a horizontal cut across the bottom of the breast. Return your knife to the top of the breastbone and cut through the length of it, gently removing it from the carcass. Do this for each breast then carve each into slices.

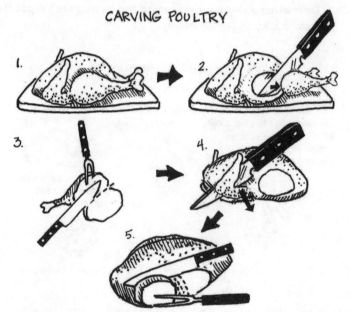

CARVING POULTRY

FIGURE 13-2: Carving a whole chicken.

Illustration by Elizabeth Kurtzman

Making Bread Crumbs

Fresh bread crumbs are easy to make and can serve multiple purposes. You can use them to coat chicken for oven-fried chicken, to bread fish, or to make breaded zucchini planks — or even for a topping for pasta or a casserole.

To make bread crumbs, simply

1. **Cut stale bread into thick slices that will fit into a food processor.**
2. **Process until you have the desired crumb.**

TIP

If you don't have a food processor, you can put the bread into a heavy-duty zippered plastic or silicone bag, seal, and then roll with a rolling pin to get rustic crumbs.

Use the bread crumbs immediately or store them in an airtight container for up to three months. It's that easy!

TIP

You can use bread crumbs plain, or season them with dried herbs like oregano, parsley, thyme, or dill and spices like paprika, cumin, and ground red or black pepper. You'll see an example of this in Baked Fish with Herbed Bread Crumbs later in this chapter.

SAFE MINIMUM COOKING TEMPERATURES

Sure, we all know that one person who orders their steak well-done, but it's perfectly safe to eat steak rare. And due to changes in how pigs are raised and cared for, pork's minimum temperature is 145 degrees. In fact, this is the ideal temperature to ensure moist, juicy meat. When you cook meats properly and to the safe minimum temperature, you won't have to chew and chew and chew. Use a food thermometer to check for safe temps (you can buy a basic, inexpensive thermometer at most grocery and big box stores).

Meat	Safe Minimum Temperature
Beef, pork, lamb, and veal chops, roasts, and steaks	145°F (let rest 3 minutes before serving)
Fish	145°F
All poultry, including ground	165°F
Ground beef, pork, lamb, and veal	160°F

Warning: Foodborne illness is no joke. The most common germs that cause illness are novovirus, Salmonella, Clostridium perfringens, Campylobacter, and Staphylococcus aureas. Cook food to proper temperatures, store it properly, and avoid cross contamination.

Whole Roast Chicken

PREP TIME: 20 MIN	COOK TIME: 55 MIN	YIELD: 6 SERVINGS

INGREDIENTS

1 teaspoon ground thyme

2 teaspoons dried rosemary, or
1½ tablespoon fresh chopped
leaves

1 whole roaster chicken (about
5 pounds)

1 tablespoon olive oil

1 lemon, cut into thin slices

1 stalk celery, washed and cut
into 3 pieces

½ large onion, cut into
4 pieces.

4 sage leaves

DIRECTIONS

1 Preheat the oven to 375 degrees.

2 Mix thyme and rosemary in a small bowl. Set aside.

3 Remove giblet bag from the chicken cavity. Pat chicken dry
and rub with olive oil, using clean hands or a basting brush.
Rub herb mixture all over the breast, back, and legs. Place all
but two of the lemon slices into the cavity along with the celery and onion.

4 Loosen the skin from the breast by sliding your fingers
between the skin and the flesh then insert sage leaves under
the skin and over the breast meat. Do the same with the
remaining two lemon slices, placing them under the skin.
Truss the chicken for roasting; refer to Figure 13-1. (Trussing
is optional, but I feel it looks nicer and still allows for an
evenly cooked bird.)

5 Roast uncovered for 40 to 45 minutes. Check the bird to ensure it's not overbrowning. If it is, cover loosely with foil and return to oven. Roast another 15 to 20 minutes, or until it's a golden brown and meat thermometer reaches 165 degrees at the thickest part of the thigh without touching bone.

6 Remove from the oven and allow to rest for 20 to 30 minutes. Transfer to a cutting board to carve (refer to Figure 13-2).

NOTE: You'll find either fryer, broiler, or roaster chickens at the supermarket. A *fryer* or *broiler* chicken is smaller (about 2 to 3 pounds). This is generally what you'll get when you purchase a cooked rotisserie chicken from the deli. A *roaster* is larger, generally around 5 pounds. These are the best choice if you're feeding a larger family or if you want leftovers.

TIP: You can store the chicken meat in a covered glass container in the refrigerator for up to 4 days. Use it to make Chicken Parmesan Stuffed Mushrooms (see Chapter 8), or Chicken with Orzo, Artichokes, and Zucchini, in this chapter.

TIP: Make stock! Remove all the meat from the bones and place the carcass (including onions, lemon, and herbs) into a large stockpot or Dutch oven. Check out the Homemade Stock recipe in Chapter 10. Pour stock into a freezer-safe container and freeze for three months, or you can store in the refrigerator for up to five days.

Chicken with Orzo, Artichokes, and Zucchini

PREP TIME: 15 MIN	COOK TIME: 15 MIN	YIELD: 2 SERVINGS

INGREDIENTS

4 ounces orzo (about ½ cup), cooked according to package directions

1 teaspoon olive oil

1 small zucchini, sliced into ¼-inch slices

Pinch of salt

Cracked black pepper, optional

One 6-ounce jar marinated artichokes, drained (reserve liquid, see Tip)

6 ounces cooked chicken, cubed

DIRECTIONS

1 While orzo cooks, heat a nonstick skillet over medium heat. Add the oil and heat through. Add the zucchini and sauté for 3 to 4 minutes. Salt and reduce heat to low.

2 Add the artichokes, chicken, and cooked orzo to the pan, stirring to combine and heat through.

3 Divide the orzo mixture between two bowls. Garnish with cracked black pepper.

TIP: Drain artichokes over a small bowl then transfer the reserved liquid back to the jar. This liquid can add a flavor boost to a rice dish, Versatile Pesto (see Chapter 11), or salad dressing. Add it for part of the liquid in the Creamy Veggie Dip (see Chapter 8), or add a tablespoon to the Lemony Salmon Patties (also in Chapter 8).

VARY IT! Substitute halved grape tomatoes, diced bell pepper, or spinach for the artichokes. Just add them to the zucchini and sauté.

Foil-pack Greek Chicken with Olives, Feta, and Peppers

PREP TIME: 10 MIN	COOK TIME: 35 MIN	YIELD: 4 SERVINGS

INGREDIENTS

4 boneless chicken breasts (20-24 ounces)

½ chopped kalamata olives (or other variety)

½ cup thinly sliced onion

½ cup sliced, roasted red peppers (jarred, or see Roasted Bell Peppers recipe in Chapter 12)

4 teaspoons olive oil

½ cup crumbled feta cheese

1½ teaspoon Mediterranean herb blend (or equal amounts of oregano and thyme)

DIRECTIONS

1 Preheat the oven to 400 degrees. Cut chicken breasts horizontally to make two thinner breast pieces from each breast.

2 Cut 4 pieces of foil, about 12-x-8 inches. Place two pieces of chicken onto each piece of foil, then divide olives, onion, and peppers evenly, topping each of the 4 chicken packets. Drizzle each packet with a teaspoon of olive oil and add feta. Fold long ends of foil together and then crimp up the other two ends, sealing loosely (see Figure 13-3).

3 Place the packets onto a baking sheet and bake for 30 to 35 minutes or until chicken is cooked through. (When you cut into chicken, juices should be clear — if they're pink, return to oven for another 5 to 10 minutes.)

4 Transfer packets to 4 plates and carefully open, avoiding steam.

NOTE: Cutting the chicken in half reduces its thickness and allows it to cook through more quickly and evenly.

TIP: You want the foil to be sealed enough so that juices don't run out of the packet but loose enough to allow the contents to steam.

VARY IT! You can stuff the foil packet with other combinations, such as onions, sliced mushrooms, and shredded Cheddar or Swiss cheese.

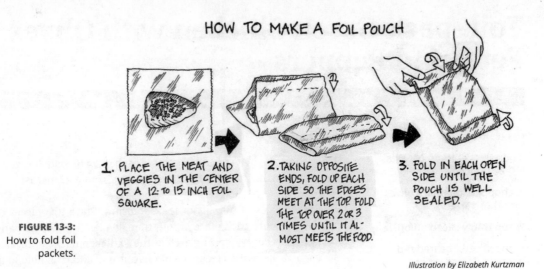

HOW TO MAKE A FOIL POUCH

1. PLACE THE MEAT AND VEGGIES IN THE CENTER OF A 12- TO 15- INCH FOIL SQUARE.

2. TAKING OPPOSITE ENDS, FOLD UP EACH SIDE SO THE EDGES MEET AT THE TOP. FOLD THE TOP OVER 2 OR 3 TIMES UNTIL IT AL- MOST MEETS THE FOOD.

3. FOLD IN EACH OPEN SIDE UNTIL THE POUCH IS WELL SEALED.

FIGURE 13-3:
How to fold foil
packets.

Illustration by Elizabeth Kurtzman

Teriyaki Chicken Tenders

PREP TIME: 10 MIN	COOK TIME: 20 MIN	YIELD: 4 SERVINGS

INGREDIENTS

⅓ cup soy sauce

½ teaspoon honey

1 teaspoon garlic powder

¼ teaspoon ground ginger

1–2 green onions, thinly sliced, divided

1 tablespoon vegetable oil

1 pound chicken tenders

DIRECTIONS

1 Mix soy sauce, honey, garlic powder, ginger, and the green onions (reserve a tablespoon for garnish) in a shallow bowl. Set aside.

2 Heat oil over medium heat in a large nonstick skillet. Add the chicken strips and brown lightly on both sides, cooking for about 3 minutes per side.

3 Reduce heat to low and add the sauce to the pan, coating chicken evenly. Cover and cook for an additional 10 minutes until chicken is cooked through.

4 Garnish with the remaining green onions.

TIP: Serve over rice or ramen noodles with Garlic Broccoli, Roasted Carrots with Honey Glaze (both in Chapter 12), or another cooked vegetable.

NOTE: You can use 2 teaspoons of grated ginger in place of ground.

VARY IT! You can add 1 cup of broccoli florets or sliced carrots to the pan with the chicken in Step 3.

Spiced Chicken over Rice

PREP TIME: 5 MIN	COOK TIME: 25 MIN	YIELD: 2 SERVINGS

INGREDIENTS

1 tablespoon canola oil

½ cup diced onion

2 cloves garlic, crushed, or 2 teaspoons jarred minced garlic

One 15-ounce can diced tomatoes

1 teaspoon turmeric

1 teaspoon curry powder

¼ teaspoon cinnamon

½ teaspoon cumin

Pinch of salt

One 8-ounce skinless, boneless chicken breast cut into 1-inch pieces

1½ cups cooked white rice (cooked according to package directions)

DIRECTIONS

1 In a large skillet, heat the oil over medium heat. Add the onion and cook for 3 to 4 minutes until onion is translucent. Add the garlic and cook another 1 to 2 minutes.

2 Add the tomatoes, turmeric, curry powder, and cinnamon to the pan. Stir to combine and cook down the tomatoes over low to medium heat for about 4 to 5 minutes.

3 Sprinkle the cumin and salt evenly over the chicken pieces and add the chicken to the tomato–onion mixture. Stir until the chicken is opaque, about 3 to 5 minutes. Cover with a lid and allow to simmer for another 6 to 10 minutes or until the chicken is cooked through. Serve over rice.

NOTE: Add a minced hot pepper to the dish in Step 1 if you'd prefer some heat.

Chicken-Stuffed Baked Potatoes

| PREP TIME: 10 MIN | COOK TIME: 55 MIN | YIELD: 4 SERVINGS |

INGREDIENTS

4 large baking potatoes

1½ cups cooked chicken, chopped or shredded

½ cup pesto

½ cup shredded mozzarella cheese

Salt and black pepper to taste

DIRECTIONS

1 Preheat the oven to 425 degrees.

2 Cut into the top of the potatoes, making a 4-x-1-inch cross. Place potatoes right on the oven rack and bake for 45 minutes or until fork easily slides through potatoes. While potatoes bake, mix the chicken with the pesto and set aside.

3 When the potatoes are cooked, set them onto a baking sheet, split them open, and evenly top with the chicken-pesto mixture, dividing cheese evenly onto each potato.

4 Return to the oven for 10 more minutes to warm all ingredients and melt the cheese.

NOTE: These make a great lunch, so consider baking extra potatoes to have ready in the refrigerator that can be stuffed with leftovers through the week.

VARY IT! Stuff these with leftover chili and Cheddar cheese; black beans, salsa, and sour cream or plain yogurt; chopped cooked spinach, jarred artichokes, and Parmesan cheese; leftover curry; or goat cheese and walnuts.

Grilled Marinated Flank Steak

PREP TIME: 2 HR	COOK TIME: 8 MIN	YIELD: 4 SERVINGS

INGREDIENTS

2 tablespoons salt-free steak spice blend

¼ cup Worcestershire sauce

¼ cup lime juice, or juice from 1 lime

2 tablespoons vegetable oil

1 to 1½ pound beef flank steak

DIRECTIONS

1 Poke the flank steak all over with a fork (to help marinade soak through and tenderize). Pour the spice blend, Worcestershire sauce, lime juice, and oil in a zippered storage bag and mix by carefully squeezing the bag until contents are blended. Add the steak and seal the bag. Rub the liquid all around the steak and refrigerate for at least 90 minutes or 2 hours (mix and turn it over halfway through marinating time).

2 After steak has marinated, preheat the grill to 450 degrees.

3 Remove the steak from the marinade and lightly pat dry. Place directly onto the hot grill. Grill for 3 to 4 minutes then turn once, grilling another 3 minutes for medium rare (145 degrees on your meat thermometer). To ensure steak doesn't stick, don't move the steak until you're ready to turn it.

4 Remove steak to a cutting board and allow to rest for 10 minutes before cutting.

5 Cut the steak into ¼-inch slices, against the grain, on a slight diagonal (see Figure 13-4). Serve with a baked potato and the Chopped Salad with Lemon Vinaigrette (see Chapter 10), or the Black Bean and Edamame Salad (see Chapter 12).

NOTE: Flank steak is lower in fat (and saturated fat), so it's a great choice if you're following a heart-healthy diet. It's also budget-friendly. Because it's lean, it does require tenderization, so give it time to marinate. If you don't have a reusable bag, you can mix the marinade in a shallow dish and place the steak in it. Turn the steak over, coating both sides before covering and refrigerating. Turn the steak over after about 2 hours of refrigeration.

NOTE: Resting the steak once you remove it from the grill allows it to finish cooking and ensures a juicier end product.

TIP: If you don't have a grill, you can use your oven's broiler. Place the steak on a broiler rack and cook for 3 minutes. Open the oven and turn the steak once, and cook for 4 more minutes for medium rare.

SLICING FLANK STEAK

REMOVE THE STEAK TO A CUTTING BOARD.

CUT THE STEAK INTO THIN PIECES AGAINST THE GRAIN, ON A SLIGHT DIAGONAL.

Illustration by Elizabeth Kurtzman

FIGURE 13-4: How to slice flank steak.

Skillet Meatballs

PREP TIME: 20 MIN	COOK TIME: 15 MIN	YIELD: 10–12 MEATBALLS

INGREDIENTS

2 pounds lean ground beef (or a "meatball" mixture of ground beef, pork, and veal)

¾ cup breadcrumbs

1 tablespoon fresh parsley, minced, or 1 teaspoon dried

2 eggs, beaten

¼ cup milk

⅛ teaspoon salt

Black pepper to taste

1 tablespoon olive oil

2 cups prepared tomato sauce (or 15-ounce can)

4 ounces shredded mozzarella cheese

DIRECTIONS

1 Add ground meat, bread crumbs, parsley, eggs, milk, salt, and pepper into a large mixing bowl. Mix well until all ingredients are evenly combined. Form into 10 to 12 meatballs.

2 Coat a large skillet with the oil over medium heat. Add meatballs, gently turning every minute to brown each side. Cook for about 5 minutes.

3 Reduce heat to low and add the tomato sauce. Simmer about 10 minutes then remove from heat.

4 Turn broiler on high. Sprinkle the meatballs with the cheese and place them in the broiler for 2 to 3 minutes (watch carefully so cheese doesn't burn). Remove from skillet and serve.

NOTE: These meatballs can keep in the refrigerator for up to four days, or you can freeze leftover meatballs with sauce in an airtight container for up to three months.

NOTE: You can buy "meatball/meatloaf" ground meat mix at some supermarkets. This mixture gives the best flavor to meatballs.

VARY IT! You can use ground turkey or substitute an equivalent amount of vegetarian meat alternative crumbles.

TIP: Meatballs or meatloaf are a great place to use up stale bread or leftover fresh herbs or tomato sauce. Serve the meatballs with a green salad and crusty bread.

Spice-rubbed Pork Tenderloin with Roasted Sliced Grapes

PREP TIME: 15 MIN PLUS REFRIGERATION TIME	COOK TIME: 30 MIN	YIELD: 4 SERVINGS

INGREDIENTS

1 tablespoon paprika

¼ teaspoon cinnamon

1 teaspoon garlic powder

1 tablespoon brown sugar

¼ teaspoon salt

1½-pound pork tenderloin

3 teaspoons olive or avocado oil, divided

1 cup seedless grapes, halved

DIRECTIONS

1 Mix the paprika, cinnamon, garlic powder, and brown sugar in a small bowl.

2 Rub the spice mixture all over the tenderloin, coating all sides. Place the meat into a glass covered container and refrigerate for an hour or even overnight.

3 When ready to cook, preheat the oven to 375 degrees. Heat 1 teaspoon oil over medium heat in a large skillet. Add the tenderloin and lightly brown all sides, cooking for about 8 minutes.

4 Transfer the tenderloin to a baking dish and arrange the grapes around it. Drizzle the grapes with remaining oil. Bake for 25 minutes, until internal temperature is 145 degrees.

NOTE: Most tenderloins are 1 to 2 pounds in weight. A rule of thumb is to cook the pork for 20 to 25 minutes per pound. Adjust cooking time accordingly, but don't overcook it! Today's pork is not your mother's pork. Cooking times have changed over the years due to improved safety of the raw product, and pork is done when internal temperature reaches 145 degrees.

TIP: Roasting is a great way to use up less-than-fresh seedless grapes before they role to the back of your fridge and shrivel up.

TIP: You can vary the spice blend. If there's a premixed spice blend you enjoy, use 2½ tablespoons of it.

Slow Cooker Pulled Pork

PREP TIME: 10 MIN	COOK TIME: 6–10 HR	YIELD: 5 SERVINGS

INGREDIENTS

One 2-pound pork shoulder or butt roast

½ cup apple cider vinegar

15 ounces salsa or one 15-ounce can diced tomatoes

1 cup fruit (pineapple chunks, mango, or dried fruit)

1 cup barbeque sauce

DIRECTIONS

1 Place pork roast into a slow cooker.

2 Mix the vinegar, salsa, fruit, and barbeque sauce in a medium bowl.

3 Pour the sauce mixture over the pork and cook on low for 8 to 10 hours or on high for 5 to 6 hours.

4 When roast is cooked, remove it from the cooker and shred the meat, using two forks. Pour some of the sauce over the shredded meat and serve.

NOTE: Roasting pork or chicken in a slow cooker is a great way to use up leftover, overripe, or drying-up fruit. The fruit cooks down and adds flavor and nutrients to the sauce mixture, and you can consume part of the cooking liquid after it's cooked.

VARY IT! If you need to reduce your saturated fat intake (due to high cholesterol or cancer risk), choose a boneless pork loin for this recipe. It'll still be tasty but won't "fall apart" like the higher fat cuts. You can also use fruit jam instead of the fruit.

TIP: There are so many ways to enjoy pulled pork. You can make pulled pork nachos; use it in place of the chicken in the Chicken-Stuffed Baked Potatoes, earlier in this chapter; or make a pulled pork egg skillet (substitute the pulled pork for the fajita filling in the Fajita Eggs; see Chapter 9).

Roast Pork Loin with Apples and Onions

| PREP TIME: 10 MIN | COOK TIME: 65 MIN | YIELD: 8 SERVINGS |

INGREDIENTS

One 4-pound boneless pork loin roast

1 teaspoon salt

Black pepper to taste

1 teaspoon dried crushed rosemary

½ teaspoon ground thyme, or 1½ teaspoons fresh

1 large onion, thinly sliced

5 apples, cored and quartered

1 cup apple cider

DIRECTIONS

1 Preheat the oven to 450 degrees.

2 Place the pork loin onto a racked roasting pan. Salt the pork on all sides. Mix the pepper and herbs together in a small bowl then sprinkle and rub them over the pork. Add the onions and apples to the pan, surrounding the roast. Pour the apple cider into the bottom of the pan. Put the roast into the oven and roast for 15 minutes.

3 Turn the oven down to 350 degrees and continue roasting the pork for another 30 to 40 minutes or until internal temperature reaches 145 degrees. Allow to rest for 15 minutes before slicing to serve.

NOTE: Roast at 350 degrees for 20 minutes per pound in Step 3, depending on the exact size of your roast, and then check internal temperature.

Broiled Salmon Fillet

PREP TIME: 10 MIN	COOK TIME: 10 MIN	YIELD: 6 SERVINGS

INGREDIENTS

2 tablespoons Dijon mustard

1 tablespoon brown sugar

2 tablespoons Worcestershire sauce

1 tablespoon oil

Black pepper to taste

One 2-pound salmon fillet, fresh or frozen and thawed

DIRECTIONS

1 Preheat the oven broiler on high and position rack 6 inches from broiler element.

2 Mix the mustard, sugar, Worcestershire sauce, oil, and pepper in a small bowl. Place the salmon on broiler rack, skin-side down. Coat the fillet with the mustard mixture.

3 Broil the salmon for 10 to 12 minutes, or until it's just opaque and flakes easily.

NOTE: You can use six 5- to 6-ounce thawed, frozen salmon fillets instead of one whole fillet and shorten cooking time to 8 to 12 minutes.

Baked Fish with Herbed Bread Crumbs

PREP TIME: 15 MIN	COOK TIME: 10 MIN	YIELD: 4 SERVINGS

INGREDIENTS

Nonstick cooking spray

½ cup bread crumbs

1 teaspoon dried dill, or
1 tablespoon fresh

1 teaspoon dried parsley,
or 2 teaspoons fresh

3 teaspoons olive oil, divided

Four 4-ounce white fish fillets
(such as cod or tilapia)

DIRECTIONS

1 Preheat the oven to 350 degrees and spray a glass 8-x-8-inch baking dish with cooking spray.

2 Mix the bread crumbs, herbs, and 2 teaspoons of the olive oil in a small bowl until blended.

3 Place the fish, closely, into the baking dish and top each with the bread crumb mixture. Drizzle evenly with the remaining teaspoon of oil.

4 Bake for 10 minutes, until fish is opaque and bread crumbs lightly browned.

NOTE: Grind your own bread crumbs using stale bread; see "Making Bread Crumbs," earlier in this chapter, for instructions.

TIP: You can use this method for any fish, including perch, grouper, mahi mahi, and flounder. If you have leftover fish try the Fish Tacos recipe in Chapter 15.

Foil-baked Tilapia with Peppers

PREP TIME: 10 MIN | COOK TIME: 10 MIN | YIELD: 2 SERVINGS

INGREDIENTS

2 tilapia fillets

Pinch of salt

Black pepper to taste

½ cup finely diced bell pepper

¼ cup finely diced onion

¼ cup salsa

½ teaspoon cumin

4 lemon slices

DIRECTIONS

1 Preheat the oven to 400 degrees.

2 Place each fillet on its own 9-x-12-inch piece of aluminum foil. Season with salt and pepper.

3 Mix the bell peppers, onion, salsa, and cumin together in a small bowl. Top each fish fillet with the bell pepper mixture and then two lemon slices.

4 Fold the long ends of the foil together and fold over twice. Fold in each end of the packet, sealing loosely (refer to Figure 13-3).

5 Place the packets on a baking sheet and put into the oven. Bake for 10 minutes.

6 Carefully remove the fish packets and plate, or you can serve these right in the foil.

NOTE: Because there often seems to be leftover salsa that's not enough for a bowl of chips, using it on fish or chicken is a good zero waste food strategy. It adds both flavor and moisture to the foil packs.

TIP: Any small fish fillet, including cod or perch, works well for this recipe. Choose tilapia that's been farmed from Peru or Ecuador. According to Seafood Watch (www.seafoodwatch.org), you should avoid any seafood from China as their regulations are loose.

Moroccan Veggie Skillet

PREP TIME: 15 MIN | COOK TIME: 25 MIN | YIELD: 4 SERVINGS

INGREDIENTS

1 tablespoon olive oil

1 cup diced bell pepper

½ diced onion

1 cup chopped or shredded carrots

1 large, sweet potato, peeled and diced

Pinch of salt

¼ teaspoon cinnamon

1 to 1½ cups vegetable stock, divided

2 cups plant-based veggie-burger crumbles

¼ teaspoon garlic powder

One 15-ounce can diced tomatoes, undrained

1 tablespoon tomato paste

One 15-ounce can garbanzo beans, drained and rinsed

½ cup chopped dried apricots or raisins

½ teaspoon paprika

½ teaspoon turmeric

1 teaspoon curry powder

2½ cups cooked couscous (cooked according to package directions)

DIRECTIONS

1 Heat the oil over medium heat in a 3-quart saucepan or Dutch oven. Add the onion-pepper mix and the carrots and cook until onions are translucent, about 3 to 4 minutes.

2 Add sweet potatoes, salt, cinnamon, and ½ cup of the vegetable stock. Cook for 5 to 6 minutes until liquid is reduced by half.

3 Add the veggie-burger crumbles, garlic powder, tomatoes, and tomato paste to the pot. Stir and cook for another 3 minutes.

4 Add the beans, dried apricots, paprika, turmeric, curry powder, and another ½ cup stock. Reduce heat, cover, and simmer for about 5 to 8 more minutes, or until broth is slightly reduced. If needed, add additional stock.

5 Plate the couscous into 4 bowls. Serve the beans and vegetables over the couscous. Refrigerate leftovers for up to four days or freeze in an airtight container for up to three months.

TIP: Adding a tablespoon (or even two) of tomato paste can really intensify the flavor of dishes like this one. Tomato paste in a tube costs a bit more but can help reduce food waste because instead of opening a 6-ounce can, you can squeeze out only what you need.

NOTE: You can use 1½ cups frozen bell pepper and onion mix in place of fresh pepper and onions.

VARY IT! Plant-based protein crumbles can be found in the freezer section; use as you would use ground meat. You can easily substitute ¾ pound of ground beef or turkey in this dish in place of the veggie crumbles.

Spicy Tofu Broccoli Bowl

PREP TIME: 30 MIN PLUS TIME TO DRAIN AND PRESS TOFU	COOK TIME: 30 MIN	YIELD: 4 SERVINGS

INGREDIENTS

1 package firm tofu, drained and pressed (see the upcoming Tip for instructions)

4 teaspoons cornstarch, divided

¼ cup soy sauce

2 tablespoons water

1 tablespoon sriracha sauce

2 cloves garlic, crushed, or 2 teaspoons jarred minced garlic

2 teaspoons honey

2 teaspoons canola oil, divided

1 large bunch broccoli, chopped, including stems

2 cups cooked rice (cooked according to package directions)

1 teaspoon red pepper flakes, optional

DIRECTIONS

1 Cut tofu into ½-inch cubes and place into a medium bowl. Sprinkle 3 teaspoons of cornstarch over it and toss well to evenly coat.

2 Mix soy sauce, water, sriracha sauce, garlic, remaining cornstarch, and honey in a small bowl. Set aside.

3 Heat 1 teaspoon of oil in a wok or large nonstick skillet. Add the tofu and brown on all sides, about 15 minutes (don't overcrowd the pan — if needed, work in batches). Remove crisp tofu from the pan and transfer to serving bowl.

4 Carefully wipe the pan with a paper towel to remove any lingering bits of browned cornstarch. Add remaining teaspoon of oil and the broccoli to the pan. Stir-fry for about 5 minutes. Return tofu to the pan and continue cooking another 2 minutes over medium-high heat.

5 Reduce heat and add the sauce to the tofu-broccoli mixture. Stir as the sauce simmers for about 2 to 3 minutes. Transfer back to serving bowl. Serve over rice and garnish with red pepper flakes (if desired).

TIP: To drain and press tofu, wrap it in a paper towel and place into a colander over a large bowl. Place a heavy small pan onto it (a small cast-iron pan works well). Allow it to sit for 15 minutes then change the paper towel and allow it to continue draining for another 10 to 15 minutes.

Lentil-stuffed Zucchini

PREP TIME: 20 MIN	COOK TIME: 45 MIN	YIELD: 4 SERVINGS

INGREDIENTS

2 small zucchini, halved lengthwise

2 teaspoons olive oil

½ cup diced onion

1 cup cooked green or red lentils (cooked according to package directions)

2 tablespoons tomato paste

½ teaspoon dried oregano

¼ teaspoon garlic powder

¼ cup water

Pinch of salt

Olive oil spray

3 teaspoons grated Parmesan cheese

2 tablespoon chopped fresh basil (or 2 teaspoons dried) for garnish, optional

DIRECTIONS

1 Scoop only the soft, seedy flesh from each zucchini (see **Note**). Place the zucchinis onto the baking sheet, cut-side up, and set aside. If zucchinis won't sit right on your pan, slice a thin layer of the skin off the bottom of each half to make it sit flat (see Figure 13-5).

2 Preheat the oven to 375 degrees. Line a baking sheet with parchment paper or a silicone mat.

3 Heat the olive oil in a medium skillet over medium-low heat. Add onions and sauté for about 3 minutes. Add the zucchini pulp and sauté another 2 minutes, or until onions are translucent. Reduce the heat to low and add the lentils, tomato paste, oregano, garlic powder, and salt. Add about ¼ cup water and stir to combine. Simmer this mixture for 2 or 3 minutes until all liquid is reduced and forms a light sauce. Remove from heat.

4 Spray each zucchini half with olive oil spray. Stuff each of them with the lentil mixture, dividing evenly. Sprinkle each half with the cheese and bake for 25 minutes until the zucchini is fork-tender. Garnish with basil, if desired, and serve immediately.

NOTE: You can sauté the zucchini pulp to include with this dish at Step 3, or reserve it to make a spread. Cook the pulp with 2 tablespoons minced onion, 1 teaspoon crushed garlic, and a diced tomato or 2 tablespoons tomato paste, in a small skillet over medium heat until the onion is translucent and soft. Serve as a spread for crackers or bread.

SCOOPING OUT ZUCCHINI

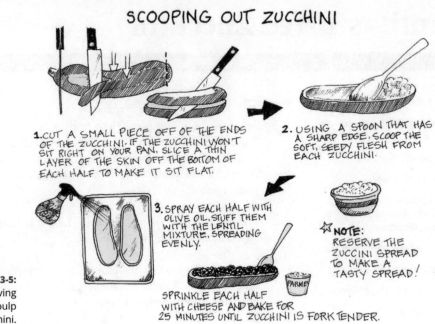

1. CUT A SMALL PIECE OFF OF THE ENDS OF THE ZUCCHINI. IF THE ZUCCHINI WON'T SIT RIGHT ON YOUR PAN, SLICE A THIN LAYER OF THE SKIN OFF THE BOTTOM OF EACH HALF TO MAKE IT SIT FLAT.

2. USING A SPOON THAT HAS A SHARP EDGE, SCOOP THE SOFT, SEEDY FLESH FROM EACH ZUCCHINI.

3. SPRAY EACH HALF WITH OLIVE OIL, STUFF THEM WITH THE LENTIL MIXTURE, SPREADING EVENLY.

☆ NOTE: RESERVE THE ZUCCHINI SPREAD TO MAKE A TASTY SPREAD!

SPRINKLE EACH HALF WITH CHEESE AND BAKE FOR 25 MINUTES UNTIL ZUCCHINI IS FORK TENDER.

FIGURE 13-5:
Removing seedy pulp from zucchini.

Illustration by Elizabeth Kurtzman

Chapter **14**

Oh, the Pasta-bilities!

RECIPES IN THIS CHAPTER

- Broccoli Bits and Bell Peppers with Linguine
- Vegetable Lasagna
- Penne Bake with Veggies
- Smoked Salmon Pasta with Asparagus
- Garlic Linguine with Clams
- Pasta with Roast Vegetables and Salmon
- Pasta with Chickpeas
- Veggie-Roast Pasta Primavera
- Bow Ties with Turkey and Peas
- Roasted Tomatoes and Bell Peppers with Penne
- Angel Hair with Shrimp and Spinach

Whether pasta began on the island of Sicily or has its roots in the Far East, I'm sharing mostly Italian-inspired dishes in this chapter, as pasta was a big part of my life growing up. Every Sunday was pasta Sunday. We usually had one large midday meal of spaghetti with a short-rib tomato sauce, or, on special occasions, homemade ravioli. Sometimes pasta would just be the first course followed by a roast chicken. We wouldn't need more than a light snack later in the day to keep us full through bedtime.

During the week, my mom would whip up an easier meal with pasta, something like the Garlic Linguine with Clams or the Pasta with Chickpeas in this chapter. Or she'd throw some leftover greens into a pasta dish. The beauty of incorporating pasta into zero waste cooking is that, like eggs, it's a blank canvas for leftovers, it's easy to prepare, and it's budget-friendly, too.

REMEMBER

Never underestimate the value of sharing an enjoyable meal with family and friends.

Over the past decade, media stories and carb-shunning dieters have tried to give pasta a bad reputation. Shocking claims that grains like pasta dull your brain or make you fat simply have no evidence to back them up (but they do sadly create viral influencer followings).

Food choices are an individual thing, and choices are steeped in culture, upbringing, and geography. While the food you eat can support or deteriorate your health, even if you have a health issue or intolerance, there's usually no reason to eliminate entire food groups from your diet. Grains provide important vitamins, minerals, and fiber, helping to balance a meal.

This chapter helps you reduce food waste with easy, delicious, and healthful pasta meals.

Pasta Basics

I'm a stickler for matching pasta to the dish and cooking it properly. As you plan your shopping trips, consider pasta shapes that work best with the type of sauces you like, and the shapes your household enjoys most. However, while I suggest specific pasta shapes for each recipe in this chapter, keep the spirit of zero waste in mind and use up what you have on hand first.

TIP

It's easy to cook more pasta than you need. Good news: it reheats well. Also, here's a quick guide to help you measure portions appropriately:

>> For long pasta, like spaghetti, fettucine, and linguine, one serving (or 2 ounces) is about the diameter of a quarter.

>> For small pasta, you can use standard measuring cups to measure it dry.

- A serving of bow ties or rigatoni would measure ¾ cup.

- A serving of elbows, penne, or rotini (springs) would measure ½ cup dry.

- A serving of ditalini would be about ⅓ cup dry.

Name that pasta shape

Here are some of my favorite pasta shapes and some tips to go along with each. Of course, you have many more types of pasta to choose from, but these are great to have on hand for everyday cooking.

>> **Penne, ziti, rigatoni, and ditali:** These tubular pastas often are ridged, which helps the sauce cling to them. Ditali is Italian for "small thimble" and can come in a few sizes, most commonly ditalini (a petite version) which is nice for soups and the Pasta with Chickpeas recipe in this chapter.

- » **Farfalle and rotini:** Better known as "bow ties" and "springs" around my house, use these noodles for pasta salads or with a chunky veggie sauce.

- » **Fettucine:** These wide ribbons work deliciously well with a cream sauce because the surface area "grabs" more saucy goodness, and this pasta is sturdy enough to not get bogged down by a heavier sauce (like an angel hair or other thin spaghetti would).

- » **Spaghetti and linguine:** These types of pasta strings are perfect to pair with a simple marinara or pesto. Linguine works well with a lighter sauce, such as a simple butter, and traditionally is used for seafood pasta dishes.

- » **Bucatini:** This noodle may look solid, but it's actually a hollow tube. Still, it stands up well to a thick and meaty tomato sauce.

- » **Angel hair and capellini:** These thin, quick-cooking pastas like to keep it light, working well with peas, veggies, a simple *aglio e olio* (olive oil and garlic sauce), or a light tomato sauce.

- » **Lasagna sheets and other special pastas for stuffing:** These special pastas are used for specific dishes. Lasagna are wide sheets of pasta (lasagna is the singular, and the American spelling, lasagne is the plural and Italian spelling). You can purchase them precut in either a boil or no-boil option. These are used in the Vegetable Lasagna recipe, and the sheets also can be filled and rolled up to make manicotti (or you can buy cannelloni tubes to fill). You'll also find large shell pasta that can be stuffed in a similar manner.

- » **Shells, orecchiette, and elbows:** These types of pasta are small, versatile shapes that are ideal for pasta salads and cheese sauces.

TIP

You can substitute one pasta shape for another in the same "pasta shape family." For instance, a recipe calling for penne could also use ziti or rigatoni. Figure 14-1 provides a visual guide to several popular pasta shapes.

Pasta cooking instructions

In my book (literally), pasta is best when it's cooked *al dente,* or slightly firm to bite. When you learn how to get that perfect al dente, you'll never go back to mushy pasta.

FIGURE 14-1:
A guide to
popular pasta
shapes.

Illustration by Elizabeth Kurtzman

Overcooking pasta also makes it more difficult to digest. Give your belly a break and learn to cook it al dente. Here's how:

1. **Fill a large stockpot with enough water to give the pasta room to cook evenly.**

   The general rule is 4 quarts of water per pound (or 16 ounces) of pasta. If you're cooking only half a pound of pasta, you can use less water, but still boil at least 3 quarts of water. Use a larger pot with more water (6 quarts) when you're cooking more than a pound of pasta.

2. **As the water begins to boil, add 1 to 2 tablespoons of salt to the stockpot.**

   Adjust the amount of salt to taste (and if using less water, use less salt), or in light of your health needs — if you have high blood pressure, easy does it, but don't skip it.

3. **Add pasta to the boiling, salted water and stir often through cooking.**

4. **Cook for 8 to 10 minutes, or until al dente.**

   Cooking time will vary on the brand, or whether a pasta is dry, fresh or frozen. Check the instructions on the package. Taste pasta around the 7- or 8-minute mark and then every minute until al dente. It should be firm and a little chewy.

   Smaller pasta (like elbows, small shells, or angel hair) takes less time to cook, while larger pasta (like rigatoni and spaghetti) may take more. And fresh pasta cooks more quickly, so reference the cook time on the package whether dry or fresh. Another strategy is to turn the pot off at 6 minutes then leave the pasta in the water while you get your bowl of sauce or other parts of the meal ready. That way it won't be overcooked. But don't forget about the pasta sitting in the water or it will get mushy!

5. **Using a glass measuring cup, scoop about a cup of pasta water from the pot to help finish your dish.**

   You may not need to use all of this reserved water, but adding some pasta water to your final dish helps thicken and give body to the sauce (it shouldn't be watery). The cooking liquid also helps the sauce stick to the pasta, so do not rinse your pasta.

6. **Strain the remaining water from the pasta.**

   Use a colander to strain smaller pasta, and use tongs to remove long pasta strands from water.

7. **Immediately transfer the drained pasta to a serving bowl with your sauce and combine.**

TIP

When it comes to pasta dishes, using freshly ground black pepper is the best choice in my opinion. When peppercorns are freshly ground, they have more of a peppery kick. When peppercorns are already ground, they've been exposed to oxygen and lose flavor. Grinding the peppercorns yourself allows you to adjust the coarseness to your preference, and it gives some texture to the dish as well. Don't overdo it, but a couple of twists of a peppermill perfectly accent most pasta dishes. If you don't have a peppermill, you can use regular black ground pepper, or skip it if you aren't a big ground pepper fan.

Despite measuring and planning your meal to perfection, you still may end up with leftover pasta. Or you may get a huge portion when dining out and bring home a to-go box full. No worries. Cooked pasta dishes refrigerate and reheat well. Microwaving is the quickest way to reheat a pasta dish and keeps the pasta moist. I recommend heating individual serving bowls one at a time for even reheating. If you are reheating a pasta dish with a light sauce or an oil- or butter-based sauce, like Smoked Salmon Pasta with Asparagus or Garlic Linguine with Clams, add a tablespoon of water per serving before heating. This helps prevent the cold pasta from sticking together. You can also freeze in an airtight container for up to three months, defrost, and then heat in the same manner.

Broccoli Bits and Bell Peppers with Linguine

PREP TIME: 10 MIN	COOK TIME: 30 MIN	YIELD: 4 SERVINGS

INGREDIENTS

3 tablespoons olive oil, divided

½ cup sliced broccoli stems and chopped florets and leaves

1 small yellow bell pepper, seeded and thinly sliced

1 small green bell pepper, seeded and thinly sliced

1 small onion, thinly sliced

2 cloves garlic, crushed, or 2 teaspoons jarred minced garlic

Pinch of salt

8 ounces linguine

Grated Parmesan cheese (optional)

Black pepper (optional)

DIRECTIONS

1 Heat 1 tablespoon olive oil in a skillet. Add broccoli, peppers, and onions to the pan, salt and sauté for 4 to 5 minutes.

2 While veggies are cooking, put about 3 quarts of water in a large stockpot on the stove to boil. When water starts to boil, add a tablespoon of salt. When at full boil, add linguine, stir, and cook for about 9 minutes until al dente or according to package instructions.

3 Meanwhile, add an additional 2 tablespoons of oil and the garlic to the pan with the veggies. Heat over low to medium heat until garlic is lightly golden, and then remove from heat.

4 Drain the pasta, reserving a cup of pasta water. Transfer the pasta to a serving dish. Add about ¼ cup of the hot pasta water, or more as needed, and toss. Add the vegetables in oil and gently toss again. Garnish with the cheese and black pepper (if desired).

TIP: Use as much or as little bell pepper as you have. You can definitely sauté the small leaves that are often left on a head of broccoli. You can also add any other wilting veggies that you need to use.

VARY IT! Try this dish with roasted grape tomatoes. Add halved grape tomatoes to the skillet in Step 1 and sauté along with other veggies.

Vegetable Lasagna

PREP TIME: 20 MIN	COOK TIME: 40 MIN	YIELD: 4 SERVINGS

INGREDIENTS

Nonstick cooking spray

6 lasagna noodles

3 bell peppers, seeded and chopped

2 small zucchinis, sliced

1 cup mushrooms, thinly sliced

4 cloves garlic, minced, or 4 teaspoons jarred minced garlic

1 tablespoon olive oil

Pinch of salt

For the sauce

2 tablespoons butter

2 tablespoons flour

2 cups milk

3 ounces cream cheese

Pinch of salt

Pinch of black pepper

For the lasagna

2 cups part skim ricotta cheese

1 egg, beaten

2 tablespoons chopped fresh parsley, or 2 teaspoons dried

1 cup shredded sharp cheese (like Cheddar or Gouda)

1 cup shredded mozzarella cheese, divided

DIRECTIONS

1 Preheat the oven to 400 degrees. Spray an 8-x-8-inch pan with cooking spray.

2 Bring 4 quarts of water to boil in a stockpot, add 1 tablespoon of salt, and cook the lasagna noodles according to package directions. Set aside.

3 Place the peppers, zucchini, mushrooms, and garlic on a baking sheet lined with a silicone mat or parchment paper for easier cleanup. Drizzle with olive oil and salt to taste. Roast the vegetables for 20 minutes then reduce oven to 350.

4 Melt the butter in a nonstick saucepan over low-medium heat. Make a roux by adding flour to the butter and stirring quickly, using a wire whisk. Cook for 1 to 2 minutes. Gradually pour in the milk, stirring constantly.

5 Stir sauce continuously for 1 to 2 minutes, and then add the cream cheese. Continue stirring until cream cheese has melted and sauce is slightly thickened. Season with the salt and pepper and keep warm.

6 In a large bowl, mix the ricotta, egg, parsley, sharp cheese, and 3/4 cup of mozzarella cheese. Mix well.

7 Add about 2/3 cup of sauce to bottom of prepared baking dish. Layer 2 of the lasagna sheets on top of the sauce. Add half of the ricotta mixture to the lasagna layer and spread evenly.

8 Top the ricotta with half of the roasted vegetables. Repeat layers (sauce, noodles, cheese, vegetables).

9 Top the second layer of vegetables with a final layer of noodles. Spread the remaining sauce over the top. Sprinkle with the remaining mozzarella cheese. Cover tightly with aluminum foil.

10 Bake for 35 minutes at 375 degrees, until bubbly. Remove foil and return to the oven for another 5 to 10 minutes or until cheese is lightly browned on top.

NOTE: If you have another favorite traditional lasagna recipe, don't be shy about adding some veggies that you have left in the refrigerator. Finely chopped carrots, onions, eggplant, and mushrooms can all easily be added to the tomato sauce. If you have leftover Roasted Veggie Trio, you can add it, too!

TIPS: You can use any mushroom, but baby portobellas offer a deeper flavor to the lasagna. You can also mix and match any sharp cheese you have on hand into the filling. If your lasagna noodles tear while cooking, don't worry. Just place them into the bottom or middle portions of the pan. It'll all bake together and be delicious anyway.

VARY IT! Instead of the roasted vegetables, you can add 4 to 5 cups of spinach. Sauté spinach in oil, add 3 minced garlic cloves, and stir until wilted. Cool then add the spinach to the cheese mixture. If you have leftover cooked chicken, you can add it to the filling as well.

Penne Bake with Veggies

PREP TIME: 10 MIN	COOK TIME: 10 MIN	YIELD: 4 SERVINGS

INGREDIENTS

Cooking spray

1 small to medium zucchini

1 teaspoon olive oil

2 garlic cloves, crushed, or 2 teaspoons jarred minced garlic

Pinch of salt

8 ounces penne

2 cups tomato sauce

1 cup ricotta cheese

¼ cup grated Parmesan cheese, divided

Black pepper to taste

3 tablespoons chopped fresh basil (optional)

DIRECTIONS

1 Preheat the oven to 350 degrees. Spray a 9-x-11-inch baking dish with cooking spray.

2 Bring 4 quarts of water to boil in a large stockpot.

3 Slice the zucchini lengthwise then cut into ¼-inch slices. Heat oil in a small pan over medium heat and add zucchini. Cook for 5 to 8 minutes then add the garlic and salt, and cook another 2 to 3 minutes.

4 While zucchini cooks, add 1 tablespoon of salt to the water. When at full boil, add the penne and stir. Cook al dente, for about 7 to 8 minutes, or according to package instructions. Reserve a cup of the pasta water.

5 Drain the pasta then transfer it to a large bowl. Stir about ¼ cup of the pasta water back into the pasta to keep it from sticking together and to allow the tomato sauce to adhere to pasta. Add the tomato sauce and gently stir to combine. Gently fold zucchini and then the ricotta cheese into the pasta.

6 Pour the pasta mixture into the prepared baking dish. Sprinkle with 1 tablespoon of the Parmesan cheese and black pepper.

7 Bake for 35 minutes. Garnish with basil (if desired). Serve the remaining grated cheese at the table with the pasta.

NOTE: Parsley works well in place of basil in this recipe.

VARY IT! Have carrots that are starting to look a little dry? Chop them up and add them to the pasta water during the last 4 minutes. You can also add small amounts of leftover chopped chicken or baked salmon to this pasta bake.

Smoked Salmon Pasta with Asparagus

PREP TIME: 15 MIN	COOK TIME: 10 MIN	YIELD: 4 SERVINGS

INGREDIENTS

3 tablespoons plus 1 teaspoon olive oil, divided

1 bunch asparagus (about 15–20 spears), cut into 2-inch pieces

Juice and zest from 1 lemon

Pinch of salt

8 ounces small pasta shells

2 garlic cloves, crushed, or 2 teaspoons jarred minced garlic

1 teaspoon Herbs de Provence or 1 teaspoon of dried thyme or tarragon

3 ounces smoked salmon, cut into strips

2 ounces feta cheese

Black pepper to taste

DIRECTIONS

1 Heat 2 to 3 quarts of water to boil in a stockpot.

2 Heat 1 teaspoon of oil in a large skillet. Add asparagus and sauté for 4 minutes until asparagus is bright green. Squeeze with lemon juice and salt, then transfer to a large serving bowl.

3 When water is boiling, add 1 tablespoon of salt to the water, add shells, stir, and cook for 7 to 8 minutes, or according to package instructions.

4 In the same pan you cooked asparagus in, add remaining oil, garlic, and herbs. Heat for 1 to 2 minutes or until garlic is lightly browned and fragrant, and remove from heat.

5 Meanwhile, drain pasta, reserving 1 cup of the pasta water. Transfer pasta to the serving bowl and add the salmon. Toss pasta, salmon, and asparagus, adding up to ½ cup of the reserved pasta water as needed, to prevent sticking.

6 Pour the hot oil and garlic–herb mixture over the pasta and toss to combine. Garnish with the feta cheese and black pepper.

NOTE: Timing is a learned skill. You want to heat the oil about 2 minutes before the pasta is done. Remove it from the heat then quickly drain the pasta and toss all ingredients together in the bowl.

TIP: This pasta dish is a great way to use any of the Broiled Salmon Fillet you may have leftover.

VARY IT! This can also work as a cold salad. Instead of heating the olive oil, toss everything with the Everyday Vinaigrette Dressing or the Go-to Honey Dijon Salad Dressing (see Chapter 11).

Garlic Linguine with Clams

PREP TIME: 15 MIN	COOK TIME: 10 MIN	YIELD: 6 SERVINGS

INGREDIENTS

16 ounces linguine

¼ cup olive oil

4 cloves garlic, crushed, or 4 teaspoons jarred minced garlic

Two 6.5-ounce cans minced clams, drained, liquid reserved

¼ cup grated Parmesan cheese

Black pepper to taste

DIRECTIONS

1 Heat water to boil in a large stockpot. Add 2 tablespoons salt. When water is at full boil, add pasta and stir.

2 While pasta cooks, heat oil in a large pan over medium-high heat. Add the clams and garlic and sauté for 2 to 3 minutes. Add reserved clam juice and heat through for another minute. Remove from heat.

3 Drain the pasta, reserving a cup of the water. Transfer to a large bowl. Add the clam mixture over the pasta and toss together until it's coated, adding a small amount of the pasta water if needed. Garnish with cheese and black pepper.

VARY IT! Add chopped leftover broccoli to this dish for a bit of color and vitamin C. At the 4-minute mark, add the broccoli to the pasta water. Then toss the pasta and broccoli with the garlic oil and clams.

Pasta with Roast Vegetables and Salmon

PREP TIME: 10 MIN	COOK TIME: 35 MIN	YIELD: 4 SERVINGS

INGREDIENTS

1 cup mushrooms, thinly sliced

1 yellow summer squash or zucchini, thinly sliced

1 bell pepper, seeded, thinly sliced

¼ cup olive oil, divided

1 lemon, sliced into ⅛-inch rounds

Pinch of salt

8 ounces rotini

6 ounces cooked salmon, broken into pieces

¼ cup grated Parmesan or Romano cheese

1 to 2 tablespoons fresh parsley, chopped (optional)

DIRECTIONS

1 Preheat the oven to 425 degrees. Place vegetables onto a baking sheet lined with a silicone mat or parchment paper. Drizzle with 1 tablespoon olive oil, top with half of the lemon slices, a pinch of salt, and roast for 25 minutes, tossing halfway through.

2 While vegetables roast, bring a large pot of water to a boil, adding 1 tablespoon of salt when boiling. When water is at full boil, add the pasta, stir, and cook until al dente, 7 to 8 minutes, or according to package instructions. Reserving a cup of the pasta water, drain the pasta and transfer to a large serving bowl.

3 In the same pot the pasta cooked in, heat the remaining oil for 2 minutes. Drizzle the oil over the pasta. Add the salmon, up to ¼ cup of the reserved pasta water (if pasta is sticky), and toss well.

4 Top the pasta with the vegetables. Garnish with grated cheese, parsley (if desired), and remaining lemon slices.

NOTE: You can also sauté the vegetables in a pan on the stove top, but roasting gives them more depth and brings out their sweetness.

TIPS: Save time by using leftover cooked salmon or canned salmon. Also, keep frozen salmon fillets on hand to make meal prep easy as well. Simply roast a salmon fillet for 15 minutes, along with the vegetables.

VARY IT! These veggies pair nicely with salmon and pasta; however, you can also use asparagus or eggplant or make this dish with leftover veggies from the Roasted Veggie Trio recipe.

Pasta with Chickpeas

PREP TIME: 10 MIN | **COOK TIME: 35 MIN** | **YIELD: 4 SERVINGS**

INGREDIENTS

8 ounces ditalini pasta or other small pasta

1 tablespoon olive oil

2 tablespoons minced onion

1 clove garlic, pressed, or 1 teaspoon jarred minced garlic

One 10-ounce can chickpeas, drained and rinsed

2 cups Quick Canned Tomato Pasta Sauce (see recipe in Chapter 11) or 2 cups jarred sauce

¼ cup grated Parmesan cheese

Black pepper to taste

DIRECTIONS

1 Bring a large pot of water to boil then add 1 tablespoon of salt. Add the pasta and stir. Cook pasta until al dente, or according to package instructions (about 7 to 8 minutes).

2 While pasta cooks, heat olive oil in a 3-quart pot over medium heat for a minute. Add the onion and garlic. Stir, and cook until onion is translucent. Reduce heat, add the chickpeas, and cook for 2 more minutes.

3 Add the tomato sauce to the bean mixture.

4 Drain pasta, reserving a cup of liquid. Add pasta into sauce and bean pot. Stir until coated, and then simmer for another 20 to 30 minutes. Add ¼ cup of the reserved pasta water if mixture seems too thick. Transfer to a serving dish and top with Parmesan cheese and some black pepper if desired.

NOTE: Unlike a traditional Pasta Fagioli soup, this comfort dish results in a rich, thick sauce mixed into the pasta and beans. Small pasta shapes work best for this dish, but you can substitute penne or orecchiette for the ditalini pasta. You can also add some red pepper flakes to the sauce, if you like a little kick.

Veggie-Roast Pasta Primavera

PREP TIME: 10 MIN	COOK TIME: 30 MIN	YIELD: 4 SERVINGS

INGREDIENTS

2 cups sliced carrots

1 zucchini, sliced

2 cups sugar snap peas, fresh or frozen

2 cloves garlic, or 2 teaspoons jarred minced garlic

Salt to taste

1 tablespoon olive oil

Basic Cream Sauce (see the recipe in Chapter 11)

8 ounces fettucine

2 tablespoons chopped basil or parsley (optional)

DIRECTIONS

1 Preheat the oven to 425 degrees. Line a baking sheet with parchment paper or a silicone mat. Spread the vegetables and garlic onto the baking sheet, salt and drizzle with oil, and toss to coat. Roast for 20 to 25 minutes, turning halfway through. Remove from oven and set aside.

2 While veggies roast, prepare the Basic Cream Sauce (from Chapter 11) and keep it warm over a very low burner, stirring occasionally. Also bring water to a boil in a large stockpot. Add 1 tablespoon of salt to the water.

3 Add the fettucine, stir, and cook until al dente, for 8 to 9 minutes, or according to package instructions. Reserve a cup of the pasta water.

4 Ladle a spoon of the Basic Cream Sauce into a large serving bowl. Drain the pasta and transfer to the bowl. Stir in 2 tablespoons of pasta water, or more if needed. Top the pasta with another spoon of the sauce, and then add the roasted vegetables. Toss gently, adding the remaining sauce. Garnish with basil or parsley (if desired).

NOTE: You can use penne or thin spaghetti in place of fettucine.

VARY IT! Change it up by using any vegetables you have in the refrigerator or freezer. Roasted cauliflower or broccoli is a great addition.

Bow Ties with Turkey and Peas

PREP TIME: 5 MIN	COOK TIME: 10 MIN	YIELD: 2 SERVINGS

INGREDIENTS

Pinch of salt

5 ounces farfalle (bow tie) pasta

½ cup peas

1 tablespoon butter

1 cup cooked, chopped, or shredded turkey

¼ cup grated Parmesan cheese (optional)

DIRECTIONS

1   Bring a large stockpot of water to boil. Add 1 tablespoon of salt to the water. When at full boil, add pasta, stir, and cook until al dente, for 9 to 10 minutes or according to package instructions. During the last 3 minutes of cooking, add peas.

2   Reserving a cup of the water, drain pasta and peas and transfer to a serving bowl. Add the butter and a few tablespoons of the reserved water, and toss until butter is melted and pasta is lightly coated. Add few spoons of reserved water as needed. Top with the turkey.

3   Garnish with the cheese (if desired) and serve.

VARY IT! Replace the turkey with cooked chicken, pulled pork, or thinly sliced steak or roast beef.

Roasted Tomatoes and Bell Peppers with Penne

PREP TIME: 10 MIN | COOK TIME: 30 MIN | YIELD: 4 SERVINGS

INGREDIENTS

2 cups grape or cherry tomatoes

1 yellow bell pepper, seeded and thinly sliced

1 green bell pepper, seeded and thinly sliced

1 small onion, thinly sliced

2 cloves garlic, or 2 teaspoons jarred minced garlic

3 tablespoons olive oil, divided

Pinch of salt

8 ounces penne

½ cup grated Parmesan cheese (optional)

Black pepper (optional)

DIRECTIONS

1 Preheat the oven to 425 degrees. Line baking sheet with a silicone mat or parchment paper and spread the tomatoes, peppers, and onions onto it. Crush one garlic clove and add to the pan. Toss together, salt, then drizzle the vegetables with 1 tablespoon of the oil, tossing to coat. Roast for 20 minutes, toss and stir them around halfway through to ensure they don't stick.

2 While veggies are roasting, put a large stockpot of water on the stove to boil. Add a tablespoon of salt to the water. When water is at full boil, add the penne, stir, and cook al dente for 8 to 9 minutes, or according to package instructions.

3 Heat the remaining 2 tablespoons of oil over medium heat in a small pan. Add the remaining garlic and heat until garlic is lightly colored.

4 Drain the pasta, reserving a cup of the pasta water. Transfer the pasta to a serving dish. Add hot garlic oil and toss. Top with the roasted vegetables and about ¼ cup of the pasta water, then gently toss again. Garnish with the cheese and the black pepper (if desired).

Angel Hair with Shrimp and Spinach

PREP TIME: 5 MIN	COOK TIME: 10 MIN	YIELD: 6–8 SERVINGS

INGREDIENTS

1 teaspoon olive oil

1 shallot, minced

One 10-ounce bag fresh spinach

Pinch of salt

1 pound cooked shrimp (thawed, with shell removed)

1 cup Quick Canned Tomato Pasta Sauce (see recipe in Chapter 11) or 1 cup jarred tomato sauce

16 ounces angel hair pasta

¼ cup grated Parmesan cheese (optional)

DIRECTIONS

1   Bring a large stockpot of water to boil.

2   Heat the oil in a large pan over medium heat. Add the shallot and sauté for 1 to 2 minutes. Add the spinach, salt, and stir until wilted, about 2 minutes. Add the cooked shrimp and sauté until heated through, about 2 minutes, then add the tomato sauce and keep warm over low heat while you cook pasta.

3   Add 2 tablespoons of salt to the boiling water. Add the angel hair pasta and stir. Check the pasta at 2 minutes (this variety cooks quickly). It should have a tender bite, not too soft. If needed, cook an additional minute, but no more. Drain the pasta, reserving a cup of the water, and transfer to large serving bowl. Add enough of the reserved water to prevent sticking.

4   Top the pasta with the shrimp-spinach mixture and toss gently. Serve with grated cheese.

VARY IT! Add a bit of heat by adding 1 teaspoon red pepper flakes to the final dish.

Chapter **15**

Creating Delicious Handhelds with What You Have on Hand

RECIPES IN THIS CHAPTER

Mushroom Turkey Burgers

**Pork Pita Pockets with
Cucumber Sauce**

Flexible Quesadillas

Fajitas with Avocado Cream

**Pork Tacos with Peppers,
Onions, and Lime Crema**

Fish Tacos

**Bagels with Smoked Salmon
and Cream Cheese**

Seafood Salad Sandwich

*H*andhelds are meals you can eat with your hands, including your go-to sandwich, taco, wrap, pita pocket, and more. Almost everyone loves a handheld because they're easy to prepare, taste delicious, and require no utensils to eat, plus the combinations of ingredients are endless. Handheld fillers easily make use of leftover items you have in the fridge, so they're great for reducing food waste.

Unfortunately, bread and other grain foods have come under criticism over the past decade. Keep in mind that balance is the most important factor in choosing foods that support health. Pay attention to your own body's needs, but be wary of extreme dietary philosophies. While we are all human, each of us has a somewhat unique physiology that's impacted by our genes, our environment, our activity, and what we eat. That said, if bread doesn't work for you, you can skip it. If you're gluten sensitive, you're in luck, because you can find more delicious choices on the market than ever.

REMEMBER

Self-proclaimed health and wellness gurus shouldn't be your go-to source for nutrition science. Speak to a registered dietitian about your diet and health to learn more about your specific nutrition needs.

In this chapter, you find recipes for delicious handhelds that you can enjoy for lunch or a quick dinner. (Don't worry, the following section provides a few easy breakfast ideas as well.)

Keeping It Fresh: Working with More than Just Sliced Bread

You can make endless creations with two slices of bread. And you can choose from a variety of bread types, including whole grain breads chock-full of healthy seeds, Italian bread, rye bread, French baguettes, or sourdough. Sure, a simple sandwich between two slices of bread works (peanut butter and jelly is a mainstay in my house), but there are lots of different types of grain products that can hold leftovers and help you reduce food waste.

Choosing the right vehicle to hold the right filling is key. You can interchange a variety of breads with some of the recipes in this chapter, but keep in mind how the filling will work with the grain product. If you have a moist or saucy filling, you won't want to use a soft bread. Whole wheat bread can make an awesome grilled cheese sandwich, but it doesn't work well for a fish sandwich or pulled pork. A sturdy bun will hold a hot filling better than a softer bun. That's why I recommend you serve the Mushroom Turkey Burger on a bun. You could get away with using an English Muffin, but regular sliced bread probably won't cut it.

Don't be afraid to get a couple of different types. Breads freeze well as long as you use an airtight bag. Plus, you'll find plenty of ways to reduce food waste using stale bread by checking out the tips in Chapter 19.

TIP

The U.S. Dietary Guidelines for Americans recommend that you try to make half of your grains be whole grains. They're healthier because they provide more nutrients (fiber, vitamins, and minerals). However, it's totally fine to choose white breads, like Italian, French, or sliced bread, part of the time. Mix it up, and remember you can also choose whole grains in the form of oatmeal, barley, and brown or wild rice.

Beyond sliced bread, there are so many other grain options for handhelds: corn and flour tortillas, bagels, buns, English muffins, flatbreads, wraps, naan, and pita. These are all grain products but not technically classified as bread.

TECHNICAL STUFF

Bread is generally defined as a leavened product that's made with flour and yeast. *Flatbread* is an unleavened bread product made without yeast, and includes pita, naan, and even tortillas.

Enjoying Handhelds for Breakfast

A breakfast handheld makes getting out the door easy on busy workdays. The key to creating a healthy breakfast handheld is balancing nutrients. Adding some protein and fat to your carbs at breakfast makes for a satisfying, balanced meal that sticks with you. When carbohydrates are eaten alone, they metabolize more quickly and will likely leave you feeling hungry sooner. Start with a bread product, then add a protein food like eggs, nut-butters, meat, or cheese. Then add a fat source, like cream cheese, butter, a plant-based spread, or avocado. The result? A balanced breakfast sandwich.

Here are just a few ideas for creating a quick, balanced breakfast using a variety of breads and other ingredients you may already have in your kitchen:

>> Spread a slice of toasted whole grain seeded bread with peanut butter and top with banana slices.

>> Make an open-face English muffin melt with cheese, sliced plum tomato, and basil. Toast in the oven until cheese is melted.

>> Mash half an avocado in a small bowl, add a squeeze of lime juice and a pinch of salt, and then spread onto half a bagel. Top with chopped nuts or sliced cucumber.

>> Top your morning toast with a dollop of ricotta cheese sprinkled with cinnamon.

>> Make a breakfast burrito by filling a tortilla or wrap with scrambled eggs, shredded cheese, chopped peppers, and a spoon of salsa.

Mushroom Turkey Burgers

PREP TIME: 15 MIN	COOK TIME: 10 MIN	YIELD: 4 BURGERS

INGREDIENTS

1 teaspoon olive oil (or other vegetable oil)

2 cups finely chopped mushrooms

8 ounces ground turkey or beef

¼ teaspoon salt

¼ teaspoon garlic or onion powder

¼ teaspoon paprika

Pinch of crushed red pepper (optional)

Black pepper to taste

1 teaspoon Worcestershire sauce (optional)

4 whole grain buns

Lettuce, tomato, and onion slices for garnish (optional)

DIRECTIONS

1 Heat oil in a large nonstick pan over medium heat. Add the mushrooms and sauté until well cooked, about 4 to 6 minutes. Drain off liquid and set aside to cool for 5 minutes.

2 In a large bowl, mix the ground turkey, cooked mushrooms, salt, spices, black pepper, and Worcestershire sauce (if desired). Mix until well blended.

3 Divide evenly and form 4 burger patties.

4 Heat a large pan or grill pan on medium-high heat. Cook burgers for about 7 to 10 minutes, turning once.

5 Place the burgers on the buns and serve with lettuce, tomato, and onion slices (if desired) and any additional favorite toppings.

NOTE: I like to use baby Bella mushrooms for this recipe, but white button mushrooms work well, too. You don't have to cook the mushrooms, but I feel it provides the best result.

TIP: You can also cook the burgers on the grill. Brush each side of burger lightly with some olive or vegetable oil using a basting brush. Heat the grill to high and cook burgers 5 to 6 minutes per side, turning once.

VARY IT! You can find a variety of pre-blended herbs and spices at the supermarket, including burger, steak, and poultry seasonings. Others are blended for a certain type of cuisine (Italian, Greek, Moroccan). They often contain salt, so adjust the added salt accordingly when you use them.

Pork Pita Pockets with Cucumber Sauce

PREP TIME: 15 MIN	COOK TIME: N/A	YIELD: 2 SERVINGS

INGREDIENTS

Cucumber Sauce

½ cup plain yogurt

⅓ cup finely chopped, seeded cucumber

Juice from half a lemon, or 1 teaspoon lemon juice

¼ teaspoon olive oil

¼ teaspoon garlic powder

1 tablespoon chopped fresh mint (optional)

Salt to taste

Pork Pita Pockets

5 ounces (or 1 cup) chopped or sliced cooked boneless pork loin or tenderloin

2 pita pockets

¼ cup chopped tomatoes (optional)

DIRECTIONS

1 Make the cucumber sauce by mixing the yogurt, cucumber, lemon juice, olive oil, garlic powder, and mint (if desired) in a bowl. Season with salt to taste.

2 Place the pork into the pita pockets and top each with the cucumber sauce. Garnish with chopped tomatoes (if desired).

NOTE: This cucumber sauce is much like Tzatziki, a classic Greek condiment. It makes a great topping for salads, sliced tomatoes, bread, rice, or pasta salads; it also goes well with meat and veggie kabobs.

TIP: You can make and use this cucumber sauce immediately, but it's even tastier when you refrigerate it for a few hours or overnight since flavors will meld. Store in the refrigerator for up to 3 to 5 days.

VARY IT! You can use leftover cooked chicken for this sandwich, too.

Flexible Quesadillas

PREP TIME: 5 MIN	COOK TIME: 10 MIN	YIELD: 2 SERVINGS

INGREDIENTS

1 cup of any cooked meat or vegetables, or a combination

½ cup shredded cheese

Nonstick cooking spray

Four medium-sized flour tortillas

¼ cup salsa (optional)

1 tablespoon fresh cilantro, chopped (optional)

DIRECTIONS

1 Heat a griddle or large nonstick pan over medium–high heat.

2 Add one tortilla to the pan, top with 2 tablespoons of the cheese, then half of the meat and/or veggies, and then 2 more tablespoons of cheese. Top with another tortilla. Spray the top of the tortilla with cooking spray. Cook the tortilla for 4 to 5 minutes, until lightly browned, then carefully flip over and cook another 3 to 4 minutes.

3 Transfer tortilla to large plate and cut into 4 wedges. Repeat with the other tortillas using the same process with the remaining meat, veggies, and cheese.

4 Serve with salsa and garnish with cilantro (if desired).

TIP: Use whatever size tortilla you have, and top it with whatever sounds good that you have in your kitchen! Some traditional options include sour cream and chile con queso (more cheese please!). Use up any extra lettuce, tomato, onion, peppers, or avocado before they go bad.

VARY IT! Don't be afraid to mix cuisines. Or get creative and try putting these leftovers in between two tortillas with cheese: beef chili, the Kitchen Sink Chicken Chili (see Chapter 10), turkey and mashed sweet potatoes, or black beans and cheese. Of course, you can also make a simple quesadilla with just cheese.

VARY IT! You can fill a quesadilla with just about anything! Beans, rice, spinach, grilled veggies, or even fruit! Use those two extra tortillas left in the package for a dessert quesadilla. Spread tortilla with a soft cheese like cream cheese or goat cheese. Top with canned pears (or sliced ripe pear), sprinkle with ¼ teaspoon cinnamon and a pinch of ground ginger, top with second tortilla and heat as instructed in Step 2.

Fajitas with Avocado Cream

PREP TIME: 10 MIN	COOK TIME: 15 MIN	YIELD: 2 SERVINGS

INGREDIENTS

Avocado Cream

1 avocado, smashed

1 lime, divided

½ cup sour cream or plain yogurt

1 teaspoon hot chili sauce (optional)

1 teaspoon canola or avocado oil

Fajitas

1 bell pepper, seeded and thinly sliced

½ cup onion, thinly sliced

1 teaspoon ground cumin

¼ teaspoon garlic powder

½ teaspoon chili powder

¼ teaspoon paprika, regular or smoked

1 tablespoon avocado oil

1 tablespoon soy sauce

1 tablespoon water

1 cup cooked shredded chicken

4 medium flour tortillas

½ cup shredded cheese

DIRECTIONS

1 Make the avocado cream by combining the avocado, juice from half the lime, sour cream, and chili sauce in a small bowl. Set aside.

2 Heat the oil in a large skillet over medium heat. Add the peppers and onions and sauté until onions are translucent and peppers are tender, about 5 to 6 minutes.

3 While vegetables cook, mix the cumin, garlic powder, chili powder, and paprika in a small bowl. Add the avocado oil, soy sauce, and water. Stir until combined.

4 Add the chicken to the pepper-onion mixture and reduce heat to low. Pour the sauce mixture over the chicken mixture, stir, then simmer for 2 minutes.

5 To prepare tortillas, stack them between two damp paper towels and heat in the microwave for 15-20 seconds until warm and soft.

6 To assemble, divide the chicken and pepper mixture evenly between the 4 tortillas. Squeeze lime juice over the filling. Top with cheese and a dollop of the avocado cream sauce.

NOTE: Use your favorite southwest seasoning blend in place of the paprika.

TIP: If you prefer to warm your tortillas in the oven, wrap them in a piece of foil and heat in a 350-degree oven for 3 minutes. Turn the oven off and keep warm.

VARY IT! Try these fajitas with canned pinto or black beans, leftover roast beef or steak, or frozen cooked shrimp (add shrimp to the pan in Step 3 and cook for 2 minutes).

Pork Tacos with Peppers, Onions, and Lime Crema

PREP TIME: 15 MIN   COOK TIME: 10 MIN   YIELD: 6 TACOS

INGREDIENTS

Pork Tacos

Nonstick cooking spray

3 cups Slow Cooker Pulled Pork (see recipe in Chapter 13)

1 cup diced bell pepper

½ cup minced sweet onion

6 flour tortillas, corn tortillas, or hard taco shells

1 cup chopped lettuce or cabbage

½ cup salsa (optional)

Lime Crema

1 lime, zested and juiced

Pinch of salt

½ cup sour cream or plain yogurt

¼ to ½ teaspoon chili powder (adjust to taste)

DIRECTIONS

1 Preheat the oven to 400 degrees. Spray a baking sheet with nonstick cooking spray. Add the pork, peppers, and onions, spreading out over the baking sheet. Bake for 10 to 15 minutes until some bits of pork are slightly crispy or caramelized.

2 Meanwhile, heat tortillas and prepare lime crema. Mix the lime zest, lime juice, salt, sour cream, and chili powder in a small bowl. Set aside.

3 To craft the tacos, place a spoon of pork mixture onto each tortilla, top with lettuce, crema, and salsa (if desired).

NOTE: There are a few ways to heat soft tortillas. You can heat them in the microwave, by covering with a damp paper towel and heating for 30 to 60 seconds. You can also wrap them in foil and heat in the oven for 10 minutes while the pork heats. Or you can heat them one at a time in a dry hot pan, for 30 to 60 seconds per side, until lightly browned.

Fish Tacos

PREP TIME: 10 MIN	COOK TIME: 15 MIN	YIELD: 4 TACOS

INGREDIENTS

8 ounces tilapia, or any white fish

¼ teaspoon paprika

¼ teaspoon chili powder

Pinch of salt

Black pepper to taste

1 teaspoon vegetable oil

⅓ cup plain yogurt or sour cream

2 teaspoons sriracha sauce

1 lime, cut into quarters

4 to 6 small flour tortillas (street taco size)

½ cup packaged slaw mix, or finely chopped cabbage or lettuce

2 tablespoons chopped cilantro (optional)

DIRECTIONS

1 Season fish fillets with paprika, chili powder, salt, and pepper. Heat oil in a nonstick skillet over medium heat. Cook fish fillets for about 10 minutes, turning once.

2 While fish cooks, mix the yogurt with sriracha and juice from half of the lime. Set aside.

3 Warm the tortillas on a microwave-safe plate, topping with a damp paper towel. Heat on high for 15 to 20 seconds.

4 When fish is cooked, flake it using a fork. Divide fish evenly between tortillas. Top with the slaw mix and the sriracha sauce. Garnish with lime wedges and cilantro (if desired).

NOTE: You can use frozen fish fillets. You can also garnish with crumbled Cotija, feta, or Parmesan cheese, chopped avocado, or salsa.

VARY IT! You can swap tortilla types, using corn tortillas instead if you prefer. Heat corn tortillas on a griddle or in a nonstick pan. Warm on each side for a minute, turning after 30 seconds to brown both sides. You want them lightly brown, but pliable.

Bagels with Smoked Salmon and Cream Cheese

PREP TIME: 10 MIN	COOK TIME: 10 MIN	YIELD: 2 SERVINGS

INGREDIENTS

2 bagels

3 ounces cream cheese

4 ounces smoked salmon, thinly sliced

DIRECTIONS

1 Slice and toast bagels until lightly browned.

2 Spread each bagel half with cream cheese. Top with salmon and enjoy.

TIP: You can add any garnish you have — fresh or dried dill, chopped pickles, minced red onions, or capers are just a few ideas.

VARY IT! You can spread bagels with fresh avocado or prepared guacamole instead of cream cheese.

Seafood Salad Sandwich

PREP TIME: 10 MIN   COOK TIME: N/A   YIELD: 2 SANDWICHES

INGREDIENTS

One 5-ounce can tuna fish packed in oil or water, drained

⅔ cup frozen cooked shrimp, thawed and chopped

1 tablespoon mayonnaise

1 tablespoon lemon juice

½ cup chopped celery

½ teaspoon dried dill or tarragon

Pinch of salt

Black pepper to taste

2 croissants, split

Romaine lettuce leaves (optional)

Sliced tomato (optional)

DIRECTIONS

1 In a small bowl, mix tuna, shrimp, mayonnaise, lemon juice, celery, and herbs until well blended. Season with salt and pepper.

2 Divide seafood mixture between two croissants. Garnish with lettuce and tomato (if desired).

TIP: You're not limited to celery. Chop cucumber or pickles or mince carrots or bell peppers to add to your seafood salad. Zero waste and added nutrition!

VARY IT! Serve open face on a toasted English muffin or in pita pocket instead of on croissants.

» **Trying no-waste dessert recipes**

» **Experimenting with alternative add-ins**

Chapter **16**

Anytime Sweets and Savory Snacks

RECIPES IN THIS CHAPTER

- 🕐 **Peanut Butter Yogurt Fruit Dip**
- 🕐 **Basic Muffins**
- 🕐 **Fruit Cobbler**
- 🕐 **Add Anything Scones**
- 🕐 **Black Bean Brownie Bites**
- 🕐 **High-Fiber Waffles**
- 🕐 **Basic Bean Dip**
- 🕐 **Roasted Pumpkin Seeds**
- 🕐 **Individual Pizzas**
- 🕐 **Pear and Goat Cheese Flatbread**

O ne of the secrets to zero waste cooking is knowing what to do with small amounts of leftover ingredients at the bottom of a jar or package. This chapter serves to help you reduce food waste by using leftover ingredients along with pantry staples to create healthy snacks and desserts that are worth having daily. Bonus: Recipes like the Fruit Cobbler serve as a fruit serving, using up overripe berries or peaches.

REMEMBER

It's important to do a weekly inventory of your refrigerator to reduce waste. It's easy for items to get crowded on the door or shoved to the back of the fridge. Taking a quick inventory helps cue you to think up a way to use them.

Zero Waste Add-ins and Swaps

While baking is more of an exact science, I like to think of most recipes as guidelines, not hard and fast rules. I know a lot of you may get a little nervous about modifying the ingredients in a recipe, but you'll see how easy it is to swap add-ins in the Basic Muffins and Add Anything Scones recipes in this chapter, and you may find you can do this with a lot of your favorite recipes. Quick-bread recipes (muffins, banana bread, pancakes, and scones) are a great way to reduce wasting sour milk, too.

I include a basic muffin recipe in this chapter because it's nostalgic for me. This recipe was one of the very first that I learned in both my high school Home Ec class and my first Foods I class in college. Everyone should know how to make a basic muffin (don't overstir the batter!). Many modern recipes are too high in sugar, which results in a gummy consistency. From this basic recipe, you can use up all sorts of leftover fruit, including the omnipresent overripe banana.

REMEMBER

When you're working toward a goal for zero waste cooking, you need to be adventurous and creative. Baked goods, however, use science to balance fat, starches, sugars, and leavening agents to create a final product that's edible. Still, you can swap some ingredients in and out. For instance, I swapped ground high-fiber cereal for part of the flour to create the High-Fiber Waffle. And you can add just about any fruit you like to a scone or a cobbler. You can also reduce the sugar in baked goods by about 25 percent without too much problem.

Baking does have a few rules. For instance, when making muffins, waffles, or pancakes, you mix the wet and dry ingredients separately then add the wet to the dry, stirring just until mixed. Overmixing will make the final product tough, and it may rise unevenly.

Peanut Butter Yogurt Fruit Dip

INGREDIENTS

½ cup plain yogurt

¼ cup creamy peanut butter

1 teaspoon honey

DIRECTIONS

1 Mix the yogurt, peanut butter, and honey in a small bowl until combined and smooth, then serve.

NOTE: Serve immediately with apple or pear slices, or store in an airtight container in the refrigerator for 3 to 4 days.

TIP: Serve with apple slices or other fruit as you like. You can also spread this dip on a slice of whole-grain toast and top with banana slices.

VARY IT! Try using other nut butters, such as almond or cashew butter. You can also try substituting sorghum syrup or maple syrup for the honey.

Basic Muffins

PREP TIME: 10 MIN | COOK TIME: 20 MIN | YIELD: 12 MUFFINS

INGREDIENTS

2 cups flour

⅓ cup sugar

1 tablespoon baking powder

¼ teaspoon salt

¼ cup vegetable oil

1 egg

1 cup milk

1 teaspoon vanilla extract (optional)

DIRECTIONS

1 Preheat oven to 400 degrees. Line a muffin pan with paper baking cups, or spray pan with vegetable spray (or use a silicone muffin tray).

2 Mix the flour, sugar, baking powder, and salt in a medium bowl.

3 In a small bowl or large glass measuring cup, mix the oil, egg, milk, and vanilla extract (if desired), beating mixture together well.

4 Add the wet ingredients into the dry ingredients and gently stir until just mixed.

5 Fill each muffin cup about ⅔ full, then bake for 20 minutes until lightly browned. A toothpick stuck into the center of a muffin should come out clean and dry.

6 Carefully remove from muffin pan to cool, then enjoy!

NOTE: These muffins will keep in the refrigerator up to 1 week, or you can freeze some in an airtight bag or container for up to 6 months.

TIP: Don't overstir the muffin batter. And be sure to remove muffins from pan as soon as they're out of the oven to avoid overbaking and excess moisture.

VARY IT! The options are endless with this recipe! Fold in 1 cup of frozen or fresh blueberries to the batter after Step 3 and reduce milk to ¾ cup. Or eliminate the milk and use 3 mashed fresh or frozen overripe bananas (about 1 cup mashed). Fold in ½ cup chocolate chips or chopped nuts in Step 3. Make whole grain muffins by using 1 cup whole wheat flour and ¾ cup all-purpose flour in place of 2 cups flour, adjusting sugar to ½ cup and increasing baking powder to 4 teaspoons. Or switch out vanilla extract for lemon, almond, or maple extract.

Fruit Cobbler

PREP TIME: 15 MIN	COOK TIME: 40 MIN	YIELD: 8 SERVINGS

INGREDIENTS

4 tablespoons butter

3 cups mixed berries

¼ cup sugar

1 tablespoon lemon juice and zest from 1 lemon

1 cup milk

1 cup flour

1½ teaspoons baking powder

1 teaspoon cinnamon

½ teaspoon pure vanilla extract

DIRECTIONS

1   Preheat the oven to 350 degrees. Melt butter in a 10-inch cast-iron pan over medium heat then remove from heat.

2   In a small bowl, mix berries with sugar and lemon zest. Set aside.

3   Add lemon juice to milk and set aside.

4   Mix flour, baking powder, and cinnamon in a medium bowl. Add the milk mixture and the vanilla. Stir until just blended.

5   Add the berry mixture to the buttered cast-iron pan. Pour the batter evenly over the berries.

6   Bake for 35 to 40 minutes until top is golden brown.

NOTE: Cast-iron pans work best, but you can also bake in a 9-x-9-inch glass baking dish. Melt butter in the glass dish by placing it into the pre-heating oven for 1 to 2 minutes. Remove, set aside, and proceed to Step 2.

TIP: You can replace the milk with a cup of buttermilk.

VARY IT! Use 2 cups of sliced peaches or any combination of peaches with berries. If you happen to have lavender in your herb garden, add it to the topping mixture with the cinnamon in Step 4 for a delightful subtle flavor.

Add Anything Scones

PREP TIME: 15 MIN | COOK TIME: 15 MIN | YIELD: 8 SCONES

INGREDIENTS

2½ cups flour

1 teaspoon baking powder

½ teaspoon salt

⅓ cup sugar

¼ cup butter or shortening

1 egg, beaten

½ cup plain yogurt

1½ teaspoons lemon juice and zest from 1 lemon

½ cup milk plus 2 tablespoons for brushing

½ cup add-ins (optional; see Note)

DIRECTIONS

1 Preheat the oven to 400 degrees. Line a baking sheet with parchment paper or a silicone mat.

2 Mix the flour, baking powder, salt, and sugar in a large mixing bowl.

3 Using a pastry blender or fork, cut the butter into the mixture until it resembles coarse crumbs. Stir in your add-ins (if desired).

4 Make a well in the center of the flour mixture. Mix the egg, yogurt, lemon zest, juice and milk in a small bowl. Add this mixture to the well in the flour mixture. Combine until it becomes a soft dough. The dough may be slightly crumbly, but don't overmix.

5 Pull dough together and turn it onto a floured surface; smooth and form into a flat, 8-inch round disk. Cut the disk into 8 even wedges.

6 Transfer to baking sheet, brush with milk, and bake for 12 to 15 minutes, until tops are slightly golden.

NOTE: You can add ½ cup of nuts, berries, dried fruit, chocolate chips, or shredded cheese. You can also sprinkle tops of scones with sugar before you place in the oven, after you brush on the milk.

NOTE: These scones freeze well for up to 6 months in an airtight bag or container.

TIP: If you don't have sour milk, you can use buttermilk. If you don't have buttermilk, then make sour milk! Simply add 1½ teaspoons of lemon juice or white vinegar to ½ cup milk.

VARY IT! Try a savory scone by adding 1 tablespoon of your favorite herb, such as dried rosemary or tarragon. Switch out the lemon rind for orange rind.

Black Bean Brownie Bites

PREP TIME: 10 MIN	COOK TIME: 25 MIN	YIELD: 24 BROWNIE BITES

INGREDIENTS

Nonstick cooking spray

One 14-ounce can black beans, rinsed and drained

½ cup sugar

2 eggs

¼ teaspoon salt

1 teaspoon vanilla extract

3 tablespoons vegetable oil

½ cup cocoa powder

½ teaspoon baking powder

½ cup chocolate chips

DIRECTIONS

1 Preheat the oven to 350 degrees. Spray a mini muffin pan with cooking spray.

2 Put the beans, sugar, eggs, salt, vanilla, and oil into a food processor. Process until smooth. Add the cocoa powder and baking powder and mix until blended. Remove blade then stir in chocolate chips with a spoon.

3 Transfer about 1 tablespoon of batter into each muffin cup, evening up with leftover batter. Bake for 12 to 15 minutes. Cool on a wire rack for 5 to 10 minutes then remove and serve.

NOTE: You can also use an 8-x-8-inch baking pan instead of a muffin pan. Bake for 20 to 25 minutes and cut into 25 small squares or 16 larger ones. These Bites can be frozen in an airtight container for up to 3 months.

TIP: Use a small cookie scoop to put batter into muffin cups.

VARY IT! You can also use a brownie mix and use the drained black beans in place of oil and egg, then bake according to package instructions.

High-Fiber Waffles

PREP TIME: 15 MIN	COOK TIME: 20 MIN	YIELD: EIGHT 4-INCH WAFFLES

INGREDIENTS

1 cup ground high-fiber cereal

1 cup flour

½ teaspoon baking powder

2 eggs, beaten

⅔ cup milk

2 tablespoons vegetable oil

Nonstick cooking spray

DIRECTIONS

1 Preheat the waffle iron.

2 Add the ground cereal, flour, and baking powder to a large mixing bowl to blend.

3 Add the eggs, milk, and oil to the dry mixture and stir until just combined.

4 Spray the waffle iron with the cooking spray. Drop ¼ cup of batter onto each waffle grid. Press the iron until the waffle is crisp and browned.

5 Serve immediately or freeze in an airtight bag or container for up to 3 months.

NOTE: Use a high-fiber cereal such as Fiber One or Bran Flakes. Add the cereal to a food processor to grind into fine crumbs.

TIP: Adjust portions of batter depending on the size of your waffle iron.

VARY IT! Make ice-cream sandwiches by adding a scoop of ice cream atop a cooled waffle. Top with another waffle to create a sandwich. Or top waffles with a dollop of yogurt and sliced berries or canned peaches then drizzle with honey and garnish with mint leaves.

Basic Bean Dip

PREP TIME: 10 MIN	COOK TIME: N/A	YIELD: 3-4 SERVINGS

INGREDIENTS

¾ cup cannellini (white kidney) beans, drained and rinsed

1 tablespoon olive oil

2 tablespoons minced onion (optional)

¼ teaspoon garlic powder

½ teaspoon dried tarragon

1 teaspoon lemon juice

DIRECTIONS

1 Mix all the ingredients in a food processor for 3 minutes.

2 Scrape into a bowl, garnish with lemon zest and additional tarragon, and serve.

NOTE: Refrigerate in an airtight container for up to 2 weeks.

NOTE: You can make this basic dip with any type of bean, so it's a great way to use up leftover canned beans from another recipe. The dip tastes better the next day, so this is a great make-ahead appetizer. If you want to use a whole 15-ounce can of beans (1½ cups), simply double the recipe.

TIP: Serve with pita chips, crackers, or crudites (raw carrot sticks, zucchini slices, pepper slices or cucumber slices).

VARY IT! You can choose any bean and herb, spice, or citrus zest you like to flavor the dip. Nice combinations include chickpeas with garlic powder and rosemary; white beans with tarragon and lemon zest; and black beans with chili powder and lime zest. Or you could add ½ teaspoon of any herb blend that you enjoy.

Roasted Pumpkin Seeds

PREP TIME: 10 MIN	COOK TIME: 40 MIN	YIELD: 6 SERVINGS

INGREDIENTS

Pumpkin seeds from one medium-size pumpkin (about 2–3 cups)

3 tablespoons avocado oil

¼ teaspoon salt

½ teaspoon pumpkin pie spice

DIRECTIONS

1 Preheat the oven to 300 degrees. Line a baking sheet with aluminum foil or a silicone mat.

2 Clean the pumpkin seeds, removing pulp and pulling all the fibrous strands from the seeds. Rinse the seeds in cool water in a strainer and remove any remaining bits of flesh. Allow to drain and dry well (about 20 minutes or more), and then transfer to a bowl.

3 Add the oil, salt, and seasoning to the dry seeds and toss well.

4 Spread the seasoned seeds evenly onto the baking sheet, making sure seeds are in one layer on the sheet.

5 Bake for 35 to 45 minutes, tossing every 15 minutes or so, until golden and crisp. If they aren't crisp by 45 minutes, then bake an additional 10 to 15 minutes.

NOTE: Pumpkin seeds are a good source of fiber, potassium, and magnesium, and they provide some protein and healthy fat to your diet. Don't waste them! They'll store in an airtight container in the refrigerator for up to 9 months.

TIP: Pat seeds dry with paper towels to quicken drying time. Use any vegetable oil, such as soybean, olive, or canola, for roasting.

VARY IT! Make these savory. Try using garlic powder, a spicy ground pepper blend, taco seasoning, paprika, or cumin in place of the pumpkin pie spice.

Individual Pizzas

PREP TIME: 10 MIN	COOK TIME: 10 MIN	YIELD: 2 SERVINGS

INGREDIENTS

2 pieces naan bread

¼ cup tomato sauce

½ cup Italian blend cheese

¼ cup sliced, sautéed mushrooms

DIRECTIONS

1 Heat oven to 350 degrees.

2 Layer naan bread with tomato sauce, cheese, and mushrooms. Bake for 7 to 10 minutes, or until cheese is melted.

VARY IT! Naan bread works great for these quick and easy pizzas, but you can also use pita bread or another flatbread for your crust. If you have meat lovers in the house, top with cooked ground sausage or sliced pepperoni (but try to sneak in a green veggie like sautéed spinach or kale, or even a few thin slices of zucchini). Or create a flatbread by using any leftover Roasted Veggie Trio or the Roasted Peppers along with any hard cheese, such as a shredded sharp Cheddar, Asiago, or Gouda.

Pear and Goat Cheese Flatbread

PREP TIME: 10 MIN	COOK TIME: 10 MIN	YIELD: 4 SERVINGS

INGREDIENTS

2 flatbreads or naan bread

2 teaspoons olive oil

1 teaspoon dried oregano

½ cup sliced canned pears

4 ounces crumbled goat cheese

DIRECTIONS

1 Heat oven to 425 degrees. Place each flatbread on a preheated pizza stone or regular pizza pan, and drizzle the flatbread with olive oil. Then top evenly with the oregano, pears, and goat cheese.

2 Bake for 10 to 12 minutes. Cut each flatbread into 6 squares to serve.

TIP: I used canned pears in this recipe because they are totally underutilized and make this recipe so easy! But if you have fresh pears on hand, go ahead and use them. Thinly slice a ripe pear in place of the canned. Ripe, soft pears will work best and don't require cooking.

NOTE: For a crisper crust, place the flatbread directly on the oven rack. Also, instead of baking this, you can grill on a hot grill for 5 minutes.

Chapter 17

Crafting Mocktails, Smoothies, and Cocktails

RECIPES IN THIS CHAPTER

- Mocktail Lemonade with Mint
- Mocktail Sangria with Citrus
- Mocktail Long Island Iced Tea
- Berry Smoothie
- Green Smoothie
- Tofu Smoothie
- Basil-infused Sparkling Water
- Cranberry-Rosemary Cocktail
- Infused Vodka
- Pimm's Cocktail
- Special Whiskey Sour Cocktail
- Vegged-Up Bloody Mary Cocktail

W ho doesn't enjoy a nice, refreshing beverage poured over or shaken with ice? This chapter shows you how to use up some ingredients or scraps to create memorable mocktails, nourishing smoothies, or enjoyable cocktails. And why not use the occasion to sneak a veggie serving in as well?

Of course, even wine can sit around too long. Don't waste it! Making a sangria gives you an opportunity to use the wine and add some of the fruit left in your fridge.

Mocktails are definitely having a moment, and there are so many advantages. You may be surprised at how much more enjoyable a beverage is when it's served in a cocktail glass. As you sub in a mocktail for a cocktail, don't forgo the fancy glass nor the garnish. You'll find the flavors and presentation of the mocktails to be just as festive as the cocktails in this chapter.

Setting up Your Bar and the Pour

You don't have to become a mixologist to enjoy this chapter, but having a few tricks up your sleeve won't hurt. The idea here is to consider ways you can reduce food waste by making fun drinks! Understanding the fundamental elements of a cocktail is a good place to start.

>> The base (spirit or alcohol, juice, or tea)

>> The balancing agent (sugar, citrus, bitters)

>> The modifier (accent flavors)

>> Water (for dilution)

Enjoying a cocktail shouldn't be about altered states, but rather taste sensations. A good cocktail or mocktail is balanced for bitterness and/or sweetness. Measuring the liquor ensures that the alcohol doesn't overpower (see the list of helpful bar tools later in this chapter). A touch of sugar or citrus helps cut through the sting, and the modifying agent applies some synergy. Modifying agents are things like the herb in the Cranberry-Rosemary Cocktail, the cucumber and mint in the Pimm's Cup, the aquafaba in the Special Whiskey Sour, or the umami of the Worcestershire in a Vegged-Up Bloody Mary. Even the herbs in the mocktails fill this bill (Basil-infused Sparkling Water and the Mocktail Long Island Iced Tea).

Water (often introduced through ice) acts as a diluting agent, taking the bite out of the alcohol or reducing the overall sweetness or potency of a drink.

It's also fun to have a variety of glasses on hand, whether you're pouring a mocktail or cocktail. Common types of glasses include rocks glass (a short glass measuring 8 to 10 ounces), a highball glass (a tall, 12-ounce glass), a martini or coupe glass (good for cocktails served "up"), or a pilsner or stein for beer (12 to 16 ounces).

REMEMBER

While an occasional glass of wine or cocktail shared with friends can have health benefits, overdoing it can lead to health problems. Alcohol consumed in moderation is best. The Dietary Guidelines for Americans and the CDC define moderate alcohol consumption as 1 serving or less per day for women, and 2 servings or less per day for men. (So unfair that men get more, but this is primarily attributed to differences in metabolism.) A *serving* is defined as 5 ounces of wine, 12 ounces of beer, or 1.5 ounces of liquor (such as whiskey, bourbon, gin, rum, tequila, or vodka).

The purpose of the Dietary Guidelines for Americans is to provide science-based recommendations on what Americans should eat and drink to promote health and prevent chronic disease. They aren't intended to be clinical guidelines for care, so you should speak to your doctor about a referral to a registered dietitian if you are dealing with a health problem such as diabetes, high blood pressure, heart disease, or other diagnosis.

Watch out for that big pour. It's a good idea to measure out some of the glasses you often use at home. Take out a sampling of your wine, beer, or cocktail glasses. Fill each with water then pour into a liquid measuring cup. You may be shocked to see that your favorite wine glass holds 3 times the amount of "one serving."

Knowing how much your wine glass holds and using standard measures helps keep alcohol consumption in moderation. Let's look at some bar tools that can help you out.

>> **A shot glass or measuring cup:** A shot glass measures a perfect pour when creating your cocktail. There is no true standard measure, but a "shot" is considered a 1-ounce measure and most glasses hold 1 to 2 ounces. You can also find measuring bar glasses that are marked for 1 to 4 ounces.

>> **A cocktail shaker:** This gem helps chill and mix your drink as well as mildly dilute it. This may bring to mind a classic "shaken not stirred" James Bond martini, but you can totally use a shaker for a mocktail, too. You can add chopped ripening fruit or a cucumber into a shaker, add ice and water, and shake vigorously. Pour through the built-in strainer and you'll have flavor infused water without the pulp.

>> **Muddler:** This little device is handy for crushing berries, herbs, or cucumber for your drinks. Place ingredients into your shaker, then use the muddler to crush them, releasing their essential oils and flavors for the drink. A pestle can work too but may be hard to reach into your cocktail shaker.

>> **A paring knife and small cutting board:** You'll use this to create your garnishes. To make a lemon or lime wheel, wash the fruit under cold water, thinly slice into rounds. Cut the round through peel just to the center so you can "hang" it on the cocktail glass.

>> **A peeler:** To create the Sugared Citrus Peel recommended later in this chapter, you need this device (which, of course, also works for peeling potatoes and other fruits and vegetables). A peeler allows you to remove thin strips of peel from citrus fruit or even create a cucumber ribbon for a garnish.

>> **A bar spoon:** This isn't a necessity but comes in handy when stirring ingredients in a tall glass. You can also use an aluminum straw.

Mocktail Lemonade with Mint

INGREDIENTS

1 cup lemon juice, or juice from 4 to 5 lemons

½ cup sugar

3 cups water, divided

1 cup sparkling water

8 ounces sparkling water

6–10 fresh mint leaves

DIRECTIONS

1 Reserving half a lemon for garnishes, squeeze the remaining lemons to make 1 cup juice.

2 Combine sugar and 1 cup water, and microwave for 30 seconds to 1 minute to dissolve sugar. Add the lemon juice and stir to blend.

3 Pour the sugared lemon juice into a large pitcher. Add the remaining 2 cups of cold water and stir.

4 Pour lemonade into 4 highball glasses filled with ice. Top each glass with about 2 ounces of sparkling water. Garnish with a lemon wheel and fresh mint leaves.

NOTE: This recipe is lower in sugar than typical lemonade recipes, helping to balance your overall sugar intake. And adding mint helps balance the tartness of the lemons.

TIP: Use the peels from the lemon for the Sugared Citrus Peel Garnish recipe (see the sidebar in this chapter).

VARY IT! If you prefer, substitute agave nectar for the sugar for a lower glycemic index. For a sugar-free version, mix lemon juice and water then add 3 teaspoons of a nonnutritive sweetener, such as stevia, aspartame, or sucralose.

VARY IT! To switch this into a cocktail, add an ounce of lemon vodka.

Mocktail Sangria with Citrus

PREP TIME: 10 MIN, PLUS CHILLING TIME	COOK TIME: N/A	YIELD: 5–6 SERVINGS

INGREDIENTS

16 ounces cranberry juice

16 ounces orange juice

1 cup orange slices

1 cup sliced strawberries

½ cup chopped apples

16 ounces sparkling water

DIRECTIONS

1 Mix juice and fruit into a large pitcher or punch bowl.

2 Refrigerate for an hour before serving to incorporate flavors of the fruit.

3 Serve over ice in wine or rocks glasses topped with about 2 ounces of sparkling water.

NOTE: Out of oranges? Lemon slices work, too. Or use any berry or apple or pear slices.

TIP: You can use any combination of juices to add up to 32 ounces. A red juice — cranberry, grape, pomegranate, or cherry juice — offers a nice color.

VARY IT! Add sliced peaches, strawberries, or pears along with or instead of the apples.

VARY IT! Traditional sangria is made with red wine, brandy, and juice. To make this into a cocktail version, reduce the 16 ounces of cranberry and orange juices to 2 ounces each, and add 14 ounces of wine and 2 ounces of brandy.

Mocktail Long Island Iced Tea

INGREDIENTS

1 lemon

½ green bell pepper, roughly chopped

4 ounces apple cider or apple juice

16 ounces sweetened iced tea

6 ounces nonalcoholic ginger beer

4 mint leaves

DIRECTIONS

1 Cut 2 lemon wheels for garnish and set aside. Squeeze the juice from the remaining lemon into a food processor. Add the bell pepper and apple cider. Process until smooth.

2 Pour half the iced tea into a cocktail shaker half filled with ice. Add half of the pepper mixture, cover, and shake vigorously. Strain into an ice-filled highball glass.

3 Repeat, pouring the remaining iced tea and pepper puree into the shaker. Shake vigorously then strain into another ice filled highball glass.

4 Pour 3 ounces of ginger beer into each glass and garnish with lemon wheel and mint.

NOTE: A Long Island Iced Tea is an alcoholic beverage that uses a variety of liquors to create a drink that tastes like iced tea. This nonalcoholic version starts out as iced tea and gets added flavor from scraps.

VARY IT! To reduce sugar, use unsweetened iced tea and diet ginger ale or diet ginger beer.

Berry Smoothie

INGREDIENTS

1½ cups fresh or frozen berries

1 ripe banana, peeled

1 cup milk

1 cup cottage cheese

½ teaspoon ground cinnamon

DIRECTIONS

1 Place fruit into a high-speed blender. Add milk, cottage cheese, and cinnamon.

2 Blend until smooth and creamy. Divide between two tall high-ball glasses.

NOTE: There are no hard and fast rules when it comes to creating a smoothie. A basic smoothie can be any combination of 1 to 2 cups of fruit to 1 cup liquid (milk, yogurt, juice). You can also use any type of milk or alternative (cow's milk, goat milk, almond milk, soy milk) or juice (orange juice, berry juice, apple juice, pineapple juice) that you prefer. You can experiment with ingredients, and you can always add more liquid if you find your smoothie to be too thick. You can also add a couple of ice cubes to make it a bit frothier and colder.

TIP: Smoothies are best consumed as soon as you make them. If you want to make one serving, half the recipes.

VARY IT! Use plain yogurt in place of cottage cheese. Or if you have ricotta, you can use that in place of cottage cheese as well.

Green Smoothie

PREP TIME: 10 MIN	COOK TIME: N/A	YIELD: 2 SERVINGS

INGREDIENTS

2 cups spinach or kale

1 apple, cored and sliced

1 avocado

½ cup chopped cucumber, seed pulp removed

½ cup chopped celery

½ cup orange juice

½ cup ice

4 mint leaves (optional)

DIRECTIONS

1 Place spinach, apple, avocado, cucumber, and celery into a high-speed blender.

2 Add orange juice, ice, and mint (if desired). Process until well blended and smooth.

3 Divide between two tall highball glasses.

NOTE: There are a lot of options with a green smoothie. Try kale and pineapple. Spinach and mango (you can use frozen or fresh mango), or spinach, avocado, and banana. To balance the bitterness of the greens, include at least ½ cup of fruit to 1 cup of greens.

TIP: Smoothies aren't an exact science but are great for dealing with aging avocadoes or leftover scraps of celery or cucumber. If you have only celery but no cucumber, no worries. Experiment with different combos and thin out with juice as needed.

VARY IT! Substitute ½ cup grapefruit juice, almond milk, or dairy milk in place of orange juice. Add ½ cup frozen mango in place of ice cubes.

Tofu Smoothie

PREP TIME: 10 MIN	COOK TIME: N/A	YIELD: 2 SERVINGS

INGREDIENTS

1 cup frozen berries

1 ripe banana, peeled

8 ounces tofu, cut into cubes

1½ cups soy milk

2 teaspoons honey

DIRECTIONS

1 Place berries, banana, tofu, milk, and honey into a high-speed blender.

2 Blend until smooth and creamy. Add additional milk to thin. Pour into two tall highball or pint glasses.

NOTE: Use frozen mango or cherries in place of frozen berries. If you use fresh fruit instead, add 3 ice cubes.

TIP: Silken tofu will give a creamier texture. You can use firm tofu but may need to add some water to blend.

VARY IT! This recipe is vegan. You can also use almond milk or regular dairy milk in place of soy milk.

Basil-infused Sparkling Water

PREP TIME: 10 MIN	COOK TIME: N/A	YIELD: 1 SERVING

INGREDIENTS

6 basil leaves

16 ounces sparkling water

1 lime wedge

DIRECTIONS

1 Gently muddle the basil leaves in the bottom of a tall highball glass. Top with ice.

2 Pour sparkling water into the glass. Garnish with a squeeze of lime juice.

NOTE: You can also infuse a pitcher of still water. Add the juice from one lime to the water. Muddle a cup of basil in a mortar or small bowl. Add it to a water infuser along with lime slices. Keep in mind that infusing water is a great way to use up old citrus.

TIP: To muddle herbs, add herbs to mortar or small bowl, and smash with pestle or muddler tool until leaves are broken.

SWEET SIDE: SUGARED CITRUS PEEL GARNISH

Sometimes the best part about a treat is the cherry on top — or in this case, the sugared citrus peel. To make these delicious peels that work for both cocktails and mocktails — and make a festive addition to charcuterie boards — you need ½ cup sugar, ½ cup water, and peel from 4 oranges, grapefruits, or lemons. Then follow these steps:

1. Preheat the oven to 170 degrees.

2. Quarter oranges (or other citrus). Cut peel off citrus with a sharp knife, following the curve of the fruit, leaving most of the white pith behind. Slice each quarter peel into ¼-inch slices.

3. Bring water to boil in a medium pot over medium heat, and add the citrus peels. Cook for about 10 minutes. Remove the peels from the water with a slotted spoon and transfer to a baking sheet lined with parchment paper or a silicone mat to dry for about 15 to 20 minutes.

4. Empty pot, then add ½ cup water and ½ cup sugar to the pot. Bring to a low boil and stir occasionally until sugar is dissolved. Return the citrus peels to the simple syrup liquid, reduce heat, and simmer for about 10 minutes, until liquid thickens and peels are more translucent.

5. Remove the peels from the water with a slotted spoon and transfer back to the baking sheet lined with parchment paper or a silicone mat, spreading so that they aren't touching each other. Save the sugar water in a jar or other airtight container (now you have a citrusy simple syrup to use in a cocktail).

6. Allow to cool for about an hour, or until dry. Toss with 2 tablespoons sugar and store in an airtight container.

Note: After using citrus fruit for juicing, salads, or other recipes, save the peels, storing in an airtight container until you have time to candy them.

Cranberry-Rosemary Cocktail

PREP TIME: 10 MIN | **COOK TIME: N/A** | **YIELD: 1 SERVING**

INGREDIENTS

2 ounces cranberry juice

1 ounce gin

1 ounce lime juice

4 ounces sparkling water

Lime wheel

1 rosemary sprig

DIRECTIONS

1 Pour juice, gin, lime juice, and sparkling water into a tall glass half-filled with ice.

2 Garnish with the lime wheel and rosemary sprig (go ahead, use it as a stir stick!).

TIP: You can use club soda in place of sparkling water.

Infused Vodka

PREP TIME: 10 MIN, PLUS INFUSING TIME	COOK TIME: N/A	YIELD: 8 SERVINGS

INGREDIENTS

2 cups cucumber slices

1 lime, cut into thin slices then halved

12 ounces vodka

DIRECTIONS

1 Add the cucumber, lime slices, and vodka to a 32-ounce, clean mason jar.

2 Seal the jar, and set in a cool, dark place for 2 to 3 days.

3 Pour the liquid through a mesh sieve that's set over a bowl.

4 Transfer the infused vodka back to the mason jar and seal. Refrigerate for up to a year.

NOTE: You can also infuse vodka with mint, citrus peels, fruit, or herbs like lavender or rosemary. For fruit, use about 1½ to 2 cups of chopped fruit per 12 ounces of vodka. Try strawberries or pineapple with 6 to 8 mint leaves. The longer it soaks, the more flavor.

TIP: There are about 25 ounces in a fifth of liquor. Double this recipe if you want to infuse a whole fifth.

VARY IT! Try substituting cubed watermelon or strawberries for the cucumber.

Pimm's Cocktail

PREP TIME: 10 MIN   COOK TIME: N/A   YIELD: 2 SERVINGS

INGREDIENTS

1 lemon

½ cup cucumber slices

½ cup strawberry slices, fresh or frozen

3 ounces Pimm's No. 1 liquor

4 ounces ginger ale

Mint and lemon wheels for garnish (optional)

DIRECTIONS

1 Slice 2 lemon wheels from the lemon for garnish. Set aside.

2 Divide the cucumber and strawberry slices evenly between two highball glasses. Add ice.

3 Juice the remaining lemon evenly into each glass. Add Pimm's. Top with ginger ale and stir.

4 Garnish with mint and lemon wheels (if desired).

NOTE: Pimm's is a gin-based liqueur that originated in England. It's lower in alcohol (25% alcohol by volume, ABV) than gin (35-55% ABV) and has a slightly bitter, citrusy flavor profile. This classic cocktail is perfect for using up overripe strawberries and cucumber.

VARY IT! Try it with basil instead of mint.

Special Whiskey Sour Cocktail

PREP TIME: 20 MIN   COOK TIME: N/A   YIELD: 2 SERVINGS

INGREDIENTS

4 ounces bourbon

Juice from ½ lemon

2 tablespoons simple syrup

¼ cup Aquafaba Fluff (see recipe in Chapter 11)

2 Maraschino cherries

Orange wheels for garnish (optional)

DIRECTIONS

1 Add bourbon, lemon juice, simple syrup, and aquafaba to a cocktail shaker filled with ice. Shake to blend.

2 Strain into two coupe glasses. Add a cherry to each glass.

3 Garnish with the orange wheel (if desired).

NOTE: Simple syrup is a common cocktail mixer that's easy to make yourself. Simply mix 1 part sugar with 1 part water. You can use a glass measuring cup to mix and microwave for 30 seconds to dissolve the sugar. Allow to cool.

TIP: Save the liquid when you drain chickpeas to use in cocktails or to make the Aquafaba Fluff (see Chapter 11).

VARY IT! You can also serve this drink over ice in a rocks glass.

Vegged-Up Bloody Mary Cocktail

PREP TIME: 15 MIN	COOK TIME: N/A	YIELD: 2 SERVINGS

INGREDIENTS

8 ounces tomato juice

¼ cup sliced carrots

¼ cup chopped bell or hot pepper

1 teaspoon Worcestershire sauce

1 teaspoon horseradish

¼ teaspoon smoked paprika

2 ounces vodka

2 stalks celery

2 lime or lemon wedges

DIRECTIONS

1 Add tomato juice, carrots, peppers, Worcestershire sauce, horseradish, and paprika to a high-speed blender. Blend until smooth.

2 Divide between two tall glasses. Add 1 ounce of vodka to each glass. Stir with a celery stick and garnish with lime wedge.

TIP: Add more or less carrots and peppers to taste. You can also blend in parsley and celery.

NOTE: Some delicious Bloody Mary garnishes include green olives, grape tomatoes, cucumber wheels, chunks of Cheddar or Swiss cheese, sweet gherkin pickles, and thawed frozen shrimp. Or try leftover Spice-Rubbed Pork Tenderloin with Roasted Sliced Grapes (see Chapter 13) cut into cubes, stuffed olives with feta cheese — or anything else you fancy! Place your favorite garnishes on a 6-inch wooden skewer and serve with your Vegged-Up Bloody Mary Cocktail.

4

The Part of Tens

Discover how to use leftover eggs, ripening produce, and other scraps.

Find new ways to consistently use stale bread.

Do more with expiring dairy.

Make the most of leftover takeout.

Chapter **18**

Ten Uses for Leftover Eggs, Ripening Produce, and Scraps

took a rough survey when I began writing this book, and several items came up that were often wasted, including egg whites or yolks and scraps of produce or herbs.

Say that you need an egg yolk to make a chocolate mousse. What can you do with the whites? Or you find some spinach at the back of your crisper drawer that isn't fit for a salad, but you can't bring yourself to scrap it. This chapter will help you out.

Feed Crushed Egg Shells to Your Plants

My grandfather never chucked eggshells into the trash; he used them to help his garden — and you can, too! Crush them and mix them into the soil for your tomato or pepper plant. The shells are rich in calcium carbonate, which is good for some plants. The shells also can serve as a natural repellent to slugs. Just spread the crushed shells around the base of the plant, and snails and slugs will stay away.

For houseplants, you can make a liquid fertilizer with the shells. Rinse the shells then allow them to dry. Crumble them up by hand or with a rolling pin. Place the crushed shells into a heat-safe glass container, and then pour boiling water over them. Let that steep for about an hour, and then transfer the cooled water into a water can, straining out shells. Use for you houseplants.

Freeze Egg Whites

Sure, you can dump an egg white down the drain, but why not let it provide you with some nutrition. Simply refrigerate leftover whites for up to 4 days. Then you can scramble a white with another whole egg for breakfast or lunch sometime over the next 4 days. You can also use them by substituting two egg whites for one egg, in recipes like Lemony Salmon Patties (see Chapter 8) or Ham Fritters (also in Chapter 8). To keep them longer, freeze egg whites for later use (to scramble or add to baked goods). Just put them in an airtight container (covered ice cube trays work, too) and freeze for up to a year. They won't beat into a meringue as well once frozen, but you can add them to a meatloaf, Skillet Meatballs (see Chapter 13), or make a foamy cocktail like the Special Whiskey Sour (see Chapter 17) with them.

Add Any Extra Egg Yolks

There are a lot of uses for egg yolks. Like egg whites, you can simply refrigerate leftover yolks then mix them into more eggs for an egg strata, omelet, a scramble, or other egg dishes you'll find in Chapter 9. Find a purpose for them quickly, as yolks keep in the refrigerator for up to 2 days only. You can also freeze yolks for up to a year. To freeze, lightly beat them with ¼ teaspoon salt before freezing to prevent them from gelling. Here are some other ideas:

>> Glaze your banana bread, pie crust, or fresh rolls with the beaten egg yolk wash, add sugar or seeds, and then bake.

>> Make a key lime pie. Beat 3 egg yolks in a mixer (or by hand) until pale yellow. Add one 14-ounce can of sweetened condensed milk and blend for another few minutes until smooth and combined. Stir in ⅔ cup key lime juice and blend well. Pour into a prepared graham cracker crust and bake for 10–15 minutes in a 350-degree oven. Cool then refrigerate (you can cover and freeze the pie for later as well). Garnish with lime zest and whipped cream if desired.

» Make a Caesar dressing, sans anchovies. In a small saucepan, whisk 1 yolk with 2 tablespoons of lemon juice until blended. Add 1 teaspoon Dijon mustard and blend well. Heat over very low heat, stirring constantly until mixture begins to bubble. Remove from heat and cool completely (about 15 minutes). Very slowly, add ¼ cup olive oil to the egg-mustard mixture, whisking until it's smooth and creamy. Stir in 1 minced garlic clove. Thin to desired consistency by adding a spoon of water at a time. Stir in 1–2 table-spoons Parmesan cheese.

WARNING

Some hens carry salmonella, which can cause a dangerous foodborne illness. Cook-ing kills the bacteria. When you choose to use raw eggs, use only pasteurized eggs.

» Use egg yolks for a special coating on oven-fried chicken. Mix 1–2 leftover egg yolks with ¼ to ½ cup mayonnaise, 1 teaspoon of Dijon mustard, and salt and pepper. Spread onto boneless chicken strips, and then press into panko or bread crumbs. Place chicken onto a cooling rack set into a baking sheet. Bake in a 375-degree oven for 20 minutes until golden brown (or bake in an air-fryer for 10 to 15 minutes, or according to appliance instructions).

» You can add egg yolks (or whites) to meatloaf, burgers, or meatballs. Adding an extra yolk into a meatloaf will make it taste even better. Adding an egg, some minced onion, and a dash of Worcestershire sauce into ground beef or turkey makes a good burger, although burger purists prefer no egg and just ground meat and spices.

» Try a hollandaise sauce. You can mix this up in a blender or small food processor. Add 3 yolks, 1 teaspoon of mustard, and 1 tablespoon of lemon juice (or juice from half a lemon) to a blender or processor. Blend for 5–10 seconds until smooth. Melt 1 stick of butter in the microwave or in a small pot on the stove. With the blender running, gradually pour the melted butter into the egg mixture. Pour over poached eggs on toast, baked salmon, steamed broccoli, or asparagus.

Seal and Gloss with an Egg Wash

Use an *egg wash* to add gloss to baked goods. An egg wash is egg whites, a whole egg, or egg yolks lightly beaten with a bit of water or milk. You can use it to seal the edges of a hand pie, or you can use a pastry brush to brush it onto the top crust to create a glossy baked finish. Using the yolk or whole egg will provide a more golden finish.

THE GLUE THAT HOLDS IT ALL TOGETHER: USING AN EGG WASH TO MAKE SPICED NUTS

Spiced nuts are a great addition to a party spread. They're a fun cooking activity to do with friends and family, too. You can even substitute aquafaba (that liquid leftover from a can of chickpeas) for the egg whites as a vegan option. These nuts can be packaged for gift-giving as well. Place nuts into airtight glass jars, tie with a festive ribbon and voila, a gift any friend would appreciate (except the ones allergic to nuts, of course). These nuts take less than an hour to whip up. You can do a single nut variety or use a mixture of nuts. All you need is a baking sheet, 2 egg whites, a whisk, and some spices.

1. Heat oven to 300 degrees. Mix ½ cup sugar, 1 teaspoon cinnamon, 2 teaspoons chili powder, 1 teaspoon turmeric, and ½ teaspoon ground red pepper in a small bowl. Set aside.

2. In a large bowl, whisk 2 egg whites with a teaspoon of water until frothy and foamy.

3. Place 3 cups walnuts, cashews, or pecans into the bowl and mix with the egg whites. Toss until coated.

4. Sprinkle the spice mixture evenly over the nuts and toss again.

5. Spread nuts onto a baking sheet lined with parchment paper and bake for 20 to 30 minutes till golden. Cool, then store in airtight containers.

You can also brush an egg wash onto the bottom of your pie crust before you add the filling. This will keep the filling from soaking through.

Mix in Finely Chopped Veggie Scraps

Add scraps like finely chopped broccoli stems, celery leaves, carrot tops, and mushroom stems to your tomato sauce. The key here is to finely chop everything. Put it all into a food processor, and then sauté in a pan with a spoon of olive oil, add tomato puree, and simmer.

Finely chopped broccoli and mushroom stems sauté up nicely for a veggie omelet. Sauté the veggie scraps in 1 teaspoon of butter and cook over low heat until tender. Remove from pan, and then add beaten eggs to the pan for the omelet. Add the cooked vegetables and grated cheese, cook, fold, and flip.

Use the drying-out carrots in your refrigerator for carrot cake or a quick bread. Chop them in a food processor and freeze for later use or add them to a carrot muffin or cake recipe.

Roast or Sauté to Stretch Wilting Veggies

When you have wrinkled or wilting veggies in the fridge, the best thing to do is cook them. Even if you don't want to eat them right away, once they're cooked, they'll last a few more days and be prepped and ready.

>> Sauté wilted lettuce and spinach together and add to cooked rice or pasta.

>> Use wrinkled tomatoes for the Roasted Grape Tomatoes with Feta dip recipe in Chapter 8. Simply cut off any bruised or moldy parts and use the rest.

REMEMBER

If your potatoes, apples, or just about anything has a bruise or bad spot, don't throw them out — trim them. You can simply trim off the eyes of rooted potatoes, the mold off of cheese, and the wilted or black ends off greens.

WARNING

Mold is a separate issue. If mold is found on soft foods like cream cheese, cottage or ricotta cheese, casserole dishes, or soft breads, it's likely that it's persisted through the whole product. In that case, you should throw it away. If you find mold on deli meats, other cooked meats, or casseroles, discard the entire package. Hard cheeses, however, can be salvaged by cutting off a 1-inch piece beneath the mold.

Use Veggie Scraps to Create New Soups

Soup was probably invented to use kitchen scraps. A bit of this, a bit of that, add water, salt, and seasoning, and you have soup. Here are a couple of ideas:

>> Add chopped carrots, celery (including tops), any bits of onion (minced), or greens (collards, spinach, cabbage). You can simmer this into a stock and strain or simply leave it and add cooked chicken or noodles to it.

>> Cook scraps and extra bits, then puree them to add to creamy soups.

>> Use a sharp knife to cut the kernels off leftover corncobs and save them for soup or a side of corn muffins.

Dry Leftover Herbs, Veggies, or Fruit

Dehydrating food removes the moisture from it and is another method to preserve it. You may notice that dried plums (prunes), grapes (raisins), or dried apricots all last longer than their fresh counterparts. The same goes for fresh versus dried herbs.

Luckily, you don't need to invest in an expensive dehydrator to dry your own herbs, fruits, or veggies. There are a lot of other options, including simply using your oven.

>> Chop any leftover green tops from green onions or scallions into small pieces. Place them on a baking sheet and dry in a 170-degree oven for 30 minutes or up to 2 hours (check every 30 minutes until they're just dry enough to crumble). Wrap in waxed paper or store in a small jar for later use.

>> Place leftover basil, parsley, or mint (separately) on a baking sheet and dry in a 170-degree oven for 30 minutes. Store in a small jar or airtight container. If you live in a dry climate, you can let lower moisture herbs like dill, rosemary, sage, and thyme airdry. Rinse fresh herbs in cool water and pat dry. Tie a bundle of 6 stems together and hang upside down until dry, over about 2 weeks.

>> To dehydrate fruit like apples or pears, first peel, core, and slice them to about ¼-inch-thick rings and then toss them with lemon juice. Arrange on a baking sheet lined with a silicone mat and bake in a low oven (140 degrees) for 6 hours. Or you can bake them for 3 hours in a hotter 225-degree oven, turning every 30 minutes.

>> Make your own fruit leather if you have a lot of peaches, apples, or pears. Preheat the oven to 170 degrees. Peel and cook the fruit and then puree. Pour puree onto a baking sheet lined with nonstick foil or a silicone mat. Spread the puree evenly over the mat with a rubber spatula. Place in the center rack of your oven and let it dehydrate for about 6 or 7 hours. When it's done (it will be darker in color), place a piece of waxed paper on it and turn it over on a flat surface. Remove the silicone mat and cut fruit leather into strips with kitchen shears.

Turn Droopy Fruits and Veggies into Slaw or Chutney

You can always make a slaw with bits of vegetables. While you may think of traditional coleslaw, you can make a slaw out of a variety of chopped fruits and veggies. Add your favorite slaw or salad dressing to these combos and mix well:

>> Scallions with cabbage or romaine

>> Kale or collard greens with a chopped cabbage slaw

>> Snap peas with a shredded red cabbage

>> Apples or mangos with cabbage slaw

>> Herbs or nuts with any slaw or salad

Chutney is a jam-type relish mixture that originated in India. It's traditionally made from chopped fruits and vegetables and served as a condiment. You can make it spicy or sweet depending on your preference and how you'd like to use it. A chutney is a nice way to use up ripe peaches or other fruit that could go to waste.

The basic process is to cook down ripe fruits and/or vegetables with some chopped onions, celery, vinegar, salt, and spices. Cook it down for 1–2 hours, depending on how many ingredients you have. For every 3 cups of fruits/vegetables, use ½ cup chopped onions, salt to taste, and 1 cup cider vinegar. You can also add ¼ cup brown sugar and lemon zest and your choice of spices.

Keep in an airtight jar for one week. Or you can transfer it to sterile jars or freeze in airtight bags for longer shelf life. You can also try these versions:

>> A peach and tomato chutney with chili powder and ground ginger

>> Mango with ginger, garlic, and raisins

>> A green chutney with 2 cups of cilantro, mint, or basil, ½ cup chopped onion, ground ginger, cumin, and lime juice

Dye Eggs with Leftover Onion Skins

Here's one for fun and function! My grandmother immigrated to the United States in the early 1900s. She and my grandfather brought with them some old-world ideas so they could get by with very little. They were definitely zero waste masters, using onion skins or beets to dye eggs for Easter and never wasting a crumb of food.

Yep, that's right — you can dye eggs with scraps. Save onion skins as you cook and use them for a natural way to dye Easter eggs to an orangish red color. Save the skins in an airtight container in the refrigerator. When you have skins from about 10 or 12 onions, you'll have enough to dye a dozen eggs. Here are the steps:

1. Soak the onion skins overnight in a medium-size pot of water. You can use a mixture of yellow onion skins and red onion skins.

2. Add 2 teaspoons white vinegar to the onion skin water. Be sure the skins are covered with water and bring to a boil and then simmer for 10 minutes.

3. Add eggs to the pot and bring back to boil. Boil for about 10 to 12 minutes for a hard-boiled egg. Remove the eggs and refrigerate. Alternatively, you can boil the onion skins and vinegar, strain the water, and cool. Then soak the previously hard-boiled eggs into the dyed vinegar water for 30 minutes or until desired color is achieved.

TIP

"Polishing" the eggs with a little olive oil will give them a lovely sheen.

Chapter **19**

Ten Ways to Use Stale Bread

I love bread and often have two to three varieties on hand. With a smaller household, it can be a challenge to keep bakery bread fresh. One strategy is to freeze half of the loaf when you buy it. Place half of the loaf into an airtight bag and immediately place it into the freezer while fresh. This way you enjoy the fresh half, and then later you can take the rest out of the freezer to enjoy in a week or two (and it'll taste surprisingly fresh if stored in the freezer at purchase).

You might sometimes take advantage of a buy-one-get-one sale at the store and buy two loaves of sliced bread. If you can't use both in a week, freezing one is a good way to preserve it. If you plan to use it in the following week or so, you can simply store it in the freezer in the bag it came in. Otherwise, to avoid freezer burn, transfer it to a more airtight bag if you plan to keep it frozen for three weeks or more.

TIP

Some people have luck reducing freezer burn by placing a paper towel into the original bread bag before freezing. I've found that's not necessary when you are planning to use the bread in a week or two, but definitely give it a try if you're storing a loaf in the freezer longer than a week!

Regardless of your freezer skills, sometimes you still end up with a stale loaf on hand. For those times when you end up with part of a stale loaf, I've got a lot of ideas in this chapter for how to give stale bread a second chance to be awesome. They're all delicious — and help avoid food waste.

If you don't have time to implement these ideas the day you find stale bread in your bread drawer, put the bread into the freezer to use for one of these zero waste options another day.

REMEMBER

Those best-by dates on bread are only guidelines. There's no food safety issue with using stale bread. It simply isn't as tasty when it's stale. If the bread has mold on it, then that's a different story. If it's just a touch of mold on the crust, you may be safe to just pitch that slice and the one next to it, but it's hard to know whether the mold is through the whole loaf, as you can't always see it. That's why it's great to utilize your freezer if you find you are not getting through your bread; otherwise you'll probably need to pitch the whole loaf. Keep in mind that it can also be toxic to birds and squirrels and other backyard critters, so don't toss moldy bread to them either.

Fresh Bread Crumbs

Fresh bread crumbs are easy to make (see Chapter 13) and you can use them in a multitude of ways, such as the following:

>> Add bread crumbs to baked macaroni and cheese to give it a golden, crunchy top layer. Mix about ¾ cup of crumbs with a teaspoon of olive oil or melted butter and a teaspoon of dried herbs, and then sprinkle the mixture over the dish during the last half of cooking.

>> Top any casserole with a bread crumb mixture to make it extra special. Just mix ½ cup bread crumbs with ¼ cup grated cheese, 1 tablespoon melted butter, and a teaspoon of dried herbs. Top potatoes, green beans, or broccoli with it before popping casserole into oven.

>> Add a bread crumb mixture to top broiled oysters. Mix ¼ cup crumbs with ½ teaspoon olive oil, a teaspoon of liquid smoke, and 1 teaspoon grated Parmesan cheese. Then sprinkle evenly onto 12 raw oysters on the half shell. Broil for 2 minutes.

>> Add a sprinkling of bread crumbs into your skillet hash brown potatoes to brown them up and give them extra crunch (then fry an egg on top!).

>> Bread chicken, fish fillets, or zucchini planks. Dredge through flour, beaten egg, then bread crumbs. Place onto baking sheet, drizzle with butter or oil, and bake according to recipe directions.

>> Use bread crumbs for meatloaf or meatballs to offer moisture and body, allowing the mixture to bind together. See the Skillet Meatballs recipe in Chapter 13, or the Lemony Salmon Patties in Chapter 8.

>> Mix with herbs or spices to give your bread crumbs a kick of flavor. Match the herbs to the cuisine, or you can simply use salt and pepper to flavor your bread crumbs. Breading fish or chicken for a TexMex style meal? Add ½ teaspoon each of chili powder and cumin and a teaspoon of dried cilantro to a cup of crumbs along with a pinch of salt. You can use Italian-inspired herbed bread crumbs to oven-fry ravioli. Season each cup of bread crumbs with 1 teaspoon dried parsley, ½ teaspoon garlic powder, a teaspoon of dried oregano, a pinch of salt, and black pepper. Buy a package of fresh ravioli, place them on a baking sheet, brush olive oil or a vinaigrette salad dressing over each of them, and then sprinkle with herbed bread crumbs. Bake at 400 degrees for 10 to 15 minutes and enjoy immediately.

French Toast

I'm pretty sure French toast was invented to use stale bread. In fact, in France, the dish is called *pain perdu*, which means "lost bread." But because this book is all about zero waste cooking, we're not losing any bread! And using stale bread to make a treat like French toast is something to feel good about.

TIP

French toast works with just about any type of stale bread — French, white, Italian, or sourdough work especially well.

French toast is simple to make. (*Note:* If your bread is a bit on the more-stale side, use an extra egg. You want to be sure the egg mixture soaks into stale bread.)

1. For 4 slices of bread, mix 2 eggs with ½ cup milk. Add ¼ teaspoon of vanilla extract and ½ teaspoon of sugar (you can also add ground cinnamon if you want). Mix eggs, milk, and flavorings well.

2. Dip the bread slices into the egg mixture, coating both sides, and soaking bread. If the bread is more stale, you might want to let it sit for a minute or two to soak up the egg mixture.

3. Heat a griddle and then spray with cooking spray when hot. Cook French toast slices for about 2 minutes on each side, until lightly browned, turning once. Serve topped with freshly sliced strawberries, blueberries, raspberries, sliced banana, or simply maple syrup.

You can also make a French toast casserole. The method is similar to the one used for strata, but instead of chunks of bread, you use slices. Layer whole slices of bread into a 9-x-13-inch buttered baking dish. Then whisk together 10 eggs, 1½ cups milk, 2 teaspoons vanilla extract, 3 tablespoons sugar (brown or white), 1 teaspoon cinnamon, and ½ teaspoon nutmeg. Pour the egg mixture over the bread slices and refrigerate for an hour or overnight. Bake at 350 degrees for 35 to 45 minutes or until set and golden. Serve with maple syrup or fresh fruit.

Crostini for Appetizers

Crostini are small slices of toasted bread. Because you toast the bread for crostini and top it with a moist topping, you can use any stale bread for these, although a stale baguette works especially well. The process is super simple:

1. Cut the bread into thin, ¼-inch slices and place on baking sheet.

2. Toast in a 350-degree oven for 2 minutes then allow to cool.

3. Top each slice with savory toppings, such as the Versatile Pesto (Chapter 11), a soft cheese, the Creamy Veggie Dip (Chapter 8), chopped tomatoes mixed with olive oil, or you can even spread leftover Lemony Salmon Patties (Chapter 8) on them.

You can make the crostini toasts ahead and store in a container on the counter or in a bread box for later use.

Pappa al Pomodoro

This is sort of the Italian version of grilled cheese sandwiches and tomato soup. This dish, however, mixes bread *into* the tomato sauce to create a classic comfort bowl. Stale bread works very well for this dish because it's soaked in tomato goodness.

1. Cook tomato sauce then stir in about 3 or 4 ounces of cubed stale bread.

    You can make the Quick Canned Tomato Pasta Sauce (Chapter 11) or use any favorite tomato sauce.

2. Add about 1 cup of chicken or vegetable stock and stir until tomato sauce, bread, and stock are combined. Simmer for 20 minutes or until bread has broken down and you have a slightly thick soup.

3. Ladle into bowls, and garnish with grated Parmesan cheese and basil if you have it.

Bread Pudding

This delicious dessert also screams comfort food. Like French toast, this recipe involves bread, eggs, and milk. It's been a popular dessert in England since the 13th century, and some food historians date it back to 11th-century Europe. You can use white or whole grain for this sweet treat.

To make bread pudding, follow these steps:

1. Cube 8 slices of bread and place onto a baking sheet. Pop into a 350-degree oven for about 10 minutes to evenly dry them out.

2. Prepare a 7x11-inch or 9x9-inch baking dish by coating with butter or cooking oil spray. Then transfer the toasted bread cubes into the dish.

   At this point, you can add some fruit, such as blueberries or chopped peaches.

3. In a medium bowl, mix 4 eggs, 3 cups of milk, ⅓ cup sugar, 1 teaspoon vanilla extract, 1 teaspoon of ground cinnamon, and a pinch of salt (a dash of ground nutmeg is also nice to add). Mix with a whisk until well combined.

4. Pour the custard mixture over the bread cubes, making sure to cover all the bread and all corners. Some of the bread will be poking up, and that's fine. Cover and refrigerate for an hour or overnight.

5. Bake uncovered in a 350-degree oven for 35 to 45 minutes, or until golden. Cut into squares and serve.

   You can garnish with whipped cream or a scoop of ice cream if desired.

Croutons for French Onion Soup

Like the Pappa al Pomodoro, stale bread makes a simple beef and onion stock extra special. You can start with the Homemade Stock in Chapter 10 or use a store-bought stock (beef or chicken). Before you make the soup, prepare the croutons.

1. Slice stale bread to the size of your soup crock or bowl and place onto a parchment-lined baking sheet. Drizzle olive oil (or butter) onto each piece of bread and then rub a clove of garlic (or sprinkle garlic powder) over each chunk of bread.

2. Bake for 5 to 10 minutes in a 350-degree oven, until lightly browned and toasted.

Next, to make the soup, in which your delicious croutons will float, follow these steps:

1. Chop about 2 or 3 large onions.

   I love Vidalia onions, but you can use any or a mixture of varieties.

2. Heat oil or butter in a large stainless or cast-iron pan. Cook the onions on low heat until they're caramelized, golden brown, and tender.

TIP

   For another layer of flavor, you can add a cup of dry white wine to the onions after they've caramelized and allow it to reduce.

3. Add the caramelized onions to a pot of hot stock along with a teaspoon or two of dried thyme or oregano.

4. To serve the soup, ladle it into ovenproof bowls, carefully float the crouton on top, and then top with shredded Swiss cheese. Place the crocks onto a baking sheet and broil in the oven for 2 minutes until cheese is browned and bubbly.

Stuffing or Southern Dressing

These terms are often used interchangeably, but *stuffing* is the term that indicates a side dish that is "stuffed" into another food (usually poultry), whereas *dressing* is served on the side. And if you live in the South, you call it *dressing*. Most chefs recommend not stuffing the turkey at Thanksgiving (because to properly cook the stuffing to food–safe temps, the meat may be overcooked and dry). Classic Southern dressing uses cornbread, but you can use any type of stale bread to create a dressing (or stuffing!).

The steps are as easy as these:

1. Spread 5 cups of bread cubes onto a baking sheet and bake for 10 to 15 minutes at 350 degrees.

2. Heat oil in a large pan and add ½ cup diced onions, ¼ cup diced carrots, and ¼ cup diced celery. Cook until celery and onion are translucent.

   This trio of veggies is called *mirepoix* (the French term for 2 parts diced onions, 1 part each diced carrots and celery).

3. In a large bowl, beat 1 egg into 1½ cups room-temperature (or chilled) chicken stock. Add the toasted bread cubes, ¼ cup chopped parsley, 2 teaspoons dried thyme (or poultry seasoning), salt, and pepper.

4. Transfer the whole mixture to a buttered or oil-sprayed 2-quart baking dish. Bake for 40 minutes in a 350-degree oven.

TIP

You can also add dried fruit, chopped apple, or browned sausage into the stuffing before baking.

Roasted Tomatoes with Bread and Cheese

Easy and delicious, this simple dish is another great way to use up a bit of stale bread.

1. Cut tomatoes into chunks and place in a glass baking dish. Drizzle with about 1 tablespoon of olive oil. Add salt and pepper and a crushed garlic clove.

2. Cut stale bread into cubes and transfer to the baking dish and mix with the tomato mixture. Add another drizzle of olive oil (about 2 teaspoons). Bake for 20 minutes in a 400-degree oven.

3. Sprinkle with ¼ cup grated cheese then return to the oven for 5 more minutes until cheese is lightly golden. Serve as a side dish.

Panzanella

Panzanella is another Italian dish inspired by stale bread. It's a salad of sorts, which traditionally uses bread cubes, tomatoes, and onions, but you can certainly also add basil, cucumbers, and peppers to it.

1. Cut stale bread into 1-inch cubes for a total of 2 cups.

2. Heat 1 tablespoon of olive oil in a large pan, add the bread cubes, and stir gently until bread is browned.

3. Cut 1 to 2 large, ripe tomatoes into chunks and transfer to a large salad bowl. Add ½ cup chopped onion and ¼ cup chopped basil leaves (add optional chopped cucumbers or bell peppers). Season with salt and pepper. Add the bread cubes and toss together.

The salad will be more flavorful if you allow it to sit for a half hour or so.

4. Before serving, pour dressing over the salad and mix gently.

Try the Go-to Honey Dijon Salad Dressing from Chapter 11.

When All Else Fails

If you don't have time or desire for the above ideas, and you find yourself left with a stale loaf or a few slices, here are a few more last-ditch efforts to avoid wasting bread.

>> A loaf of French bread or other artisan style bakery loaf can get stale rather quickly. You can revive it in the oven by wetting it. Take the hard, stale loaf and run the crusty sides under clean water. Wrap it tightly in foil and place it into a 300-degree oven for 5 to 10 minutes. The result is a "new" warm, crusty loaf to be enjoyed immediately.

>> Like all rotting food, you can add stale or moldy bread to the compost bin.

>> Bake the Basic Egg Strata in Chapter 9.

>> I mention using stale bread for French Onion Soup earlier in this chapter, but you can also make smaller salad croutons using a similar method. Slice stale bread into bite-sized pieces, about ½ inch in size. Toss with about a teaspoon of olive oil (or melted butter) per cup cubes. Sprinkle with a teaspoon of garlic or onion powder. Place onto a parchment-lined baking sheet and bake in a 300 degree oven for 5 or 10 minutes or until golden brown.

>> Let's say you have two extra last-minute guests coming over for burger night. You can stretch your ground meat with some bread crumbs! Add 1 cup of bread crumbs per pound. So if you planned on getting four burgers out of that pound of beef, you'll now be able to get six out of it. Bonus: They may even be moister and tastier burgers!

>> I warn against feeding moldy bread to wildlife earlier in this chapter, but stale bread is fine on occasion. If you don't have time or a need for bread crumbs, take a mental health break by walking to the park to feed the birds (and if you have backyard chickens, by all means share some of your stale bread with them, too).

Chapter **20**

Ten Ways to Use Up Dairy Before It Spoils

There are many good ways to incorporate slightly sour milk into recipes. Hear me out: There's a difference between slightly sour milk and spoiled milk. By all means, if it's yellowish, really foul smelling, clumpy, or growing mold, send it down the drain — that milk is spoiled! However, if it's within a week of its best-by date and smells just slightly off, maybe a little acidic, it actually has some culinary use left in it. Don't think of this sour milk as "spoiled" but rather "lightly fermented."

This chapter gives you ten uses for that sour or lightly fermented milk that we all find in our fridge from time to time. Don't throw it out! Find a use for it and continue on your zero waste journey.

TECHNICAL STUFF

Sour milk is part of the fermented milk category that includes yogurt and kefir. These products are produced by fermentation that occurs when bacteria naturally start to form in the milk. The difference between them is the type of microorganisms present. We know that fermented products like kefir are really healthy for our gut because they are probiotic (meaning they contain microbes that have health benefits). Soured milk is actually a quite common product in the Balkan peninsula in Europe as well as Germany and Sweden. Cultured buttermilk you buy at the store is milk with extra microbes added to it to speed up the fermentation of it.

TIP

You may not have time to apply some of the tips in this chapter when your milk is starting to sour. No worries, you can freeze it for later use. To freeze, transfer the milk from its original container to another airtight plastic or glass container, being sure to leave at least one or two inches from the top of the seal (the milk will expand when frozen). You'll notice that the fat separates from the rest of the milk when you freeze. When you thaw the milk, the protein and minerals in the milk are the first to thaw, and then the water, and the fat may separate out. That's normal, so just allow the milk to thaw completely before using, and then stir or shake it to blend. Use the milk within a day or two, once thawed.

Replacing Buttermilk

If a recipe calls for buttermilk, you can substitute sour milk. Recipes that may call for buttermilk include pancakes, waffles, biscuits, mashed potatoes, cakes, brownies, or some quick or yeast breads. Sour milk will make your pancakes extra fluffy. And who doesn't love a fluffy pancake?

TIP

However, if your milk isn't sour and you don't have buttermilk, you can "sour" milk yourself by adding 1 tablespoon of lemon juice or white vinegar per cup of milk. Then use an equal substitution, sour milk for buttermilk.

Making Oatmeal

Milk that is a sniff away from perfect partners well with a bit of sugar. Just like using it for pancakes or baked goods, sour milk creates a nice bowl of oatmeal, too, if you sweeten it with brown sugar or maple syrup. Cooking oats with milk (even souring milk) rather than water improves the nutrition of your bowl, too, so it's a win-win.

Thickening Stews and Sauces

Use sour milk to thicken stews and create cream sauces (see Chapter 11 for Basic Cream Sauce). When any stew or gravy recipe calls for milk or buttermilk, you can stir in sour milk.

Baking

Sour milk works well for baking because the acid reacts with the baking soda, making your cakes extra moist and delicious. Adding sour milk to biscuits, Bundt, pound, or other cakes, or quick breads is a great use for it.

TIP

Sour milk is a great addition to scones, so when you have sour milk on hand, try whipping up the Add Anything Scones recipe found in Chapter 16.

Breading Foods

When recipes call for breading an ingredient (usually a meat, fish, or vegetable) into flour, egg/milk, and bread crumbs, you can use sour milk in place of the eggs.

TIP

Buttermilk and sour milk act as a tenderizer, so using sour milk is perfect for oven fried chicken.

TIP

Try making oven-baked zucchini planks. Slice a small to medium zucchini long-ways into ⅛-inch slices. Dredge them through seasoned flour, dip in sour milk mixed with an egg, and then dredge in bread crumbs. Place onto an oil-sprayed baking sheet. Spray the tops of zucchini planks with more cooking spray, and bake for 20 minutes in a 400-degree oven. Then watch them get gobbled up!

Making a Soft Cheese

You can use sour milk to make a soft cheese (similar to cottage cheese).

To make a cheese, you'll need a saucepan, 4 cups of sour milk, 4 teaspoons white vinegar, cheesecloth, a colander, and salt and fresh milk to taste. Then follow these steps:

1. Pour the sour milk into a saucepan. Heat over medium heat until milk is 195 degrees (this will kill any harmful bacteria that may be present).

2. Remove from heat and add the white vinegar. Stir until curds form then pour through a cheesecloth-lined colander (over a bowl). The curds will remain (the liquid whey will seep through).

3. Rinse the curds in water, squeeze, and drain out the liquid again. Transfer curds to a bowl and crumble. Add salt to taste and a small amount of fresh milk to moisten.

TIP

Instead of crumbling the cheese, you can omit the addition of salt and milk and keep the cheese in a soft ball to make a cheese to spread on crackers.

Tenderizing Raw Chicken and Other Meats

Soaking chicken in sour milk tenderizes it. Simply place chicken pieces in a bowl filled with about ½ inch of sour milk and soak in the refrigerator for 4 hours (no longer than overnight).

To make a marinade for chicken, mix 2 cups sour milk, 1 tablespoon Worcestershire sauce, 1 teaspoon salt, 1 teaspoon paprika, 2 teaspoons garlic powder, and black pepper. Marinate for 4 to 12 hours then cook the chicken as you normally would for your recipe. Or you can simply grill the chicken. Discard the marinade.

TIP

You can also use sour cream to make a tender and juicy chicken. Instead of the typical dredging through flour, egg, and bread crumbs, simply spread about a tablespoon of sour cream over the top of chicken cutlets. Press seasoned bread crumbs onto it and bake at 350 for 35 minutes.

Yogurt Helps Ensure Crispy, Moist Chicken or Fish

Yogurt is generally safe a month after the best-by date. Like sour milk, yogurt is a super ingredient to marinate chicken. You can use plain yogurt in a similar way that you'd use sour cream — in dips or cakes.

You can also use souring yogurt to coat chicken or fish before breading and baking. It tenderizes the meat, and adds moisture like no other. Place your seasoned bread crumbs or panko in a shallow dish. To make 4 chicken breast cutlets, season about ½ cup sour cream with a tablespoon of chopped parsley or a teaspoon of dried. Spread the sour cream over each side of each cutlet, one at a time, then dredge it through bread crumbs or panko, pressing to be sure coating generously adheres. Heat 1 tablespoon of oil in a nonstick skillet and pan-fry cutlets for about 3 to 4 minutes per side.

For baked fish, spread 2 tablespoons of yogurt over the top of each fish fillet. Sprinkle about 3 tablespoons seasoned panko or bread crumbs onto each fillet over the yogurt in a generous mound. Bake the fish for 15 minutes (you can use this method for chicken pieces too, but bake for 30 minutes).

Once you coat chicken or fish in yogurt, you'll never go back. The chicken will be juicier and more delicious than ever, and the fish will be moist and tasty.

Beyond Cooking: Milk Baths and Facials

Aside from cooking, you can even use sour milk for a soothing bath or facial! The enzymes in the milk are great for your skin, so why not give it a go?

Just pour 1 to 2 cups of sour milk into your warm bath water and soak.

TIP

The lactic acid in the milk can soothe skin and may even help brighten it and soothe fine lines. Try this facial recipe with your sour milk and an overripe banana you may have on the counter:

> Mix the banana with ½ cup sour milk and a teaspoon of honey. Spread mixture over face and leave it on for 5 to 10 minutes. Rinse away and blot skin dry.

Feed Me, Seymour: Fertilizing Plant

Instead of dumping your quart of sour milk, feed you plants with it! The calcium in milk is good for most plants. Simply make a mixture of equal parts sour milk and water and then water your plants with it.

Chapter **21**

Ten Ways to Reduce Waste from Restaurant Meals

Restaurants typically serve large portions. I often find myself ordering an appetizer for "dinner" or sharing plates, but sometimes I go for all the courses and generally end up not being able to finish everything. Whether you go out to eat, pick up takeout, or have food delivered, you may end up with leftovers. Sure, you can just reheat them for lunch the next day, but having some other tricks up your sleeves to be sure the food doesn't go to waste is a good idea, and this chapter is a great start.

In this chapter, I present ten ways to reduce waste and use those delicious leftovers from someone else's kitchen to make them just as — if not more — exciting than the original meal.

Order Wisely

Just like buying less food when grocery shopping is a zero waste strategy, so is ordering less food when dining or ordering out. Here are some strategies:

>> Try not to order food when you're famished. Try to plan ahead. Chomp on an apple or grab some baby carrots to snack on before you go out to eat or place your takeout order. Decide what you'll order — and actually eat — before you get too hungry. Or if you know you're going to get takeout for dinner, place your order after lunch and schedule your pickup time for after work.

>> Look over the entire menu before you start ordering. Gauge your hunger and then choose. For example, in lieu of a full entrée, consider enjoying an appetizer for your meal and add a side salad.

>> Share an entrée if you can and if you have a willing partner. This is sometimes a great strategy that not only reduces food waste but also supports a healthy waistline.

>> If possible, order by phone instead of using an app. This might help you order less (and therefore waste less) and save money. By calling the restaurant for pickup or delivery, and talking to an actual person, you're less likely to overorder than you would by mindlessly clicking too many items on an app.

Box Up Leftovers Big and Small

When you're so full but you look at your plate and see you still have food left, what do you do? What seems like a small amount of food compared to the original portion may not look worth it when you're stuffed to the gills, but that leftover may taste really good the next day when you're hungry again at lunchtime, or as a snack if it's a smaller portion. Most restaurants are more than happy to send you home with your leftovers. So even if it looks like a small portion, have them box it up and then put it right into your fridge when you get home.

TIP

Don't feel bad about asking your server to box up the bread, too.

Actually Eat What Food You Bring Home

It's surprising how good intentions sometimes can go wayward. To make sure you actually eat your leftovers, have a plan for them. Make sure they don't get left in the back seat or trunk of the car — or at the restaurant! When you get home (within 60 to 90 minutes), label your leftovers with the contents and date and refrigerate them right away, putting them on a shelf where you can see them. Then be sure to eat them within 4 days.

TIP

If you have time, transfer your leftovers into a reusable glass container so you can either pack them in the morning for your lunch or pop them directly into the microwave when you're ready to eat them. It will keep them fresher longer, too!

Combine Leftovers to Create a New Meal

Instead of just eating leftovers as is, you can also make other creations with them. If you're out with the family, box up everyone's leftovers. Maybe your daughter got a huge side of broccoli but ate only two florets. Box them up. Or maybe you have several different dishes with just a little bit of leftovers. Box them all up and create a new meal that everyone can enjoy.

TIP

A simple stir-fry is an easy way to use up leftover veggies. Cook up 2 servings of rice (or better yet, use leftover rice from another take-out meal). Slice a chicken breast and sauté it in oil in a medium pan. Once the chicken is cooked, add the variety of leftover veggies and heat through. Serve over the rice.

Turn Extra Takeout into a One-Bowl Wonder

I don't know about you, but we almost always end up with a lonely box of plain white rice when we order Chinese takeout. Usually one box is enough, among the other dishes, and we share that. Of course, you can simply use the rice as a side dish for another meal during the week and easily get four servings from that side of plain rice. However, why go plain when you can go Power Bowl? What's a Power Bowl, you ask? It's a one-bowl meal that includes a variety of food that provides a balance of nutrients.

TIP

Make a Power Bowl by adding other ingredients to the rice, and you'll easily be able to make three to four bowls from that one container of plain rice.

Follow these steps to create a basic Power Bowl and then put your own twist on it:

1. Put about ½ cup of a carbohydrate (a grain, like the rice) into a small bowl (cereal or rice bowls work well).

2. Layer sliced tomatoes, avocado, and other vegetables on top.

3. Add a protein — leftover chili, chicken, fish, tofu, beans, or nuts.

4. Add a sauce (like sriracha, teriyaki, or barbeque) or a salad dressing or a sprinkle of cheese.

The options are endless. You can mix and match proteins, and everyone in the household can add the veggies and sauces they enjoy to their own bowl.

TIP

Power Bowls are a great way to use up a variety of leftovers, not just leftover rice. You prep and serve the whole meal in individual bowls, so cleanup is easy.

Fill Omelets with Leftover Meats or Veggies

Remember those leftover veggies I advised you to pack into a doggie bag? You'll be happy you did when you can quickly whip up a Saturday morning omelet or frittata. Use the guidelines in Chapter 9 to create a delicious frittata or try adding the veggies or leftover meats to the Egg Muffin Cups.

Add Pasta to Leftover Restaurant Sauces

Pasta entrées are often quite large. In fact, I've joked at times that my restaurant serving has been enough to feed a family of four.

TIP

When you get served a giant plate of pasta, ask for your to-go container before you even start eating. That way, you won't overeat, and you can preserve the pasta to share with others at home.

In addition to the large portion of pasta, there's often a lot of sauce served with it. Whether it's a tomato-based sauce or a cream sauce, take advantage of that delicious chef's creation and extend it at home by simply adding more pasta to it. Boil 2 more servings of the same or a similar pasta at home (for instance, if your leftovers are penne, make penne or rotini — if it's fettuccine, make fettucine or linguine). Heat the leftover pasta with sauce in a large saucepan over low heat until heated through. Once the additional pasta is cooked, add it to the pan with the leftover pasta, and toss until the sauce coats all of it. Transfer to two to three bowls to serve.

Stuff a Baked Potato with Doggie Bag Goodies

Like omelets and pasta, potatoes are a great vehicle to hold leftovers. All varieties are nutritious, providing complex carbohydrates, vitamins C and B6, and minerals like potassium.

TIP Even though your doctor may recommend bananas for potassium, your dietitian (that's me) will tell you that a medium-size potato actually has quite a bit more potassium than a banana. The potato provides about 620 milligrams, while the banana has only 420 milligrams potassium. Go potatoes!

You may as well bake 4 or 5 potatoes, so then you can refrigerate the ones you don't use to save time another day. To make a stuffed potato, you want one big enough to create a meal with (those mixed bags of mini potatoes are delicious roasted, but for stuffing, you want a medium to large baking potato). You can use either a white baking potato or a sweet potato to create this simple lunch or quick meal with leftovers. All you have to do is bake the potato, split it open, and place warmed leftovers on top of it. Garnish a white potato with a little shredded cheese, salsa, or sour cream (or plain yogurt), or garnish a sweet potato with salsa or spiced honey yogurt (plain yogurt mixed with a small drizzle of honey and cinnamon or chili powder), and you've got a quick, nutritious zero waste meal.

TIP To bake the perfect baked potato, use a russet or Idaho potato. Scrub the outside of the potato and rinse with water. Dry it and pierce with a paring knife. You can either make four stabs or slice it, making a cross. Place the potato directly on the rack of a preheated 425-degree oven and bake for 45 to 55 minutes until tender when stabbed. If you want a crispy skin, brush oil or butter over the potato and return to the oven for another 10 minutes. Don't wrap potatoes in foil to bake. This steams them, resulting in a moister, less fluffy texture (plus the foil just adds more waste to landfills).

Make Takeout Leftovers into Tasty Nacho Toppings

You can make any leftover more fun by turning it into nachos! First, create a base of tortilla chips, and then top with leftover chili, shredded rotisserie chicken, pulled pork, beans, or roasted vegetables. Sprinkle evenly with shredded cheese, and then bake in a 350-degree oven for 10 to 15 minutes, or until cheese melts. Add salsa or guacamole and garnish with sour cream or plain yogurt.

REMEMBER

Don't be afraid to mix cuisines. Sure, serving leftover Kung Pao Chicken over tortilla chips (or that baked potato) isn't tradition, but why not go for it? Throw some leftover macaroni and cheese on there. The goal here is to reduce your food waste and create quick meals.

TIP

Speaking of nachos, you can also make fruit "nachos," subbing apples for chips when you have extra apples that need to be eaten. Start by coring the apples then slice them on a cross section (so you have rings). Place apple rings onto a platter, and top with nut butter, crushed cereal, or granola. Drizzle with caramel sauce for some decadence.

Level Up Grilled Cheese Sandwiches with Yummy Bits of Leftovers

Sometimes cheese just makes everything better, right? Cheese really is the glue in this scenario. Throwing bits of leftovers onto the cheese can instantly up your grilled cheese sandwich game.

Here's how you do it! For each sandwich you'll need two slices of bread. Butter one side of each slice. Heat a griddle or nonstick pan over medium-high heat and place one slice of the bread, buttered-side down, onto it. Add cheese to the bread, add your leftovers on top of the cheese, and then top with the second slice of bread, buttered-side up. Flip the sandwich after about 3 minutes, or when the bread is toasted and golden.

Here are a few ideas:

>> Cheese with sliced apples or pears is a delicious combination. Did you get a side of cooked apples with your breakfast? Bring some of it home to add to a grilled cheese. Pair apples with cheddar, or pears with brie.

>> Sneak some leftover fajita filling into your grilled cheese.

>> Add some salsa to leftover corn and top with pepper jack cheese.

>> Instead of adding cheese to your grilled cheese, put leftover macaroni and cheese between two hearty slices of bread and grill it up (or you can get fancy and use a waffle maker).

>> Have a bit left from your steakhouse steak? Slice it very thinly, and you can add it to your grilled cheese sandwich. Want to mix it up? Then add a crumble of bleu cheese.

>> Did your pasta Bolognese have extra sauce? Scoop it up and add it to a grilled provolone or Asiago cheese sandwich.

The options are endless! You can really use any cheese you enjoy, or whatever you have on hand.

Appendix

Metric Conversion Guide

Note: The recipes in this book weren't developed or tested using metric measurements. There may be some variation in quality when converting to metric units.

Common Abbreviations

Abbreviation(s)	What It Stands For
cm	Centimeter
C., c.	Cup
G, g	Gram
kg	Kilogram
L, l	Liter
lb.	Pound
mL, ml	Milliliter
oz.	Ounce
pt.	Pint
t., tsp.	Teaspoon
T., Tb., Tbsp.	Tablespoon

Volume

U.S. Units	Canadian Metric	Australian Metric
¼ teaspoon	1 milliliter	1 milliliter
½ teaspoon	2 milliliters	2 milliliters
1 teaspoon	5 milliliters	5 milliliters
1 tablespoon	15 milliliters	20 milliliters
¼ cup	50 milliliters	60 milliliters
⅓ cup	75 milliliters	80 milliliters
½ cup	125 milliliters	125 milliliters
⅔ cup	150 milliliters	170 milliliters
¾ cup	175 milliliters	190 milliliters
1 cup	250 milliliters	250 milliliters
1 quart	1 liter	1 liter
1½ quarts	1.5 liters	1.5 liters
2 quarts	2 liters	2 liters
2½ quarts	2.5 liters	2.5 liters
3 quarts	3 liters	3 liters
4 quarts (1 gallon)	4 liters	4 liters

Weight

U.S. Units	Canadian Metric	Australian Metric
1 ounce	30 grams	30 grams
2 ounces	55 grams	60 grams
3 ounces	85 grams	90 grams
4 ounces (¼ pound)	115 grams	125 grams
8 ounces (½ pound)	225 grams	225 grams
16 ounces (1 pound)	455 grams	500 grams (½ kilogram)

Length

Inches	Centimeters
0.5	1.5
1	2.5
2	5.0
3	7.5
4	10.0
5	12.5
6	15.0
7	17.5
8	20.5
9	23.0
10	25.5
11	28.0
12	30.5

Temperature (Degrees)

Fahrenheit	Celsius
32	0
212	100
250	120
275	140
300	150
325	160
350	180
375	190
400	200
425	220
450	230
475	240
500	260

Index

A

Add Anything Scones, 246
agriculture
  conservation along food supply chain, 25–28
  ecological management of pests, 26
  food production, 31–32
  organic, 32–33
  regenerative, 24
  role in greenhouse gas emissions, 28, 29
  sustainability in, 22–25
  technology in, 27, 33–34
agroecology, 26
agronomy, 33
al dente pasta, cooking, 213, 215
alcohol consumption, 254. *See also* cocktails
allergies, food, 37, 38–39
almond milk, 100
ancient grains, 91–92
angel hair pasta
  overview, 213
  with Shrimp and Spinach, 228
animal agriculture, 34–36
animal feed, 28
animal rights, 35
animal welfare, 17, 34–35
antibiotics in poultry, 97
appetizers. *See* starters
apples
  Apple-Ginger Chutney, 169
  Baked, 183
  choosing for ripeness, 93
  making fruit nachos with, 298
  Roast Pork Loin with, and Onions, 203
  storing, 55, 69, 70, 71
Aquafaba Fluff, 168
arborio rice, 91

artichokes
  Chicken with Orzo and, 192
  Chickpea Grain Bake, 178
asparagus
  choosing for ripeness, 93
  Smoked Salmon Pasta with, 221
avocado
  choosing for ripeness, 93
  Cream, 235
  freezing, 71
  growing plants from pits, 73–74

B

bacon, freezing, 72
Bagels with Smoked Salmon and Cream Cheese, 238
bags, reusable, 64–65, 70, 72
Baked Apples, 183
Baked Fish with Herbed Bread Crumbs, 205
baked potatoes, stuffing, 197, 297
baking. *See also* desserts
  egg wash for, 273–274
  eggs, 132
  pantry staples for, 80
  using sour milk in, 289
  zero waste add-ins and swaps, 242
balanced eating, 15–16, 104
bananas, 55, 69, 70, 71, 93
bar codes on produce, 56
barley, 92
Basic Bean Dip, 249
Basic Cream Cheese Dip, 124
Basic Cream Sauce, 160, 165
Basic Egg Strata, 139
Basic Frittata, 140
Basic Muffins, 242, 244
Basil-infused Sparkling Water, 262

basmati rice, 90

batch cooking, 104–105, 172, 186

beans

    Basic Dip, 249

    Beef Chili, 148

    Black Bean and Edamame Salad, 182

    Black Bean Brownie Bites, 247

    healthy eating tips, 87

    Kicked-Up Cannellini Bean Salad, 181

    Kitchen Sink Chicken Chili, 149

    Layered Dip, 121–122

    Nutty Mixed Salad with, 157

    in plant-based eating, 16

    and Rice, 183

    in side dishes, 171, 172

    Soup with Diced Pork, 151

    storing, 65

    Texas Caviar, 126

beef

    Chili, 148

    greenhouse gas emissions related to, 40

    Grilled Marinated Flank Steak, 198–199

    healthy eating tips, 95–96

    Skillet Meatballs, 200

    Stew with Potatoes, Carrots, and Peas, 147

beeswax wrap sheets, 66

beets

    Nutty Mixed Salad with, 157

    regrowing, 74

bell peppers

    Broccoli Bits and, with Linguine, 217

    choosing for ripeness, 94

    Foil-pack Greek Chicken with Olives, Feta, and, 193–194

    grain-stuffed, 176

    Pork Tacos with, 236

    Roasted, 175

    Roasted Tomatoes and, with Penne, 227

    Roasted Veggie Trio, 173

Berry Smoothie, 259

best-by dates

    eggs, 99

    first in, first out system, 66

    knowing how long to keep what, 72–73

    meaning of, 55–58

    as reason for waste, 19

beverages. *See* drinks

big box stores, shopping at, 83–84

bioengineering (genetic engineering), 31

birds, feeding eggshells to, 134

Black Bean and Edamame Salad, 182

Black Bean Brownie Bites, 247

Bloody Mary Cocktail, Vegged-Up, 268

bow ties

    overview, 213

    with Turkey and Peas, 226

BPA safety, 64

bread

    Basic Egg Strata, 139

    defined, 231

    for handhelds, 230

    healthy eating tips, 92–93

    Individual Pizzas, 251

    mold on, 280

    Pizza Rolls, 127

    stale, using, 279–286

    storing, 55, 65

    Stuffed Greek, 129–130

    waste related to, 52

bread crumbs

    Baked Fish with Herbed, 205

    making, 188–189, 280–281

bread pudding, 283

breading foods with sour milk, 289

breakfast, 106–111, 231. *See also specific recipes*

broccoli

    adding to Garlic Linguine with Clams, 222

    Bits and Bell Peppers with Linguine, 217

    choosing for ripeness, 94

    Garlic, 174

    Spicy Tofu Bowl with, 208

    storing, 76

Broiled Salmon Fillet, 204

broiler chickens, 98, 191

brown rice, 90, 91

Brownie Bites, Black Bean, 247

budget-conscious shopping. *See* shopping

Buettner, Dan, 16

bulk buys, 44, 62, 63, 83–84

burgers, 232, 286

butter, 71, 100

buttermilk, replacing, 288

"buy local", 94–95

buying food. *See* shopping

C

cabbage, regrowing, 74
Caesar dressing, 273
cage-free chickens, 97
cage-free eggs, 98
canned foods
  beans, 87
  as pantry staples, 80
  produce, 85–86
  tips for purchasing and storing, 57
cannellini beans
  Basic Bean Dip, 249
  Kicked-Up Salad, 181
caramelized onions, 172, 177
carbon capture, 28
carbon footprint labels, 40
carrots
  Beef Stew with, 147
  regrowing, 74
  Roasted, with Honey Glaze, 179
carving poultry, 187–188
cattle feed, 28
cauliflower, choosing for ripeness, 94
celery, regrowing, 74
celiac disease, 93
cereal, buying in bulk, 83
chalk, making with eggshells, 134
cheese. See also specific cheeses; specific recipes
  bulk buys, 83
  cooking tips, 100, 101
  freezing, 71
  mold on, 275
  soft, making, 289–290
Cheesy Herbed Rice, 180
Cheesy Veggie Crustless Quiche, 138
chicken
  coating with yogurt, 291
  Empty-the-fridge Vegetable Soup with Egg Noodles, 146
  Foil-pack Greek, with Olives, Feta, and Peppers, 193–194
  healthy eating tips, 97–98
  Kitchen Sink Chili, 149
  Liver Pâté, 98
  with Orzo, Artichokes, and Zucchini, 192
  oven-fried, 273

Parmesan Stuffed Mushrooms, 117–118
  sheet pan dinners, 105
  Spiced, over Rice, 196
  Stuffed Baked Potatoes, 197
  tenderizing with sour milk, 290
  Teriyaki Tenders, 195
  whole, preparing, 186–188
  Whole Roast, 190–191
chickpeas
  Aquafaba Fluff, 168
  Artichoke Grain Bake, 178
  Pasta with, 224
chilis
  Beef, 148
  Kitchen Sink Chicken, 149
chilling food, 57
Chimichurri, 167
cholesterol, 132
choline, 132
Chopped Salad with Lemon Vinaigrette, 155
chutneys
  Apple-Ginger, 169
  turning droopy fruits and veggies into, 277
circular bio-economy, 28
citrus fruits, storing, 55, 69, 70, 71
citrus peel
  storing, 76
  sugared, 263
Citrus-mustard Salad Dressing, 161
Clams, Garlic Linguine with, 222
cleanliness, in kitchen, 57
climate change, 17, 28
closed dating food labels, 56
cloth produce bags, 70
cocktail shaker, 255
cocktails. See also mocktails
  bar, setting up, 254–255
  Cranberry-Rosemary Cocktail, 264
  Infused Vodka, 265
  Lemonade with Mint, 256
  overview, 253
  Pimm's Cocktail, 266
  Sangria with Citrus, 257
  Special Whiskey Sour Cocktail, 267
  Vegged-Up Bloody Mary Cocktail, 268

coconut milk, 100

cold composting, 59

community-supported agriculture (CSA) systems, 14

composting, 47, 58–59

condiments, 52, 81

conscientious omnivores, 18

conservation along food supply chain, 25–28

containers
  airtight, 65
  for kitchen organization, 54
  repurposing, 63–64

conventional farming, 32–33

"cook from the freezer" day, 73, 86, 105

"cook once; eat thrice", 186

cooked foods, freezing, 71

cooking temperatures, safe minimum, 189

countertop, taking inventory of food on, 54–55

cover crops, 24, 27

Cranberry-Rosemary Cocktail, 264

cream cheese
  Bagels with Smoked Salmon and, 238
  Basic Dip, 124
  for dips, 122

Creamy Veggie Dip, 123

crop rotation, 27

cross contamination, 57

crostini, 282

croutons
  for French onion soup, 283–284
  for salad, 286

CSA (community-supported agriculture) systems, 14

cucumbers
  Pork Pita Pockets with Cucumber Sauce, 233
  storing, 55, 71

cycles, sale, 85

dairy foods. *See also specific dairy foods*
  alternatives to, 100, 101
  best-by dates on, 56
  grocery lists for sample meal plans, 107, 109, 110, 111
  healthy eating tips, 95, 99–101
  storing, 69
  using before spoiling, 287–288
  waste related to, 52

dairy-free labels, 38

DASH Diet, 100

decanting dry items, 66–67

deep frying, 128

dehydrating food, 276

desserts
  Add Anything Scones, 246
  Basic Muffins, 244
  Black Bean Brownie Bites, 247
  Fruit Cobbler, 245
  High-Fiber Waffles, 248
  key lime pie, 272
  overview, 241
  quesadillas, 234
  zero waste add-ins and swaps, 242

dietary cholesterol, 132

Dietary Guidelines for Americans (DGA), 39, 254–255

digital lists, 79

dinners, in sample meal plans, 106–111. *See also* main dishes; *specific recipes*

dips
  Basic Bean, 249
  Basic Cream Cheese, 124
  Creamy Veggie, 123
  Layered Bean, 121–122
  Peanut Butter Yogurt Fruit, 243
  Texas Caviar, 126
  using leftovers in, 122

"Dirty Dozen" list, 26

donating food, 54, 67

dressings
  for Black Bean and Edamame Salad, 182
  Caesar, 273
  Citrus-mustard, 161
  Everyday Vinaigrette, 162
  Go-to Honey Dijon, 163
  for Kicked-Up Cannellini Bean Salad, 181
  Lemon Vinaigrette, 155
  and marinades, 160
  overview, 143–144, 159–160
  for Salmon Spinach Salad with Sliced Grapes, 154
  Southern, 284–285

dried beans, 87

dried fruit, storing, 65

D

drinks
   bar, setting up, 254–255
   Basil-infused Sparkling Water, 262
   Berry Smoothie, 259
   Cranberry-Rosemary Cocktail, 264
   Green Smoothie, 260
   Infused Vodka, 265
   Mocktail Lemonade with Mint, 256
   Mocktail Long Island Iced Tea, 258
   Mocktail Sangria with Citrus, 257
   overview, 253
   Pimm's Cocktail, 266
   Special Whiskey Sour Cocktail, 267
   sugared citrus peel garnish for, 263
   Tofu Smoothie, 261
   Vegged-Up Bloody Mary Cocktail, 268
droopy fruits and veggies, using up, 277
dry goods
   analyzing, 20
   storing, 66–67
drying herbs/veggies/fruit, 276
dyeing eggs with leftover onion skins, 278

E

Easy Basic Marinade, 164
Easy Cheese Soufflé, 142
ecological management of pests, 26
edamame
   Black Bean and Edamame Salad, 182
   overview, 88
egg-free labels, 38
eggplant
   choosing for ripeness, 94
   Roasted Veggie Trio, 173
eggs
   Basic Frittata, 140
   Basic Strata, 139
   Cheesy Veggie Crustless Quiche, 138
   dyeing with leftover onion skins, 278
   Easy Cheese Soufflé, 142
   egg wash, using, 273–274
   Fajita, 136
   as food waste saviors, 131
   healthy eating tips, 98–99
   Leftover Steak and, 137

   Muffin Cups, 135
   nutrition, 132
   omelet basics, 133–134
   Potluck Bake, 141
   shells, uses for, 134, 271–272
   Tuna "a la Niçoise" Salad, 156
   ways of cooking, 132–133
   whites, using extra, 272
   yolks, using extra, 272–273
"empty the refrigerator" day, 73
Empty-the-fridge Chicken Vegetable Soup with Egg
   Noodles, 146
environment
   conservation along food supply chain, 25–28
   effect of meat consumption on, 34–36
   impact of food waste, 28–30
   nutrition and, 40
   and plant-based versus animal-based eating, 101
   sustainability in agriculture, 22–25
   zero waste cooking and, 17–18
Environmental Working Group (EWG), 26
Everyday Vinaigrette Dressing, 162
extra servings, preparing, 104–105

F

facials, 291
factory farming, 17, 35
Fajita Eggs, 136
Fajitas with Avocado Cream, 235
farmers' markets, 84–85
farming, conventional versus organic, 32–33. See also
   agriculture
farm-raised poultry, 97
farro
   Mixed Produce Salad with, 152
   overview, 92
Feeding America, 13, 67
fennel, regrowing, 74
fermented milk, 287. See also sour milk
fertilizers, 33
feta cheese
   Foil-pack Greek Chicken with, 193–194
   Roasted Grape Tomatoes with, 125
fiber, 87
first in, first out system, 54, 66–67

fish. *See also* salmon
  Baked with Herbed Bread Crumbs, 205
  coating with yogurt, 291
  Foil-baked Tilapia with Peppers, 206
  healthy eating tips, 99
  safe minimum cooking temperatures, 189
  Tacos, 237
  Tuna "a la Niçoise" Salad, 156
Flank Steak, Grilled Marinated, 198–199
flatbreads, 231, 251, 252
Flexible Quesadillas, 234
flour, storing, 65, 67
Foil-baked Tilapia with Peppers, 206
Foil-pack Greek Chicken with Olives, Feta, and Peppers, 193–194
Food Allergen Labeling and Consumer Protection Act, 38
food allergies, 37, 38–39
food banks, 13, 54, 67
food coverings, reusable, 66
food insecurity, 13, 30, 67
food intolerances, 39, 100, 288
food labels
  carbon footprint, 40
  free-from, 37–39
  overview, 36
  plant-based products, 39
  USDA Organic, 36–37
food safety, 57
food scraps. *See* leftovers; scraps
food supply chain
  conservation along, 25–28
  overview, 21
  sustainable, 24–25
  understanding, 31–36
food thermometers, 189
food waste. *See* waste; zero waste cooking
foodborne illness, 189, 273
free-from labeling, 37–39
freekeh, 92
free-range chicken, 98
free-range eggs, 98
freezer
  biweekly check of, 52
  bread, freezing, 279
  considering food in when meal planning, 79
  "cook from the freezer" day, 73, 86, 105

  efficient use of, 67–68
  egg whites, freezing, 272
  general rules for storage in, 68
  knowing what freezes well, 71–73
  making most of items in, 75
  product dating for items in, 57–58
  sour milk, freezing, 288
  staple ingredients, 80
  taking inventory of food in, 53
  as tool in zero waste cooking, 46
  what not to freeze, 73
French onion soup, 283–284
French toast, 281–282
fresh bread crumbs, 280–281
freshly ground black pepper, 216
frittatas, 133, 140
frozen foods, 80, 85–86. *See also* freezer
fruit. *See also specific fruits*
  avoiding waste of, 52
  bar codes on, 56
  buying at farmers' markets, 84–85
  canned and frozen, 85–86
  chutney, making with, 169
  dehydrating, 276
  droopy, using up, 277
  freezing, 71–72
  frozen, 86
  grocery lists for sample meal plans, 107, 109, 110, 111
  healthy eating tips, 93–95
  Peanut Butter Yogurt Dip for, 243
  prepping ahead, 105
  production of, 32
  regrowing, 73–74
  ripeness, choosing for, 93–94
  roasting meat in slow cooker with, 202
  saving money on, 14
  storing, 45, 55, 69, 70–71
Fruit Cobbler, 245
fruit leather, making, 276
fryer chickens, 191
frying oil, storing or reusing, 128

G

garden care, 81–82, 271–272, 291
garlic

Broccoli, 174
Linguine with Clams, 222
regrowing, 74
storing, 70
garnishes, for drinks, 255, 263, 268
genetic engineering (bioengineering), 31
genetically modified organisms (GMOs), 31, 98
glasses, for drinks, 254
gluten-free labels, 38, 93
GMO-free labels, 38
goat cheese
Flatbread, 252
Nutty Mixed Salad with Beans, Beets, and, 157
Go-to Honey Dijon Salad Dressing, 163
grains. See also specific grains
Chickpea Artichoke Grain Bake, 178
healthy eating tips, 89–93
as pantry staples, 80
Power Bowl, creating, 295–296
vegetables stuffed with, 176
Grandin, Temple, 34–35
grapes
choosing for ripeness, 94
Salmon Spinach Salad with Sliced, 154
Spice-rubbed Pork Tenderloin with Roasted Sliced, 201
Greek Stuffed Bread, 129–130
green marketing, 36
Green Smoothie, 260
greenhouse gas (GHG) emissions, 28, 29, 30, 34, 40
greens, 70, 94. See also salads; specific greens
greenwashing, 36
grilled cheese sandwiches, 298–299
Grilled Marinated Flank Steak, 198–199
grocery apps, 79
grocery list. See also shopping
based on schedule for week, 78
basic ingredients to keep on hand, 80–81
pantry staples, 80–81
perishable items, 81
for sample meal plans, 106, 107–108, 109, 110,
111–112
as step in meal planning, 77–78
tips for making and sticking to, 79–81
when shopping for needs, 11

H

habits, analyzing current, 51
Ham Fritters, 120
handhelds
Bagels with Smoked Salmon and Cream Cheese, 238
for breakfast, 231
creativity with, 230–231
Fajitas with Avocado Cream, 235
Fish Tacos, 237
Flexible Quesadillas, 234
Mushroom Turkey Burgers, 232
overview, 229–230
Pork Pita Pockets with Cucumber Sauce, 233
Pork Tacos with Peppers, Onions, and Lime Crema, 236
Seafood Salad Sandwich, 239
hands, washing, 57
healthy eating
balanced eating, 15–16, 104
canned or frozen produce, 85–86
dairy foods, 99–101
eggs, 132
and environment, 40
grains, 89–93
legumes, 86–89
meat, 95–99
overview, 86
plant-based eating, 16
produce, 93–95
well-balanced zero waste diets, 12
zero waste cooking and, 14–16, 144
heme iron, 96
herb garden, planting, 81–82
herbicides, 26
herbs. See also spices
dehydrating, 276
for Easy Basic Marinade, 164
mixing with bread crumbs, 281
as pantry staples, 80
regrowing, 74
Versatile Pesto, 167
high blood pressure, 100
High-Fiber Waffles, 248
hollandaise sauce, 273

Homemade Stock, 46, 144–145, 191

Honey Dijon Salad Dressing, 163

Honey Glaze, Roasted Carrots with, 179

hormones, in poultry, 97

hot composting, 59

humane slaughter, 34–35

hydrogenotrophs, 28

I

ice-cream sandwiches, 248

impulse buys, 79, 83

Individual Pizzas, 251

infant formula, product dating on, 56

Infused Vodka, 265

intolerances, food, 39, 100, 288

inventory of food, taking, 52–55, 241

iron intake, 96

isoflavones, 89

J

jasmine rice, 90

K

key lime pie, 272

Kicked-Up Cannellini Bean Salad, 181

kitchen, setting up for zero waste. See also freezer; pantry; refrigerator

  cleanliness, 57

  composting, 58–59

  overview, 51

  product dating, 55–58

  taking inventory of food, 52–55

  trash bin, analyzing, 19

Kitchen Sink Chicken Chili, 149

L

labels. See food labels

lactose intolerance, 100

lamb, 95–96

landfills, food waste in, 17, 28, 30

lasagna, 213, 218–219

Layered Bean Dip, 121–122

leeks, 74, 76

Leftover Steak and Eggs, 137

leftovers. See also restaurant meal leftovers

  analyzing waste of, 42

  creative use of, 105–106

  in dips, 122

  making most of, 11–12, 46–47, 73

  often wasted, uses for, 271–278

  pasta, 216

  in sample meal plans, 106

  in starters, 115–116

  using one ingredient in multiple recipes, 104

legumes, 86–89. See also beans; specific legumes

Lemon Vinaigrette, 155

lemon zest, storing, 76

Lemonade with Mint, Mocktail, 256

Lemony Salmon Patties, 119

lentils

  healthy eating tips, 88

  Stuffed Zucchini, 209–210

lettuce, 70, 74. See also salads

Lime Crema, 236

linguine

  Broccoli Bits and Bell Peppers with, 217

  Garlic, with Clams, 222

  overview, 213

liver, chicken, 98

locally grown produce, 14, 84–85, 94–95

Long Island Iced Tea, Mocktail, 258

lunches, in sample meal plans, 106–111. See also specific recipes

M

main dishes

  Baked Fish with Herbed Bread Crumbs, 205

  bread crumbs, making, 188–189

  Broiled Salmon Fillet, 204

  Chicken with Orzo, Artichokes, and Zucchini, 192

  Chicken-Stuffed Baked Potatoes, 197

  Foil-baked Tilapia with Peppers, 206

  Foil-pack Greek Chicken with Olives, Feta, and Peppers, 193–194

  Grilled Marinated Flank Steak, 198–199

  Lentil-stuffed Zucchini, 209–210

  Moroccan Veggie Skillet, 207

  overview, 185–186

  Roast Pork Loin with Apples and Onions, 203

safe minimum cooking temperatures, 189

Skillet Meatballs, 200

Slow Cooker Pulled Pork, 202

Spiced Chicken over Rice, 196

Spice-rubbed Pork Tenderloin with Roasted Sliced Grapes, 201

Spicy Tofu Broccoli Bowl, 208

Teriyaki Chicken Tenders, 195

whole roast chicken, preparing, 186–188, 190–191

marinades

Easy Basic, 164

overview, 160

with sour milk, 290

meal planning

based on schedule for week, 78

basic ingredients to keep on hand, 80–81

getting creative with leftovers, 105–106

ingredients already in kitchen, 79

making grocery list and sticking to it, 79–81

overview, 12, 77–78, 103–104

perishable items, 81

prepping and cooking extra servings, 104–105

sample meal plans, 106–112

to use up food in refrigerator and freezer, 68

using one ingredient in multiple recipes, 104

meat. *See also specific meats; specific recipes*

bulk buys, 83

conscientious omnivores, 18

environmental effects of eating, 17, 34–36

filling omelets with leftover, 296

greenhouse gas emissions related to, 40

healthy eating tips, 15, 95–99

iron intake from, 96

organic, 37

product dating on, 56

safe minimum cooking temperatures, 189

tenderizing with sour milk, 290

meat packing industry, 34–35

Meatless Monday movement, 35

melons, choosing for ripeness, 94

meringues, 168

milk. *See also* sour milk

alternatives to, 100, 101

cooking tips, 100, 101

freezing, 72

nutrition in, 99, 288

milk baths, 291

minimum cooking temperatures, 189

mirepoix, 284

Mixed Produce Salad with Farro, 152

mocktails

bar, setting up, 254–255

Lemonade with Mint, 256

Long Island Iced Tea, 258

overview, 253

Sangria with Citrus, 257

modifying recipes. *See also specific recipes*

main dishes, 185

overview, 79

side dishes, 172

snacks and desserts, 242

starters, 116

with stock, 144

mold, 275, 280

morality, unlinking food from, 89

Moroccan Veggie Skillet, 207

muffins

Basic, 244

Egg Muffin Cups, 135

zero waste add-ins and swaps, 242

mushrooms

Chicken Parmesan Stuffed, 117–118

Roasted Veggie Trio, 173

Turkey Burgers, 232

N

nacho toppings, turning leftovers into, 298

natural resources, efficient use of, 24

nectarines, choosing for ripeness, 93

needs, shopping for, 10–11, 43–45

Niçoise salad, 156

Non-GMO eggs, 98

Non-GMO Project Verified label, 37, 38

noodles. *See* pasta

"nose to tail" philosophy, 98

no-till farming, 24, 27

nut-free labels, 38

nutrition. *See* healthy eating; *specific foods*

nuts

    bulk buys, 83

    freezing, 71

    Nutty Mixed Salad with Beans, Beets, and Goat Cheese, 157

    spiced, 274

O

oat milk, 100

oatmeal, using sour milk in, 288

oils

    in marinades and dressings, 160

    as pantry staples, 80

    storing or reusing frying, 128

    testing temperature of for frying, 120

omega-3 fortified eggs, 99

omelets

    basics of making, 133–134

    filling with leftover meats or veggies, 296

    overview, 133

    veggie scraps, using in, 274

omnivores, 15, 17, 18

onions

    caramelized, 172, 177

    choosing for ripeness, 94

    dyeing eggs with leftover skins, 278

    French onion soup, 283–284

    Pork Tacos with, 236

    regrowing, 74

    Roast Pork Loin with Apples and, 203

    storing, 69, 70, 71

    tops, storing, 76

online shopping, 82

open dating food labels, 55–56

organic chicken, 98

organic eggs, 98

organic farming, 32–33

organic food labels, 36–37

Orzo, Artichokes, and Zucchini, Chicken with, 192

oven-baked zucchini planks, 289

oven-fried chicken, 273

P

package labels. *See* food labels

packaging, choosing less, 62–63

pantry

    analyzing waste in, 20, 42

    biweekly check of, 52

    considering food in when meal planning, 79

    monthly check of, 67

    staple ingredients, 80–81

    storing food in, 62–67

    taking inventory of food in, 53–54

Panzanella, 285

paper products, buying, 83

Pappa al Pomodoro, 282

pasta

    adding to leftover restaurant sauces, 296–297

    Angel Hair with Shrimp and Spinach, 228

    Bow Ties with Turkey and Peas, 226

    Broccoli Bits and Bell Peppers with Linguine, 217

    with Chickpeas, 224

    cooking instructions, 213, 215

    Empty-the-fridge Chicken Vegetable Soup with Egg Noodles, 146

    Garlic Linguine with Clams, 222

    healthy eating tips, 91

    measuring portions appropriately, 212

    overview, 211–212

    Penne Bake with Veggies, 220

    Quick Canned Tomato Sauce, 166

    with Roast Vegetables and Salmon, 223

    Roasted Tomatoes and Bell Peppers with Penne, 227

    shapes, 212–213, 214

    Smoked Salmon Pasta with Asparagus, 221

    Vegetable Lasagna, 218–219

    Veggie-Roast Pasta Primavera, 225

pasture management, 27

pasture-raised chickens, 97

pâté, chicken liver, 98

peaches, choosing for ripeness, 93

peanut butter

    storing, 55, 68

    Yogurt Fruit Dip, 243

Pear and Goat Cheese Flatbread, 252

pearled grains, 92

peas
  Beef Stew with Potatoes, Carrots, and, 147
  Bow Ties with Turkey and, 226
  frozen, 86

penne
  Bake with Veggies, 220
  overview, 212
  Roasted Tomatoes and Bell Peppers with, 227

peppercorn, freshly ground, 216

peppers. *See* bell peppers

perishable items, buying for week, 81

pesticides, 26, 33, 36–37

pesto, 167

pests, ecological management of, 26

phytoestrogens, 89

pickle juice, storing, 76

Pimm's Cocktail, 266

pineapples, choosing for ripeness, 94

Pizza Rolls, 127

Pizzas, Individual, 251

planning meals. *See* meal planning

plant-based eating, 16, 39, 101

plant-based products
  milk products, 100, 101
  protein crumbles, 207
  use of term on labels, 39

plants, feeding, 271–272, 291

plastic bags, reusing or replacing, 64–65

plastic containers, repurposing, 63–64

plastic items, single-use, 44–45

plastic safety, 64, 65

pork
  Bean Soup with Diced, 151
  Ham Fritters, 120
  healthy eating tips, 96–97
  Pita Pockets with Cucumber Sauce, 233
  Roast Loin with Apples and Onions, 203
  Slow Cooker Pulled, 202
  Spice-rubbed Tenderloin with Roasted Sliced
      Grapes, 201
  Tacos with Peppers, Onions, and Lime Crema, 236

potatoes
  Beef Stew with, 147
  Chicken-Stuffed Baked, 197
  growing plants from sprouted, 74
  sheet pan dinners, 105
  storing, 69
  stuffing baked, with restaurant leftovers, 297
  Tuna "a la Niçoise" Salad, 156

Potluck Egg Bake, 141

poultry. *See also specific poultry; specific recipes*
  carving, 187–188
  healthy eating tips, 97–99
  safe minimum cooking temperatures, 189
  trussing, 187
  whole, preparing, 186–188

Power Bowl, creating, 106, 295–296

prepping food, 104–105, 172

processed foods, 73

produce bags, reusable, 70

product dating. *See* best-by dates

protein crumbles, plant-based, 207

Protein-packed Waldorf Salad, 153

Pulled Pork, Slow Cooker, 202

pulses, 86, 87. *See also* beans

Pumpkin Seeds, Roasted, 250

Q

Quesadillas, Flexible, 234

quiches, 133, 138

Quick Canned Tomato Pasta Sauce, 166

quinoa, 92

R

recipes. *See also* modifying recipes;
      specific recipes
  conventions used in, 2
  using one ingredient in multiple, 104

recycling
  food into compost, 58–59
  grain products, 89
  used oil, 128

red meat, 95–96. *See also* beef; meat

reduce, reuse, recycle, 47–48

refrigerator

    analyzing waste in, 19, 42

    biweekly check of, 52

    efficient use, 67–68

    food safety tips, 57

    general rules for, 68

    knowing what freezes well, 71–73

    making most of items in, 75

    optimizing storage zones, 69–71

    taking inventory of food in, 53, 241

    as tool in zero waste cooking, 46

regenerative agriculture, 24

regrowing food, 73–74

repurposing containers, 63–64

restaurant meal leftovers

    adding pasta to leftover sauces, 296–297

    boxing up, 294

    combining to create new meal, 295

    eating what you bring home, 295

    filling omelets with meats or veggies from, 296

    grilled cheese sandwich additions, 298–299

    in meal planning, 105

    as nacho toppings, 298

    ordering wisely, 294

    overview, 293

    Power Bowl, creating, 295–296

    remembering to eat, 73

    stuffing baked potato with, 297

reusable bags, 64–65, 70, 72

reusable food coverings, 66

reusing frying oil, 128

rice

    Beans and, 183

    Cheesy Herbed, 180

    healthy eating tips, 90–91

    Power Bowl, creating, 295–296

    storing, 65

Roast Pork Loin with Apples and Onions, 203

Roasted Bell Peppers, 175

Roasted Carrots with Honey Glaze, 179

Roasted Grape Tomatoes with Feta, 125

Roasted Pumpkin Seeds, 250

Roasted Tomatoes and Bell Peppers with Penne, 227

Roasted Tomatoes with Bread and Cheese, 285

Roasted Veggie Trio, 173

roaster chickens

    defined, 98, 191

    whole, preparing, 186–188, 190–191

roasting vegetables in big batches, 172

roux, 165

S

safety

    food, 57

    minimum cooking temperatures, 189

    plastic, 64, 65

salads. *See also* dressings

    Black Bean and Edamame, 182

    Chopped, with Lemon Vinaigrette, 155

    croutons, making for, 286

    Kicked-Up Cannellini Bean, 181

    Mixed Produce, with Farro, 152

    Nutty Mixed, with Beans, Beets, and Goat Cheese, 157

    overview, 143–144

    Protein-packed Waldorf, 153

    Salmon Spinach, with Sliced Grapes, 154

    Tuna "a la Niçoise", 156

sales, shopping, 85

salmon

    Bagels with Smoked, and Cream Cheese, 238

    Broiled Fillet, 204

    Lemony Patties, 119

    overview, 99

    Pasta with Roast Vegetables and, 223

    Smoked, Pasta with Asparagus, 221

    Spinach Salad with Sliced Grapes, 154

sandwiches. *See also* handhelds

    grilled cheese, adding leftovers to, 298–299

    overview, 230–231

    Seafood Salad, 239

Sangria with Citrus, Mocktail, 257

saturated fat, 15

sauces

    adding pasta to leftover, 296–297

    Apple-Ginger Chutney, 169

    Basic Cream, 160, 165

    for creative side dishes, 172

hollandaise, 273
overview, 160
Quick Canned Tomato Pasta, 166
thickening with sour milk, 289
for Vegetable Lasagna, 218
veggie scraps, using in, 273
Versatile Pesto, 167
saving money, 14
schedule, meal planning based on, 78
scones, 246
scrambled eggs, baking, 132
scraps. *See also* leftovers
composting, 58–59
making most of, 11–12, 14, 46–47
storing, 75–76
veggie, using up, 274–275
seafood. *See also* fish; *specific seafood*
healthy eating tips, 99
Salad Sandwich, 239
seasonal foods, 14, 94–95
sheet pan dinners, 105
shelf life. *See* best-by dates
shopping. *See also* grocery list
adjusting to changes in household or schedule, 52
analyzing wasteful, 42
bulk buys, 83–84
buying less to prevent waste, 75
canned and frozen produce, 85–86
deciding where to shop, 84–85
impulse buys, 79, 83
overview, 82–83
specials and sales, 85
for what you need, 10–11, 43–45
shot glasses, 255
shrimp
Angel Hair with, and Spinach, 228
overview, 99
side dishes
Baked Apples, 184
Beans and Rice, 183
Black Bean and Edamame Salad, 182
Cheesy Herbed Rice, 180
Chickpea Artichoke Grain Bake, 178
creativity with, 172

Garlic Broccoli, 174
grain-stuffed vegetables, 176
Kicked-Up Cannellini Bean Salad, 181
overview, 171
Roasted Bell Peppers, 175
Roasted Carrots with Honey Glaze, 179
Roasted Veggie Trio, 173
Zucchini with Caramelized Onions, 177
sidewalk chalk, making, 134
silicone bags, 72
single-use items, 44–45, 62–63
Skillet Meatballs, 200
slaws, making, 277
Slow Cooker Pulled Pork, 202
smart farming, 27, 33–34
smoked salmon
Bagels with, and Cream Cheese, 238
Pasta with Asparagus, 221
smoothies
basics, 259
Berry, 259
Green, 260
Tofu, 261
snacks. *See also* starters
Add Anything Scones, 246
Basic Bean Dip, 249
Basic Muffins, 244
Black Bean Brownie Bites, 247
High-Fiber Waffles, 248
Individual Pizzas, 251
overview, 241
Peanut Butter Yogurt Fruit Dip, 243
Pear and Goat Cheese Flatbread, 252
Roasted Pumpkin Seeds, 250
in sample meal plans, 106–111
zero waste add-ins and swaps, 242
sodium, in canned foods, 85
soft cheese, making, 289–290
soil conservation, 27
sorghum, 92
soufflés
Easy Cheese, 142
overview, 133

soups
  Bean, with Diced Pork, 151
  Beef Chili, 148
  Beef Stew with Potatoes, Carrots, and Peas, 147
  Empty-the-fridge Chicken Vegetable, with Egg Noodles, 146
  homemade stock, 144–145
  Kitchen Sink Chicken Chili, 149
  overview, 143–144
  veggie scraps, using in, 275
  Wedding, with Spinach, 150
sour cream, 101, 290
sour milk
  baking, 289
  breading foods, 289
  feeding plants with, 291
  in milk baths and facials, 291
  in oatmeal, 288
  overview, 287–288
  replacing buttermilk, 288
  soft cheese, making, 289–290
  tenderizing meat, 290
  thickening stews and sauces, 289
Southern dressing, 284–285
soy products, 88–89, 100. See also tofu
Sparkling Water, Basil-infused, 262
Special Whiskey Sour Cocktail, 267
specials, shopping, 85
specialty stores, 84
spent grain, 89
Spiced Chicken over Rice, 196
spiced nuts, 274
Spice-rubbed Pork Tenderloin with Roasted Sliced Grapes, 201
spices. See also herbs
  Italian spice blend, 166
  mixing with bread crumbs, 281
  as pantry staples, 80
  storing, 65
Spicy Tofu Broccoli Bowl, 208
spinach
  Angel Hair with Shrimp and, 228
  fresh versus frozen, 86
  Salmon Salad with Sliced Grapes, 154
  Wedding Soup with, 150
spoiled foods, taking inventory of, 53

squash, choosing for ripeness, 94
stains, removing with eggshells, 134
stale bread, using
  bread pudding, 283
  crostini, 282
  croutons for French onion soup, 283–284
  French toast, 281–282
  fresh bread crumbs, 280–281
  last-ditch efforts, 286
  overview, 279–280
  Panzanella, 285
  Pappa al Pomodoro, 282
  Roasted Tomatoes with Bread and Cheese, 285
  stuffing or Southern dressing, 284–285
staple ingredients
  grocery lists for sample meal plans, 108, 109, 110, 112
  in meal planning, 106
  tips for, 80–81
starters. See also snacks
  Basic Cream Cheese Dip, 124
  Chicken Parmesan Stuffed Mushrooms, 117–118
  Creamy Veggie Dip, 123
  crostini for, making, 282
  Ham Fritters, 120
  Layered Bean Dip, 121–122
  Lemony Salmon Patties, 119
  overview, 115–116
  Pizza Rolls, 127
  Roasted Grape Tomatoes with Feta, 125
  Stuffed Greek Bread, 129–130
  Texas Caviar, 126
steak
  Flank, Grilled Marinated, 198–199
  Leftover, and Eggs, 137
stews
  Beef, with Potatoes, Carrots, and Peas, 147
  thickening with sour milk, 289
stir-fry, simple, 295
stock, homemade, 46, 144–145, 191
storing food
  analyzing waste related to, 42
  on countertop, 54–55
  for food safety, 57
  frying oil, 128
  making most of food by, 75

overview, 61

in pantry, 54, 62–67

properly, 10–11, 45–46

in refrigerator and freezer, 53, 67–73

scraps, 75–76

stratas

Basic Egg, 139

overview, 133

Stuffed Greek Bread, 129–130

stuffing, 284–285

substituting ingredients in recipes. *See* modifying recipes

sugar, storing, 65

sugared citrus peel, 263

sunny side up eggs, baking, 132

sushi rice, 91

sustainability

in agriculture, 22–25

defined, 22

household, 47–48

overview, 21

role of technology in, 33–34

swapping ingredients. *See* modifying recipes

sweets. *See* desserts; *specific recipes*

T

tacos

Fish, 237

Pork, with Peppers, Onions, and Lime Crema, 236

tapas, 115

technology in agriculture, 27, 33–34

temperature

of refrigerator and freezer, 68

safe minimum cooking, 189

tenderizing meat, 290

tenderloin, pork, 201

Teriyaki Chicken Tenders, 195

Texas Caviar, 126

Texmati rice, 90

Tilapia with Peppers, Foil-baked, 206

tillage, 27, 33

tofu

overview, 88

Smoothie, 261

Spicy Broccoli Bowl, 208

tomato icon, explained, 2

tomato paste, 72, 207

tomatoes

Panzanella, 285

Pappa al Pomodoro, 282

Quick Canned Pasta Sauce, 166

Roasted, and Bell Peppers with Penne, 227

Roasted, with Bread and Cheese, 285

Roasted Grape, with Feta, 125

storing, 55, 69, 70

tortillas, 234, 235, 236, 237

trash bin, analyzing, 19, 43

trussing poultry, 187

Tuna "a la Niçoise" Salad, 156

turkey

Bow Ties with, and Peas, 226

Burgers, 232

U

upcycling, 27–28

USDA Organic label, 36–37

V

veal, 95–96

vegan labels, 38

vegan meringues, 168

Vegetable Lasagna, 218–219

vegetables. *See also* salads; *specific recipes; specific vegetables*

avoiding waste of, 52

bar codes on, 56

buying at farmers' markets, 84–85

canned and frozen, 85–86

dehydrating, 276

droopy, using up, 277

filling omelets with leftover, 296

freezing, 71–72

grain-stuffed, 176

grocery lists for sample meal plans, 107, 109, 110, 111

healthy eating tips, 93–95

prepping ahead, 105

production of, 32

regrowing, 73–74

vegetables *(continued)*
    ripeness, choosing for, 93–94
    saving money on, 14
    scraps, using up, 274–275
    in side dishes, 171
    stir-frying leftover, 295
    storing, 45, 55, 69, 70–71
    wilting, using, 275
vegetarian dishes, 185–186. *See also specific recipes*
Vegged-Up Bloody Mary Cocktail, 268
Veggie-Roast Pasta Primavera, 225
Versatile Pesto, 167
vinaigrettes, 155, 162
vinegars, 80, 160, 164
Vodka, Infused, 265

W

Waffles, High-Fiber, 248
Waldorf Salad, 153
washing hands when cooking, 57
waste
    analyzing habits, 42–43
    defined, 28–29
    environmental impact of, 28–30
    overview, 1, 9, 13
waxed cotton wrappers, 66
Wedding Soup with Spinach, 150
weekly inventory, 241
weekly schedule, meal planning based on, 78
weekly shopping, 78
wheat, 92, 93
Whiskey Sour Cocktail, Special, 267
white cream sauce, 160, 165
whole grains, 230

whole roast chicken, 186–188, 190–191
wild rice, 91
wilting veggies, using, 275
World Economic Forum, 25
wrappers, reusable, 66

Y

yogurt
    cooking tips, 101
    Peanut Butter Fruit Dip, 243
    souring, using up, 290–291

Z

zero waste cooking. *See also* meal planning; shopping;
    specific foods; *specific recipes*; storing food
    analyzing food waste habits, 42–43
    benefits of, 13–18
    defined, 10
    environmental friendliness of, 17–18
    getting started with, 19–20
    and healthy eating, 14–16, 86
    mindset behind, 12–13
    overview, 1–5, 41
    realistic attitude toward, 47
    saving money through, 14
    using food and ingredients wisely, 10
    using scraps and leftovers, 11–12, 46–47
zest, storing, 76
zucchini
    with Caramelized Onions, 177
    Chicken with Orzo, Artichokes, and, 192
    Lentil-stuffed, 209–210
    oven-baked planks, 289

About the Author

Rosanne Rust is an internationally recognized nutrition expert and author with a passion for facts. She created her Chew the Facts® blog, as an antithesis to pseudoscience, to help consumers decipher nutrition fact from myth so they can enjoy life. Rosanne is the owner of Rust Nutrition Services (rustnutrition.com) where she's a sought-after communicator known for her unique insight as well as her unflappable communication style in tackling tough topics. A researcher and writer at heart, her most popular consumer books include the *DASH Diet For Dummies*, 2nd Edition; *DASH Diet for Two Cookbook*, and the *Glycemic Index Cookbook For Dummies*. Rosanne also served as both an editor and chapter coauthor for the Academy of Nutrition and Dietetic's book (Spring 2020) *Communicating Nutrition: The Authoritative Guide*. Rosanne is happily married and the mother of three sons. She practices what she preaches: A well-balanced life, that includes food and beverage splurges, caring for the environment, along with an active lifestyle. Follow her on social media @chewthefacts or contact her at her website or Facebook Author Page (www.facebook.com/RosanneRustAuthor).

Dedication

This book is dedicated to my parents, the king and queen of zero waste. Having grown up during the depression, my folks did not waste anything. Food was procured, prepared, preserved, and used wisely. My paternal grandfather was a butcher, so my father learned early on how to gratefully use the animal from nose to tail. My maternal grandfather's green thumb provided loads of fruits and vegetables for us to enjoy, while my grandmother and mother preserved some of them to use all year long. This foundation of a no-waste philosophy was imprinted upon me, and I have always done my best to keep kitchen waste minimal. My hope is that by rethinking your kitchen workspace, as well as your food shopping and storage habits, you can do your best to reduce your food waste footprint, bringing more purpose and happiness to your life.

Author's Acknowledgments

I'd like to thank my agent, Matt Wagner, and Tracy Boggier, Senior Acquisitions Editor at Wiley, for her interest in helping me bring this title to you. Since this book couldn't have come together without an excellent editing team, I send my sincere gratitude to Project Editor Alissa Schwipps, Copy Editor Jennette ElNaggar, Technical Editor Marianne Smith Edge, and Dummies Coach Vicki Adang for her input on the table of contents.

Publisher's Acknowledgments

Senior Acquisitions Editor: Tracy Boggier

Project Editor: Alissa Schwipps

Copy Editor: Jennette ElNaggar

Technical Editor: Marianne Smith Edge

Proofreader: Debbye Butler

Senior Managing Editor: Kristie Pyles

Illustrator: Elizabeth Kurtzman

Cover and Other Images: Rosanne Rust